Profit and Enterprise

Profit and Enterprise

The Political Economy of Profit

Edited by

David Parker
Cranfield School of Management

Richard Stead
Leeds Business School

St. Martin's Press
New York

First published in the United States of America in 1991

Printed in Great Britain

ISBN 0-312-05684-2

Library of Congress Cataloging-in-Publication Data
Parker, David, 1949–
    Profit and enterprise : the political economy of profit / by David
Parker, Richard Stead.
    p. cm.
    Includes bibliographical references and index.
    ISBN 0-312-05684-2
    1. Profits—History. 2. Entrepreneurship—History. 3. Economics—
History. I. Stead, Richard. II. Title.
HB801.P25 1991
338.5'16—dc20   90-48084
                                                          CIP

To the generations of economics scribblers
who made this book possible

Contents

Preface

Today there is new interest in profit and enterprise. In the United Kingdom and the United States this has been matched by the election of governments which have given unequivocal support to the 'entrepreneurial spirit'. Other Western countries too have introduced policies to cut taxes, rein in the growth of public spending, cut red tape and restore free markets. Nor has this trend occurred only in the West – the Communist East has witnessed some of the most startling conversions to reliance on individual initiative.

Paradoxically this interest in profit and enterprise is reflected neither in most mainstream economics textbooks nor in economics courses in our universities and schools. Few books and syllabuses include more than a passing reference to enterprise, while profit is usually treated as little more than an *assumption* in highly stylised economic theories. This is because economics teaching centres upon neoclassical equilibrium models in which markets are shown to adjust to exogenous changes in a manner which is smooth, mechanical and predictable. This approach, however, has the effect of obscuring the dynamic, evolving conditions of real markets. It thus under-emphasises the 'prime mover' of economic life – the entrepreneur. In consequence, there is an obvious danger that students gain little insight into the real processes of markets in which entrepreneurs seek out market advantage, under conditions of high uncertainty, motivated by profit. Little wonder that generations of policy-makers and business and trade union leaders can leave universities and colleges, highly competent in abstract economic model building but at best only vaguely aware of the importance of enterprise. What a shock it must be to discover that competition in practice has very little to do with 'normal' profits but everything to do with entrepreneurial initiative, skill and imagination!

This book has two broad purposes. First, it attempts to answer the question: why are profit and enterprise so neglected in much of economics teaching? To answer this question we have traced the way generations of economists have viewed profit and enterprise in each of the major schools of economic thought. Inevitably this has meant looking in some detail at their different approaches to the creation of value, income distribution and competition.

The second purpose of the book is to examine the major policy prescriptions of these various schools. Different conceptions of profit and enterprise lie at the heart of current debates about the 'free market' versus central planning, state regulation and state ownership. Implicit in the book is the view that the new attention to individual enterprise on the part of policy-makers and the rediscovery of free market ideas by economists are not coincidental. We refrain, however, from evaluating cause and effect – though as economists we do have a leaning towards the notion that the scribblings of economists do, eventually, impact on policy.

In this we draw comfort from the oft-quoted words of the Cambridge economist John Maynard Keynes:

> Practical men, who believe themselves to be quite exempt from any
> intellectual influences, are usually the slaves of some defunct economist.
> Madmen in authority, who hear voices in the air, are distilling their frenzy
> from some academic scribbler of a few years back. I am sure that the power
> of vested interests is vastly exaggerated compared with the gradual
> encroachment of ideas.

The book should appeal especially to students of economic thought, economic policy and industrial economics who need to understand why economists differ in the emphasis they place on individual enterprise. But we hope that it will also be of interest to the general reader who wants to understand the current reassessment of the role of the market and planning in resource allocation.

The structure of the book is as follows. In Chapter 1 we introduce profit and enterprise and consider why they are now fashionable as subjects for study. Chapter 2 traces the development of attitudes to profit and enterprise from the earliest times down to the end of the mercantilist period in the 1770s. Chapter 3 follows this development into the classical economics of Adam Smith to John Stuart Mill, while Chapter 4 examines the views of the neoclassical economists who shaped the teaching of economics in the political West. The book then proceeds to look at approaches to profit which lie outside the mainstream. Chapter 5 considers the Austrian tradition, which places entrepreneurship and profit-seeking at the centre of its analysis of markets. Though perhaps less well known than the other schools of thought reviewed, Austrian economics has exercised an important influence on economic policy during the 1980s in both the United States and the United Kingdom. Chapter 6 then examines theories of profit propounded by radical or critical economists, whose views have heavily influenced the nature of economic policies of the interventionist governments in democratic countries as well as the planning policies of the Communist bloc.

Chapter 7 explains why the various theories of profit have survived all attempts to disprove them. Chapter 8 then critically examines the policies which, drawing upon the advice of economists, governments have pursued in the post-war era. The concluding chapter (Chapter 9) provides an overview of the controversy surrounding profit and enterprise and suggests that they could usefully be incorporated into the teaching of introductory economics.

Many people have indirectly contributed to the contents of this book in discussions over a long period of time. But we would especially like to record our thanks to Professors John Burton and Mike Campbell at Leeds Polytechnic, who read and commented on parts of the manuscript; and to Martin Anderson, formerly of the Institute of Economic Affairs, London, who commented upon, edited and published the article (Parker, 1986/7) which led to the commissioning of this book. The usual disclaimers apply. And we owe, of course, a great debt to our wives and families who tolerated our moods and absences during another long period of writing.

1

Economics, profit and enterprise

After decades of neglect, policy-makers in every continent are re-awakening to the importance of profit and enterprise. In the West, governments have sold off state-owned businesses, cut direct taxes and deregulated markets – putting into reverse decades of interventionism, high taxation and state ownership. In the Soviet Union and China too, central controls have been relaxed, allowing state enterprises more autonomy. Variously termed 'liberalisation', 'privatisation', 'supply-side economics' or, in the socialist states, *perestroika* or *gaige*, these policies share a single objective: the encouragement of individual enterprise.

This reappraisal of the profit motive can be traced to the mid-1970s. Before then, it had been thought that economies could suffer either from inflation or from unemployment but not both at the same time. Following the oil shock of 1973–4, however, the economies of the West experienced a steep rise in both. This 'stagflation' led to a questioning of the theories which had dominated economic thinking in much of Europe and the United States since the end of World War II. Keynesian demand-management came under particular attack. The first assault came from monetarism, which linked inflation through lax monetary control to high state borrowing. The second wave of criticism was supply-side economics, which questioned the beneficence of interventionism and high taxation. Its policy prescriptions were deregulation, privatisation and tax cuts. By the mid-1980s policy-makers (if not economists) were emphasising the importance of profit and enterprise for economic development.

Changes of attitude are also under way in the Communist bloc, where economic performance for long lagged behind that of the West. Despite heavy investment and an abundance of natural resources, the ambitious targets set by government planners were frequently missed. Output was held back by low productivity, shortages of materials and waste. In Hungary in the 1960s, China in the late 1970s and finally in the USSR in the 1980s, economic reform – meaning the liberalisation of markets – came to the fore.

The struggling economies of Europe, North America and the Communist bloc presented a sharp contrast to the economic success of Japan. In the space of a few decades Japan rose from being a medium-sized economy to an economic superpower, with net overseas assets of $250 billion – more than any other nation. The spearhead of Japan's economic advance was its export industries, whose success raised that country's share of world trade by a factor of five between 1955 and 1986.

The search for an explanation of Japan's success occupied analysts for many years. The discipline and effort of Japanese workers and their willingness to submerge their personal ambitions in the objectives of their employers were among the ideas canvassed, as were the competitive education system and the Japanese habit of thrift. It was also suggested that Japan's success rested upon cooperation between industry and government through the offices of the Ministry of International Trade and Industry (MITI). In time, however, it came to be appreciated that although these elements had contributed to Japan's success, they would have been of little use by themselves. The simple fact is that Japan's resources have been directed with the utmost accuracy towards the production of the goods and services which consumers want to buy. The realisation dawned that the vital resource of the Japanese economy is the ability of its businessmen to identify and exploit market opportunities. In a word, the Japanese have shown enterprise.

Japan's search for market opportunities has been guided by the profits to be gained. Anticipation of profit dictates decisions about the markets to be entered, the products to be redesigned, the training to be undertaken and the research programmes to be pursued. Indeed, 'market opportunities' may be described more informatively as 'profit opportunities'. What has distinguished Japan – and Asia's 'little dragons' like Taiwan, South Korea, Hong Kong and Singapore – from Western Europe and the Communist bloc has been both the energy with which they have undertaken this search for profit and their outstanding success. It is this winning formula which other nations now seek to emulate.

1.1   Economics – a paradox

The paradox of economics is that, given that both market equilibrium and enterprise are important topics, economics courses tend to focus upon the former virtually to the exclusion of the latter. For example, at a colloquium in 1979 held by the London-based Institute of Economic Affairs, P. D. Henderson, Professor of Political Economy at University College, London, made the following admission:

> . . . I give a course of lectures which is concerned particularly with government policies in Britain towards industries and enterprises, mainly those which are in the public sector but with some consideration also of the private sector. In these lectures I have never made any reference to the problems of the entrepreneur or to the role of the entrepreneur; and in making no such reference I did not take a conscious decision to exclude the subject – it simply never crossed my mind to refer to it. Moreover, I suspect that if I had sent my lecture notes for comments to a representative group of fellow-economists who were likewise interested in this range of topics, while I would have received a wide variety of criticisms and suggestions for improvement, probably no-one would have remarked: 'There's one important omission: you've said nothing about entrepreneurship.' (Kirzner *et al.*, 1980, p. 103)

Professor Henderson's comments appear to apply quite widely. A perusal of the contents of many economics textbooks suggests a widespread lack of interest in enterprise and profit. For example, Richard Gill's *Economics: A text with included readings* (1973) provides, in its 846 pages, discussions of poverty, industrial concentration, ecology, the mixed economy, Marxism and other topics in addition to the standard fare of equilibrium models. According to the index, profit and enterprise receive relatively scant treatment, not appearing until page 200. *Economics* by Professor Tony Culyer (1985) is a more extreme case, making no mention whatever of the entrepreneur or enterprise in the index. Nor is there any coverage of enterprise in the chapter on uncertainty and risk. Profit is first discussed (as opposed to being mentioned in passing) in Chapter 12 on profit-maximising behaviour in markets – markets which move smoothly from one equilibrium to another. In Baumol and Blinder's *Economics: Principles and policies* (1988) enterprise is, according to the index, deferred until page 770 and merits but two references in a work of over 900 pages. Finally, the authors of one of the most widely used texts – Begg, Fischer and Dornbusch (*Economics.*, 1987) – confine themselves, like Culyer, to discussions of equilibrium models of markets. There is no reference to enterprise or the entrepreneur in the index to their text.

In some texts, such as McConnell (1981) or Samuelson and Nordhaus (1985), entrepreneurship is given fuller consideration. These works contain chapters, typically located in a section on factor rewards, which explain the role of profit, showing that it acts as an incentive for businessmen to try new ventures. These chapters are, however, quite separate from the analysis of markets which are, as in other texts, shown to be either in equilibrium or to be moving swiftly towards it. Importantly, entrepreneurship is not integrated into the theory of competition.

The more advanced microeconomic texts are little better. Indeed, progression to higher levels of sophistication in economics is often measured primarily in terms of an increasing reliance upon mathematical techniques, whose use appears to vary inversely with the attention devoted to enterprise and profit. A. Koutsoyiannis' *Modern Microeconomics* (2nd edition, 1979) omits all mention of enterprise in the index, confining discussion õf profit largely to equilibrium models. Fred Glahe and Dwight Lee in their *Microeconomics: Theory and applications* (1981) appear from the index to delay mention of profit until page 208 and, like Koutsoyiannis, to eschew all discussion of enterprise. David Laidler (1981) follows the same approach.

The core of these texts – and hence of economics courses – is formed by models of different sorts of markets such as perfect competition, oligopoly and monopoly. In these models, markets are depicted as being in equilibrium, with firms maximising their profits by selecting the optimum level of output. When supply or demand changes, a new equilibrium is established smoothly and mechanically.

These models have two notable features. One is that they normally contain the implausible assumption that economic agents (producers and consumers) are fully informed. A second feature is that producers are generally *passive* – they react to changes in market conditions but they rarely initiate change. The method of maximising profits in the models is by adjusting production levels so that marginal costs and marginal revenues are equal; there is rarely a reference to the commonplace tactics of business life by which firms seek to earn profit, such as designing new products, seeking new markets, diversifying into new industries, cutting costs and prices by installing new machinery, advertising or a host of other business strategies. These practices are of course different forms of enterprise.

The failure to emphasise enterprise in mainstream economics in the United States and the United Kingdom is no accident but arises directly from economists' concern with market equilibrium. Equilibrium has been defined as 'a state of rest . . . characterised by the fact that there exists no feeling of urgency on the part of buyers and sellers to change their behaviour' (Hardwick, Khan and Langmead, 1982, p. 7). When a market is in equilibrium, the implication is that producers are not acting entrepreneurially to disturb matters. In other words, enterprise and equilibrium are, in large measure, mutually exclusive states of affairs: markets may display one or the other but not both at the same time.

The justification for this focus upon equilibrium is that it allows economists to assess the effect of changes in conditions, like a fall in demand or the imposition of a tax, upon price and output. This method is termed 'comparative statics' since it involves the comparison of one static equilibrium (the situation before the change) with another (the situation after). The great advantage of this procedure is that in principle it allows economists to make predictions about the effects of various changes. The approach does, however, involve many assumptions which often appear unrealistic, like the idea that economic decision-makers possess perfect information (or are at least able to measure the risks which face them). Professor Milton Friedman (1953) has strongly defended this method, arguing that the benefits in terms of predictions outweigh the disadvantages in terms of lack of realism. This issue is pursued in Chapter 7; for the present it suffices to note that the focus upon equilibrium has a rather serious effect: it obscures the dynamic, evolving conditions of real markets which do not usually move swiftly towards equilibrium but which constantly veer from one temporary position to the next under the continuing impact of new initiatives by businessmen. In short, the conventional approach underemphasises the 'prime mover' of economic life – the entrepreneur.

The result of this failure to include enterprise in discussions of markets is that the analysis of profit is incomplete or contradictory. When it is included, the chapters on profit demonstrate its role as an energiser of the market economy, an incentive to innovate or to risk one's capital in uncertain ventures. In the chapters on markets themselves, however, profits (or more precisely supernormal profits) normally arise as a result of outside forces such as an unexpected increase in demand. The only actions which profit is shown to influence are the decisions to enter an industry or to alter the level of output. Firms are not shown to be deliberately seeking profit through enterprise. In other words, in the equilibrium models the introductory texts fail to show any strong, direct link between profit and enterprise and the behaviour of firms in markets.

Clearly there is a paradox. On the one hand, enterprise in the pursuit of profit has been the locomotive force of free market economies for at least three centuries. On the other, it is apparent from a review of economics texts that the overwhelming concern in economics teaching is with theoretical abstractions in which enterprise merits little or no attention. This raises the question of why economists take this particular stance. Put differently, why do students of economics and thus future generations of managers and policy-makers learn so little about enterprise and profit through their study of economics?

1.2   The nature of enterprise

In the seventeenth century the provider of enterprise was known as a 'projector' and later as an 'adventurer' or 'undertaker'. In the nineteenth century the term 'capitalist' was initially popular but, in the face of socialist agitation, it fell from common use and the French word 'entrepreneur' became widespread. The *Oxford English Dictionary* traces this word back to the late fifteenth century and defines it in terms which reflect its ancestry as 'someone who undertakes; a manager, controller; champion'. Although 'businessman' and 'business executive' are terms used today to describe someone who runs a business, most economists would agree that there is an important distinction between routine management and the provision of enterprise. The latter implies more dynamism or risk-taking: it suggests that the entrepreneur is a force for change or the 'prime mover' of the free market economy. Indeed, the idea of the entrepreneur as a 'champion' accords with the more popular notion of the entrepreneur as a somewhat exceptional individual like the celebrated entrepreneurs of history – e.g. Richard Arkwright, the eighteenth-century pioneer of steam-powered cotton spinning in Britain; Henry Ford, the first to mass-produce the motor car; IBM's Henry Watson, who turned the computer from an invention into a commercial success; or Akio Morita, who built Sony into a worldwide producer of electrical equipment. Alongside the famous there has been an untold number of lesser figures who have enticed customers with improved designs, more competitive prices and new methods of producing or marketing. The feature common to all these entrepreneurs has been an ability to find and exploit market opportunities. Thus for our purposes, enterprise may be defined as the *activity of seeking out new business*.

Ludwig von Mises (1881–1973), a leading economist of the Austrian school, took a more extreme position, arguing that all individual action – not simply business life – is in some sense entrepreneurial. The implication is that people can be entrepreneurial in trade unions, political parties, churches or sports clubs. Certainly this argument can be accepted if the only components of enterprise are risk-taking and the exploitation of opportunities, since everyone does this on a daily basis to some degree at work and in managing personal finances. While there may be some merit in defining enterprise so widely, von Mises' approach does draw attention away from the contribution of enterprise to the operation of markets and competition. Accordingly, most economists prefer to use a narrower, more functional interpretation and this approach is followed here.

The essential feature of new business ventures is that they involve uncertainty. This must be clearly distinguished from risk. The latter relates to events which have a known (or knowable) probability of occurring which can be measured by the use of historical data. For example, the risk that a city-centre shop will be burgled can be broadly determined by looking at the number of past burglaries. It is consequently possible to take out insurance against the risk. Uncertainty, by contrast, relates to events whose probabilities of occurring are not measurable and for which historical data provide no guidance. New business ventures typically fall under the heading of uncertainty: a new magazine, for example, may sell – but equally well it may not. The success of other magazines may be of little guidance since all publications differ. Even with the assistance of market research and pilot sales, the uniqueness of the decision to launch the magazine means that a degree of uncertainty must surround the outcome. There is thus no means of knowing in advance whether the venture will succeed. Many economists, but especially those of the new Austrian school, associate entrepreneurship with uncertainty, arguing that all truly entrepreneurial decisions involve uncertainty (as distinct from risk).

This Austrian perspective, which is examined in detail in Chapter 5, has important implications for the assumptions which are made in economics about information. Conventional economics texts – particularly when dealing with equilibrium models – tend to assume that the participants in markets are perfectly informed. Although modern economic thinking (Stiglitz, 1985) has attempted to accommodate the fact that people invariably operate with limited information, these extensions to mainstream theory have yet to percolate to the level of most student texts and, moreover, tend to concentrate upon risk as opposed to uncertainty. Austrian economists however argue that these assumptions about information are insufficient because economic decisions often have to be made under conditions of uncertainty. It is, they argue further, this very uncertainty which provides scope for entrepreneurs to operate. Their argument is that if everyone were endowed with perfect information (or were able to quantify the risks they faced), decisions about pricing, investment and the launching of new products could be taken with total certainty (or a reliable probability of success) and there would simply be no role for enterprise. In the real world, however, there is uncertainty and therefore much scope for enterprise.

In consequence of these views on enterprise and information, Austrian economists tend to be critical of the equilibrium models which fill the textbooks. While conceding that these models and the associated procedure of comparative static analysis provide insights into the likely reactions of markets to exogenous shocks like higher sales taxes, Austrian economists believe that these models of conventional textbooks are deficient because, as noted above, they neglect the role of enterprise.

1.3 The emergence of enterprise

While the decision to strike out on new business ventures is made by individuals, several writers have attempted to analyse the social and economic conditions which stimulate entrepreneurship.

The first is the legal framework. Although the private ownership of assets is now the norm, this was not always the case. In medieval Europe, property rights were far more complex. Villages normally farmed their lands cooperatively in large fields (the two-field or three-field systems), each family having a certain share of the strips in each field. Serfs were bound to the land, and the wealth of the nobility was measured by the size of their estates. These estates, however, were not usually theirs to buy and sell, for they were hereditary fiefs to be held in perpetuity by the grace of God and the monarch. Eventually this feudal system of quasi-collective ownership of land began to move over to private ownership, with peasant households beginning to buy and sell farms as if they were private property (MacFarlane, 1978). Other peasants migrated to areas in which the writ of the feudal lords did not run – the 'wastes' – so that their farmsteads were effectively private property. Others again moved to the towns where feudal obligations were weaker and market relationships were more prevalent. Finally, the great fields of feudal Europe were 'enclosed' into private farms and the transition from feudal property rights to private ownership was complete.

The importance of this change in property rights is that it was essential for the development of a market economy and for the exercise of enterprise. This is because enterprise is undertaken primarily in pursuit of private gain. If the benefits of the action are not to be retained by its initiator but are to be dispersed among a group, then it is unlikely that individual enterprise will be forthcoming.

It has also been argued that a major factor in the emergence of enterprise is the prevailing attitude to work and saving. Earlier this century, historians like R. H. Tawney and sociologists like Max Weber debated the contribution which Protestantism might have made to the emergence of capitalism by encouraging thrift and hard work. The basic evidence for such a connection is the strong link between the Reformation and the more commercially developed areas of Europe like the Low Countries and Britain.

Although the early idea of a simple relationship between Protestantism and business success is now discredited, it is clear that Quakers and Congregationalists were overrepresented among the early entrepreneurs of the English commercial and industrial revolutions. What is not so clear is the causal relationships at work: although the attitudes of these groups to work and thrift may well have helped them, it is also possible that they were driven into business by the legal disabilities which faced them in other walks of life such as public office (Mathias, 1969, p. 159). More generally, many entrepreneurs have been drawn from disadvantaged minority groups which find themselves on the margins of a society, sometimes as a result of migration (Bannock and Doran, 1978). Examples include the Jewish- and Chinese-Americans.

Alongside the entrepreneurs from marginal groups are those born into positions of wealth and influence (Westergaard and Resler, 1975). Moreover, certain social groups carry traditions of entrepreneurship which provide role-models for the younger generation. Thus the sons and daughters of business people are more likely to enter business themselves than the population at large (Mokry, 1988, p. 17). Other important factors may be the values imparted to children by upbringing (McClelland, 1961). Roberts and Wainer (1971), for instance, claim to have found a relationship between religion, home circumstances and enterprise, though their conclusion must remain tentative due to the small sample of entrepreneurs investigated.

The personal qualities which successful entrepreneurs possess have also attracted attention. These are difficult to identify, though successful entrepreneurs seem to have imagination, knowledge, foresight and the ability to perceive new opportunities. They also have skills in negotiation, organisation, delegation and quality control (Casson, 1982). Some would add the personal qualities of self-confidence, perseverance and 'guts'. The economist Israel Kirzner, who has taken a special interest in this topic, has identified such factors as a 'restive temperament, a thirst for adventure, ambition and imagination'. At the same time, and less flatteringly, the entrepreneur has been labelled an 'eccentric', 'an egotist' and even someone who 'needs to be slightly nutty' (Kirzner *et al.*, 1980).

These separate factors are of course difficult to isolate, and in general researchers have had little success in obtaining conclusive evidence on the sources of enterprise. As the historian Peter Mathias in his study of British industrialisation concludes: 'It is difficult to make any valid generalisations about the social origins of the entrepreneurs. They arrived from every social class and from all parts of the country' (Mathias, 1969, p. 156).

Just as social attitudes can encourage enterprise, they may also discourage it. Although part of Britain's failure in the late nineteenth century to adopt new technologies, like the open-hearth process in steelmaking or the Solvay method of alkaline production, may have been no more than a rational response to low anticipated profits (McCloskey 1981), it has also been argued that in Victorian Britain there was a hostility to industrialism. For example, Wiener (1981) has linked

Britain's relative economic decline to a cultural preference for the life of the gentleman as against the world of business. Again McKendrick (Kirzner *et al.*, 1980, p. 49) has drawn attention to the frequent portrayal in contemporary literature of the entrepreneur as greedy and cold-hearted. This prejudice, some argue, continues to this day in Britain in the forms of an education system which favours the humanities and a widespread preference for careers in the professions rather than business.

A final factor stimulating the emergence of enterprise is naturally the rewards which it can bring, that is, profit. Many economists stress the connection between profit and enterprise, and in the 1980s enterprise-conscious governments in the United Kingdom and the United States have taken steps to raise the rewards to entrepreneurship by reducing rates of taxation upon both companies and individuals. Others, however, have at times toyed with the idea that non-pecuniary rewards should be sufficient to encourage enterprise: for example, in the late nineteenth century Professor Alfred Marshall of Cambridge, England speculated on the possibility of public honours for entrepreneurs, and during the 1960s the British government instituted a system of Queen's Awards for Industry for achievement in the fields of exports and technology. However, experience in the Communist countries, which rely heavily upon appeals to patriotic or ideological sentiments to raise the rate of economic progress, indicates that such methods have but limited value.

Critics of the idea of enterprise sometimes argue that while it might have applied to business life in the nineteenth century, the notion of entrepreneurship is of little relevance today. The argument is that the concept of the self-made man is out of place in the modern economy which is dominated by large corporations in which decisions are made by professional, salaried managers working in bureaucratic hierarchies. This idea has, however, been vigorously contested. Many economists maintain that enterprise is still required in the direction of large firms as it is in the control of small ones for the simple reason that change and uncertainty are no respecters of size. To these economists, the growing professionalism of management is simply a sign of the increasing complexity of business affairs. Many would also point to the example of Japan, where corporate size and enterprise seem to be positively rather than inversely related.

The idea that enterprise has been superseded by bureaucracy in the modern economy has been extended to the suggestion that modern corporations now pursue goals other than profit maximisation. These alternative goals have included sales–revenue maximisation (Baumol, 1959) and growth (Marris, 1964). The rationale for these hypotheses lies in the fact that the ownership of large firms is vested not in identifiable individuals but in myriads of small shareholders – none of whom, it is argued, can exercise control over management. Management therefore may be as well served by pursuing non-profit goals as by making profit. This view, however, often neglects the point that the wealth and incomes of managers and directors are often linked to the performance of the corporations they control through share ownership, share options or profit-related bonuses. Although possibly small in relation to the total number of shares issued, such holdings are usually large in relation to the total wealth of the directors themselves. Managers may thus have a direct interest in the maximisation of profits and hence in the entrepreneurial success of the corporation. Another objection is that the power of shareholders is still very real. The ultimate sanction of the small investor who is discontented with management is to sell his or her shares. Such a move would tend to depress the value of the company's shares, rendering it vulnerable to takeover by new management.

The debate on the continued existence of enterprise in the modern corporation is important because of its implications for public policy. Those economists who argue that business companies – whatever their size – still display enterprise are able to draw a sharp distinction between public and private provision. They argue that state agencies are inherently less efficient in the provision of services because there is no profit to act as an incentive for the seeking out of new forms of service or methods of delivery. State bureaucrats are more likely to follow established procedures than to be dynamic risk-takers (Dunsire *et al.*, 1988). On the other hand, if it were accepted that business firms had somehow dispensed with enterprise, then the distinctiveness of the private sector would disappear and there could be no economic objection to full state control. These debates clearly underlie current policy issues such as Britain's programme of turning state-owned businesses over to private hands in pursuit of greater efficiency.

A final issue in the analysis of entrepreneurship is the question of the relationship between enterprise and capital. In the Marxist tradition, the entrepreneur and the capitalist are one – no distinction is made. By contrast, other economists – particularly those of the Austrian school – stress the special decision-making qualities of the entrepreneur and argue that this, rather than the ownership of capital, is the distinguishing feature of the entrepreneur. Although they recognise that entrepreneurs need capital to begin in business, they maintain that the provision of capital can be separated from the provision of enterprise. In practice, of course, the work of persuading the owners of capital to subscribe to a new and uncertain venture is not always easy and there can be no doubt that an entrepreneur with wealth of his or her own is at an advantage. While Marxists may obscure an important distinction between enterprise and capital, others may equally underplay the contribution which wealth can make to becoming an entrepreneur.

1.4   Profit trends

Many economists would hold that, whatever the social and institutional background, the surest sign of enterprise is the making of profit. This section accordingly examines recent trends in profit in the United States and Britain. First, however, it is necessary to examine the procedures for assessing and recording levels of profit.

Profit is distinguished from other rewards to factors of production in that it is non-contractual. While rent, interest and salaries are normally specified in advance of payment, profit can be computed only when the transactions are complete. It is essentially the residual left over when costs of production have been met, and is set out in a company's profit and loss account. There are, however, several ways in which profits may be presented, and Table 1.1 shows, from the accounts of British Airways (BA) for 1987–8, the distinctions between (i) operating profit, (ii) profits on ordinary activities before tax and interest, (iii) profit on ordinary activities after interest but before taxation, (iv) profit after tax, (v) profit after extraordinary items and (vi) retained profits (after payment of dividends to shareholders).

Table 1.1   British Airways PLC 1987–8 Group Profit and Loss Accounts (Summary)

	£m
Turnover	3,756
Operating expenditure	3,520
Operating surplus (i)	236
Other income	12
Profit before interest payable and taxation (ii)	248
Interest payable (and similar charges)	(20)
Profit on ordinary activities before taxation (iii)	228
Taxation and minority interests	(77)
Profit for the year after taxation (iv)	151
Extraordinary items	nil
Profit after extraordinary items (v)	151
Dividends	(50)
Retained profit for the year (vi)	101

Source: British Airways Annual Report and Accounts 1988

Many analysts proceed to relate one or more of these definitions of profits to capital employed. For example, in 1987 British Airways' profit on ordinary activities before tax and interest as a percentage of net capital employed (including loans) was 16.7 per cent. In general terms, the formula for the rate of profit is

$$Pt = (Rt - Ct)/Kt$$

where P is profit, R is revenue, C is cost and K is capital employed, all in period t.

Tax and interest payments are itemised in company accounts since investors are concerned with profit both before and after interest and tax. Profit before tax and interest conveys an impression of the profitability of the company's operations, while profit after interest and tax shows how much money is available for the payment of dividends and for reinvestment without reducing the net worth of the business. These alternative ways of presenting profit can give widely differing results. For example, given identical profits and tax liabilities, a company which was financed largely by borrowing (one which was 'highly geared') would have a lower figure for profit after tax and interest than one with little loan finance. In 1987–8, partly because of the acquisition of the UK airline British Caledonian, British Airways' gearing rose considerably. Outstanding loans increased from £297 million to £848 million. The full impact on profit did not show until the following year.

In compiling these figures, problems arise in relation to revenue, cost, profit and capital. With regard to revenue, it is conventional to focus upon normal trading income and to exclude money raised from the sale of assets like land and buildings, these being classed separately in a company's accounts as 'extraordinary items'. With regard to cost, decisions again have to be made over which items are to be included in the profit and loss statement. It is conventional to include the costs of resources directly associated with production such as the labour involved in the project and the materials used. Thus an airline, when computing the cost of a particular service, would include the costs of staff, fuel and similar items which may be termed the 'direct costs' or 'variable costs' of production; for BA in 1987–8 this amounted to £3,413 million. The cost of long-lived capital items like the aeroplanes is also included even though such a cost only recurs at infrequent intervals. The convention is to count a proportion of the value of these assets as a cost of production every year. This is known as a 'depreciation allowance', and there are several different ways of computing such figures, ranging from counting the entire value of the asset in its first year of operation to averaging the depreciation charge at a fixed rate over a number of years. Thus the cost to an airline of running a service with a single plane for a year might be counted as, perhaps, one-fifteenth of the purchase price of the plane for each of the first fifteen years of the service. After that, the plane would be counted as being fully depreciated or 'fully written down' and its use would no longer appear as a cost. British Airways depreciates its fleet assets at rates calculated to write down their cost or valuation to an estimated residual value over the course of their planned operational lives (usually twelve to sixteen years).

Conventions like these have attracted criticism from economists who would prefer to see the use of assets costed at rates which reflect not a mechanical formula but the actual loss in value which the asset suffers. For example, a new aeroplane may lose in its first year of operation not one-fifteenth of its value but 25 per cent or more. Conversely, in times of rapid inflation the cost of using a capital asset should not, they argue, be linked to its purchase price perhaps eight years before, but to the current price of similar equipment. This could of course be much higher. In other words, the argument is that 'replacement' costs rather than 'historic' costs should be used in the calculation of depreciation charges. These ideas are of course counsels of perfection which accountants feel neither able nor willing to implement in full.

Further problems attend the calculation of profit itself. For the accountant, profit is simply the residual after the computation of costs and revenues. For the economist, however, such a definition ignores the costs of resources which, though they appear to be free, nevertheless impose costs on the user. These costs normally relate to resources which are owned and which do not therefore have to be paid for. Let us take the example of a family which owns a corner store. Let us assume that they have financed the purchase of the shop and its inventories with their savings and that they serve behind the counter themselves. For such a business, the accounts would show profit as being the difference between sales (say £80,000) and expenses like light, heat and replacement stock (say £35,000). Profit would thus be £45,000. An economist, however, might note the potential rental value of the shop (perhaps £6,000), the interest which the savings could have earned on deposit in a bank (say £4,000) and the fact that the members of the family could have gone out to work and earned (perhaps £15,000). All these sources of revenue from the family's land, capital and labour – a grand total of £25,000 – are forgone in running the shop. Economists would class these forgone earnings as opportunity costs, arguing that although no money changes hands these costs are no less real. The implication of the economists' logic is that the shop's true profit is not £45,000 but £45,000 less £25,000, i.e. £20,000. Moreover, since opportunity costs are excluded from most business accounts, those accounts generally overstate profits. Again, these ideas are counsels of perfection which rely upon accurate foresight about, in the example of the corner store, the level of rents, the probability of gaining employment and interest rates. Estimates of opportunity costs are therefore conjectural, and accountants prefer to use proven, receipted costs when drawing up business accounts.

Despite the difficulties in compiling and interpreting reports of company profits, economists and statisticians keep records of profit trends in most countries. Their work reveals that during the 1960s and 1970s, both the rate of profit and the share of profit in national income declined in most advanced industrial countries, Japan included. According to estimates by Armstrong, Glynn and Harrison (1984) the share of profits in 1973 as a proportion of the levels in the best post-war year was 74 per cent in the United States, 77 per cent in Europe and 78 per cent in Japan. In the seven major Western industrial countries, the rate of profit fell by about one-fifth in this period and the share of business profits in national income, which had peaked at an average of 23 per cent in the early 1960s, had fallen to 19.9 per cent by 1973. Although these trends were often moderated by taxation policies so the post-tax profits fell less steeply than their pre-tax counterparts, the overall trend was plainly downward.

The oil price hikes of 1973 and 1979 and the stagflation of the 1970s played further havoc with profitability, as did the recession of 1979–82. In Britain in the early 1980s exporters were caught between domestic inflation and a soaring exchange rate as sterling appreciated by 21 per cent. Partly in consequence, average post-tax returns in non-oil industries dropped to a calamitous 2.9 per cent in 1981. In such circumstances it was more rewarding for firms to place money on deposit with a bank than to invest it in plant and equipment. American business suffered from similar pressures, with corporate profits after tax falling to historic lows between 1980 and 1982. (See Figures 1.1 and 1.2.)

The damaging effects on market economies of this 'profits crisis' could not escape from public concern for long. As James Callaghan, Britain's Labour Prime Minister, put it bluntly, 'Today's profits must be tomorrow's jobs' (*Financial Times*, 17 May 1976). At the turn of the decade, when Ronald Reagan and Margaret Thatcher took office in their respective countries, the need to restore profitability moved decisively up the political and economic agenda.

1.5 Conclusion

As world markets become increasingly competitive, demanding more effort and ingenuity from business people, enterprise and the pursuit of profit gain in importance. On the one hand the rewards of successful

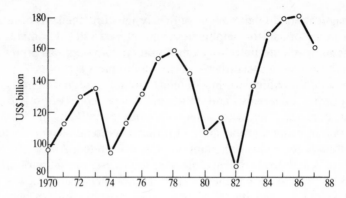

Figure 1.1 US corporate profits after tax with IVA and CCADJ, 1970 (Source: Datastream)

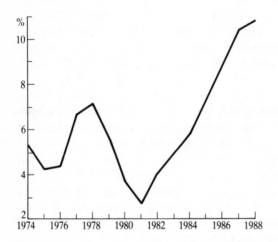

Figure 1.2 UK companies' net rates of return on capital (* estimate) (Source: *Economic Progress Report*, HM Treasury, June 1989)

entrepreneurship are evident in the prosperity of Japan and the 'little dragons' of Asia. On the other, the poverty and indebtedness which result from a failure to be competitive can be seen in many other countries. These pressures have led the established industrial economies of Europe and North America and many developing countries, as well as former Communist states, to step up their reliance upon market forces and enterprise to generate wealth and employment. This trend has been particularly evident in the United States and the United Kingdom, where President Reagan and Prime Minister Thatcher began to revitalise their nations' economies by stimulating entrepreneurship.

In the context of these trends, economics teaching displays a rather curious feature. While many economics texts acknowledge in passing the importance of the entrepreneur in the market economy, the focus of interest in such books falls squarely upon the idea of equilibrium. The net effect is a relative neglect of enterprise.

The critical point is that this neglect is by no means inevitable. The theories of profit and enterprise contained in the typical contemporary textbook are not the only ones which are available. Quite the reverse – economists have developed a multiplicity of perspectives on these topics. The standard textbooks, however, make little or no allusion to this diversity of approaches. While there are exceptions (Stead and Wisniewski, 1988), the general pattern is for such works to confine themselves to an approach which gives little prominence to enterprise – neoclassical economics.

Perhaps the principal issue over which supporters of the different theories of profit and enterprise divide is that of the contribution of profit to the well-being of society at large. At one extreme, profit is seen as the result of exploitation either by oppressive capitalists or rapacious monopolists; at the other, it is portrayed as a beneficent instrument for stimulating the technological advances and commercial innovations which bring new and cheaper products to the consumer. These differing attitudes to profit are manifest in conflicting views over the balance which should be struck between the market and the state in economic affairs. The debates here relate to issues like the optimum extent of regulation, state ownership of industry, tax levels and tariffs. The question of the function of profit and enterprise is thus no mere academic discussion: it is one of the foremost economic issues today in the United States, the United Kingdom and other Western nations – and even, more surprisingly, in the Communist states.

Further reading

To confirm the view that economics texts underemphasise profit and enterprise, it would clearly be useful to browse through a sample. A good starting-point is Begg, Fischer and Dornbusch (1987).

On the contribution of enterprise to the success of Japan, see Morita *et al.* (1987). For a good general introduction to the debate on profit and enterprise, see Kirzner *et al.* (1980). For the Austrian view of the nature of enterprise, Kirzner (1973, ch. 1) and Shand (1984) are good introductions, while Loasby (1982) provides a short comparative study of different economic perspectives on entrepreneurship. With regard to the emergence of enterprise, MacFarlane (1978) offers a penetrating insight into the development of market relationships in medieval England, while Weber (1976) and Tawney (1936) are of course the classic works on the relationship between Protestantism and capitalism. Mathias (1969, pp. 151–65) examines the origin of early British entrepreneurs; Wiener (1981) looks at the decline of enterprise in Great Britain during the nineteenth and twentieth centuries. McClelland (1961) discusses the psychological attributes of entrepreneurs, Casson (1982) offers a theory which includes economic and sociological factors, and Jacobs (1985) stresses the importance of an information-rich urban environment in stimulating new business. Mokry (1988, ch. 2) provides a short overview. For an introduction to profit from a financial point of view, see Wood (1975). Glynn and Sutcliffe (1972), Panic and Close (1973) and King (1975) discuss the decline in profit in the United Kingdom during the 1960s and 1970s. Interesting on the 'British disease' is Allen (1979).

2
Profit and enterprise before Adam Smith

This chapter traces the evolution of conceptions of profit and enterprise from the earliest times to the publication of Adam Smith's *The Wealth of Nations* in 1776. This span of time includes a watershed in ideas about profit. Prior to the sixteenth century, the world was seen primarily in terms of metaphysical principles, and trading at profit was looked upon as verging on the immoral. With the Reformation, however, these attitudes – at least in Europe – underwent substantial change. Although religious and moral precepts continued to permeate daily life, the pursuit of profit was no longer held in disdain. At the same time, the abandonment of traditional principles forced European thinkers to develop new approaches to profit and enterprise; this chapter reviews the work on this issue of the first economists of modern times – the mercantilists and the physiocrats. A crucial question was the relationship between profit-seeking and the public good; only gradually, as the chapter shows, were European economists reconciled to the idea that the entrepreneur could bring benefits to other members of society as well as to himself.

2.1   Profit and enterprise in antiquity and the Middle Ages

The pursuit of material gain is an enduring theme of human existence. For example, when offered a wish by Dionysus, King Midas requested the power to turn all he touched to gold, while one of the greatest sagas of northern Europe concerns the pursuit of the gold of the Niebelung. The recurrence of such themes in myth and fable is nevertheless no indication that the pursuit of profit through trade was thought of in the same ways in former times as now. Indeed, the differences are unmistakable. Attitudes to work, enterprise and profit in the great traditional civilisations of the past, from Central America to the Far East (including medieval Christendom) were dictated by the religious or metaphysical principles which permeated every aspect of daily life in those societies. While these principles differed widely in many respects, they contained a common core which has been termed the 'eternal philosophy' (Coomarawami, 1977, p. 43) of traditional peoples everywhere. Simply stated, it is the view that true reality is to be found not in the material world but on a higher plane. Worldly wealth is therefore a mirage and those who quest for it are chasing a shadow. Thus Midas' wish becomes a curse and the pursuers of the gold of the Niebelung are all murdered.

The implication of this philosophy in the traditional civilisations was broadly that a person's livelihood – whether farming or kingship – was a divinely ordained vocation. People were thus born into (or, less often, chose) a station in life which was to be occupied for life. Crafts and professions were not mere jobs so much as destinies to be fulfilled. Moreover, these vocations were imbued with spiritual meaning, through which men and women could find their ways to salvation or enlightenment: 'It is by intense devotion to his own vocation that Everyman attains perfection' the *Bhagavad Gita* tells us (Coomarawami, 1977, p. 47). The best-known manifestation of these ideas is of course the caste system of Hindu India, which divided the populace into priests, rulers, merchants and workers. It is nevertheless of significance that these divisions run parallel to the classes in Plato's *Republic*, while the parson in Chaucer's *Canterbury Tales* remarked 'God has ordained that some folk should be more high in estate and in some degree, and some folk more low, and that everyone should be served in his estate and in his degree.'

The antithesis between such attitudes and profit-seeking can be seen in three ways. First, enterprise creates the possibility that a person can escape his ordained station in life and rise into a different class. Second, profit-seeking can indicate a preoccupation with the riches of this world, whereas traditional doctrine teaches that true riches – enlightenment or salvation – are to be found elsewhere. Although it was necessary in the view of the philosophers of ancient times to have sufficient wealth, the pursuit of money for its own sake was the sin of avarice. Third, and perhaps most important, enterprise opens up the possibility that traditional crafts might be destroyed by imports or by new techniques of production.

The traditional attitude to trade, enterprise and profit is captured in this passage from Aristotle's *Politics*. The assumption that economic life is a zero-sum game is plain:

There are two sorts of wealth-getting, as I have said; one is a part of household management, the other is retail trade: the former is necessary and honourable, while that which consists in exchange is justly censured; for it is unnatural, and a mode by which men gain from one another. The most hated sort is usury, which makes a gain out of money itself. (Barnes, 1985, p. 1997)

Usury was the charging of interest on loans, and was held to be morally wrong. Because borrowing was often induced by distress such as a crop failure, it was felt that to take advantage of such circumstances was unjust.

The result of these traditional principles was that economic behaviour was – like other aspects of life – governed by moral and social considerations: economics was subordinate to ethical and political precepts. The prime examples are the notions of the 'Just Price' and the 'Just Wage' which were first discussed by early Hebrew writers. The Just Price was one which reflected, but did not exceed, production costs. In charging the Just Price, the vendor was in no way exploiting the buyer. Similarly, the Just Wage was one which did not reduce the hired workman to poverty but which allowed him to maintain a standard of living commensurate with his station. Clearly the two principles were interdependent: products made by labour which was paid the Just Wage should sell for a Just Price. Thus a lawyer should sell his labour at a higher rate than a locksmith because of his higher social status, but neither should profiteer: 'To sell a thing dearer or to buy it cheaper than it is worth is itself unjust and illicit' (Aquinas, *Summa Theologica*, cited in Ekelund and Hebert, 1975, p. 27).

These ideas were broadly endorsed by the philosophers of early and medieval Europe, notably St Augustine and the later schoolmen like Duns Scotus (d.1308). They examined trade and finance in the light of both Christian teaching and the intellectual heritage of the ancient world. The result was a set of attitudes in which reason and faith, philosophy and religion were inseparable. These attitudes were notably antipathetic to trade, enterprise and finance: 'Trade can scarcely, if ever, be pleasing to God' ran one of the canons of the Church, while in *The Inferno*, Dante assigns usurers along with blasphemers and sodomites to 'a bleak and sandy plain rained upon by great flakes of flame'!

Daily life in medieval Europe was influenced by these attitudes in two major respects. First, craft production was regulated by guilds. These organisations ensured the quality of production and controlled prices. The effect was that competition between craftsmen was minimised. Second, usury by Christians (though not by Jews) was prohibited in many states. This made it difficult for entrepreneurs to raise capital by borrowing.

Partly in consequence of such practices, economic innovation in medieval Europe was restricted for several centuries. Nevertheless, markets and commerce began to grow. In north-west Europe, particularly the Low Countries and England, cloth production expanded. Land was enclosed for sheep-farming, thus ending traditional common grazing rights. In consequence, a class of landless labourers began to appear. As these workers found employment, often in the towns, the separation of different factors of production (land, labour and capital) became more apparent than in feudal times. To the south, Venice and the other Italian cities began to trade extensively with the East for spices, silks and other luxuries, and banking and other financial institutions evolved to finance these trading ventures. One innovation was the *colleganza*, in which investors lent funds to a trader. This was an early example of the separation of entrepreneurship from the provision of capital. To handle more complex commercial relationships, new laws and new methods of accounting, notably double-entry bookkeeping, also developed.

Parallel with these economic and social changes came intellectual developments which had the most profound consequences for attitudes towards profit and enterprise. These changes centred upon the Reformation which began in the sixteenth century. The Protestants, led by Luther, Zwingli and Calvin, rejected the notion that salvation could only be found through the ministry of the Church. They held, rather, that individuals could find salvation through their own faith. This led to a subtle but important shift in wider attitudes: the focus of European thought moved away from the individual conceived as standing at the centre of a network of social relationships and obligations, and towards the idea that the individual was responsible before God and his own conscience for his own destiny. Thus Protestantism undermined the principles upon which the medieval economy was based: if the intercession of the Church was no longer needed, it was difficult to assert that guilds and hereditary social positions were essential either. Indeed, for the Calvinist churches, success in a person's freely chosen occupation came to be looked upon as a sign of God's blessing. To most Protestants, there was therefore no conflict between competition, enterprise and the pursuit of wealth through commerce on the one hand and religious conviction on the other. In enjoining frugality and hard work, moreover, Protestantism encouraged habits which aided business. Many of these attitudes were, in time, adopted by the Roman Catholic Church. In one of the most remarkable intellectual changes in history, Western Christianity, having condemned the pursuit of profit in business for a millennium, came to accept and legitimise the practice.

In terms of political philosophy, the focus of European thought underwent a similar transformation, with attention moving from a concern with the just relationship between buyer and seller to the autonomous individual. The idea of individual, inalienable rights – which the English political philosopher John Locke identified as the 'right to life, liberty and property' – played an important role in the American and French Revolutions of the late eighteenth century.

It is nevertheless important not to exaggerate the speed with which these new moral, political and social values were assimilated. Changes in attitudes occurred only slowly and hesitatingly, the pace varying from place to place. For example, in 1644 in Boston, Massachusetts, the Puritan merchant Robert Keayne could still be successfully prosecuted for usury. Keayne's defence was not that usury was acceptable, but that he had been falsely accused. Keayne indeed opposed usury: his outlook was still 'a balance as heavily weighted with medieval business ethics as with Protestant worldly asceticism' (Bailyn (ed.), 1964, p. xi).

In addition to the Reformation, a second factor influencing religious, social and economic attitudes was the rise of science. Following the work of the Polish astronomer Nicolaus Copernicus (1473–1543), the physical universe came to be understood as obeying certain laws which could be described by observation and experiment. This was exemplified by the work of Sir Isaac Newton (1642–1727), whose mathematically formulated laws of motion were published in 1687. This scientific approach to nature had a significant effect upon the treatment of social and economic phenomena. It served to undermine the notion that the world was shaped by an omnipotent, intervening Deity. By extension, this approach introduced the possibility that economic and social affairs could be governed by similar natural laws, which could likewise be used to describe and predict events. This led, for example, to John Locke's view that natural laws governed such matters as the value of coins and the rate of interest. This approach seemed to suggest that natural laws (rather than moral concepts such as the Just Price) should govern prices and other economic matters. It also seemed to follow that human action which attempted to defy those laws was doomed to fail. For thinkers of the seventeenth and eighteenth centuries, the discovery of these social and economic laws became an important task.

2.2   Mercantilism

From the sixteenth to the mid-eighteenth century there was, especially in Britain and France, a flood of pamphlets on economic questions. In part this outpouring was prompted by the dissolution of traditional, feudal economic institutions as more and more goods were produced for sale at a profit. It also represented an effort to develop a framework of understanding which could replace the ideas of the medieval schoolmen and which was in some way consistent with the new philosophies of natural laws and inalienable individual rights. Many of these writings explored the relationship between individual and public welfare and the related question of the optimum level of state intervention in markets – enduring themes in the debate about the nature and role of profit and enterprise.

In these writings no single idea can be found which embraces all contributions: there was no coherent 'school of thought'. Nevertheless certain themes can be discerned, and Adam Smith coined the term 'mercantilism' to describe the general approach. Like the view of the ancient Greeks, mercantilism in its crudest form is a zero-sum interpretation of economic affairs; as the French essayist Michel de Montaigne wrote in 1580, 'The profit of one man is the damage of another . . . No man profiteth but by the loss of others' (Oser, 1970, p. 10).

Mercantilism and trade

At that time, the size of a nation's money supply was broadly related to the stock of bullion, and the mercantilists reasoned that the more bullion a nation possessed, the greater would be the total purchasing power and thus the higher would be the level of production and prosperity. It followed that internal trade could not increase national wealth since no extra bullion was thereby acquired. Also, mercantilists argued that domestic trade in aggregate merely transformed inputs into outputs of the same value. The argument was that since the value of production was simply the sum of the costs of production, no net surplus was created. It followed that profit or gain by any trader must imply a loss for someone else.

The mercantilists, sharing with the medieval schoolmen a distrust of merchants, anticipated a direct conflict of interest between private profit-seeking and the public good. Thus Bernard de Mandeville (1670?–1733) and Charles Davenant (1656–1714) claimed that state regulation of business was essential to protect the commonwealth from individual avarice. Profit-seeking could be ruinous to a nation unless directed along 'suitable channels' by the dextrous management of government. Although a few mercantilists, like Antoyne de Monchretien in 1615 in his *Traicte de l'oeconomie politique*, argued of merchants that 'one ought to allow them the love and collection of profit' (Routh, 1975, p. 33), others would have approved of the policy of Colbert, Louis XIV's minister of finance from 1661 to 1683, who brought many aspects of trade and production in France under state control (Oser, 1970, p. 20).

The mercantilist analysis carried rather different implications for overseas trade, for here they saw no conflict between the activities of a nation's merchants and the public good. Since they understood that one country's export surplus was some other country's trade deficit, the mercantilists argued that export surpluses and the resultant inflows of bullion ought to be promoted. In accordance with these tenets, from the sixteenth century to the eighteenth century European governments actively regulated trade so as to maximise net exports. Britain instituted the well-known Navigation Acts in 1651 and 1660 which stipulated that imports into England or its colonies could only be shipped in English or colonial ships or those of the country of origin. England's trade was thus effectively reserved for the English merchant fleet. Furthermore foreign imports were restricted and colonial manufacturing was curbed to favour English suppliers. At the same time, the British government promoted agriculture, mining and industry with subsidies and tariffs.

Mercantilism and value

Attitudes to the source and nature of value have had an important bearing on the debate in economics about profit and enterprise. Central to this has been the idea that labour, whether directly employed or 'embodied' in tools, plant and machinery (capital), is the source of all value. Although usually associated with the classical economists like David Ricardo (Chapter 3) and Karl Marx (Chapter 5), the antecedents of this idea can be found in mercantilist writings.

The need for an explanation of value was created by the abandonment of the schoolmen's belief that prices should be just sufficient to provide producers with adequate incomes. This need the mercantilists attempted to meet. In mercantilist theories – as well as in later classical writings – the distinction was commonly made between the observed 'exchange' (or market) value of a commodity and its 'natural' value. The former was seen as changing from day to day, whereas the latter was perceived as being the underlying average to which price tended to gravitate. While modern economists explain all price movements by reference to consumers' willingness to buy and the readiness of producers to supply, mercantilist writers tended to see these forces as operating only upon exchange value. (An interesting exception here is Etienne de Condillac (1714–80), who introduced a subjective approach to value, thus foreshadowing late-nineteenth-century price theory.) For most mercantilists, supply and demand could not provide a satisfactory explanation of long-term natural value. This they believed to be determined by a more fundamental force, namely a commodity's cost of production. For many, this was interpreted to mean the labour inputs required for production of any given commodity.

In the writings of Sir William Petty (1623–87), the role of labour in value is well developed. Petty seems to have been one of the first to attempt to explore in a systematic fashion the determinants of value and income determination from the assumption that land and labour are the sources of production. To appreciate why Petty and subsequent writers chose to focus upon land and labour as the vital inputs in the creation of value, it is necessary to remember that before the Industrial Revolution Europe was predominantly agricultural and production was labour-intensive. Labour was especially important because, although land was essential to production, the benefits of nature could only be tapped by human effort. Also, capital at this time largely took the form of stocks of goods for sale or work-in-progress – indeed, the word 'stock' was often used instead of 'capital' until well into the nineteenth century. Capital was thus predominantly working capital rather than fixed plant and equipment. Since goods were produced primarily by labour, it appeared a simple step to reason that capital was merely 'embodied' or indirect labour, i.e. that it was the product of past labour. It thus followed that all output could be viewed as the product of direct or indirect labour.

Petty's view was that the natural value of a commodity was related to the labour time involved in its supply. Thus the value of a bushel of corn would in general be equal to that of an ounce of silver if the labour necessary to produce them was the same. If it were not, it would pay to shift labour between silver and corn production depending on the output of each per unit of time.

Mercantilism and wages, profit and interest

Those mercantilists who suggested that labour time entered into the determination of prices recognised that the cost of labour would affect the profits of farmers and merchants or 'undertakers'. It was therefore necessary for these writers to comment upon the level of wages. Their theories concentrated upon average levels of real wages (that is, the purchasing power of the average wage) rather than upon wage differentials between occupations. The mercantilists' view of wages, like their perception of value, left its mark upon later classical economics.

The mercantilists' attitude to wages reflects the waning popularity of the traditional doctrine of the Just Wage. Rather than being determined by moral considerations, wages were now perceived as being the outcome of the forces of supply and demand in the short run, with their 'natural' level being set by the underlying forces of population dynamics and the availability of food. The mercantilists argued that average real wage rates would be linked to the cost of subsistence, that is, the commodities necessary for bare existence. If, for example, good harvests made food cheaper, real wages would increase. This, however, would lift the natural constraints on population growth. In the words of Richard Cantillon (1680?–1734), a mercantilist of Irish origin who made his fortune in share and currency speculation in Paris, 'Men would multiply like rats in a barn if they have unlimited means of subsistence' (Cantillon, 1931 edn). It followed that higher real wages would lead within a generation to a larger working population as the greater competition between workers for jobs pushed real wages back down to subsistence level. Were real wages to fall below this level, an analogous mechanism would come into operation: a falling birth-rate and perhaps starvation would lead to a shortage of workers and real wages would rise until their 'natural' level was restored. The corollary of the mercantilists' perception of wages was that there was no prospect of a permanent rise in the living standards of the mass of the population.

In addition, a number of mercantilists concluded that as leisure is pleasant and work arduous, and since workers tend to be indolent by nature, they would be unlikely to work hard if wages were high. Once they had met their subsistence needs, the argument ran, they would cease to exert themselves. It was therefore necessary, if production was to be maximised, that wages be kept low. Certainly there is evidence that workers did not take easily to the discipline of factory life and there are numerous records of factory owners in the eighteenth and early nineteenth centuries complaining of unreliable timekeeping (Pollard, 1968, pp. 189ff). The mercantilists' recommendation that wages be kept low to maintain incentives was, in such a context, not without some logic from an economic standpoint. More generally, success in competitive markets was felt to require low costs and abundant supplies of labour. In Britain Bernard de Mandeville argued that 'in a free nation where Slaves are not allowed of, the surest Wealth consists in a Multitude of laborious poor,' and in France in 1666 Colbert, introduced tax reforms to promote a higher birth-rate.

The gradual abandonment of moral precepts in economic matters in favour of market forces was also evident in the treatment of interest. In 1691 John Locke published a spirited attack on a move in Parliament to restrict interest rates to a range between 4 per cent and 6 per cent. Defending free market outcomes, Locke argued that such measures would not succeed because, if lenders and borrowers were prepared to agree on rates above those limits, transactions would simply be driven underground. Just as importantly, however, Locke asserted that as a matter of *principle* people should be allowed to conduct their affairs without government interference. The proposal to limit interest payments was duly abandoned, and across Europe during the eighteenth century usury laws fell into disuse or were repealed. Locke's contentions that state intervention is at once unlikely to succeed and an unwarranted interference in the affairs of the individual have become axioms of economic liberalism.

Locke's defence of free market outcomes was complemented by the more detailed rationale advanced by Sir William Petty. His view was that interest was justified because it compensated the lender both for waiting for the use of his funds and for the risk of default. Since Petty was primarily concerned with an agricultural economy in which investment was undertaken by landlords, it is understandable that his analysis failed to distinguish clearly between interest as a return to capital and rent as a return from landowning. Despite such shortcomings, Petty's insight was important in drawing attention to the role of interest in rewarding suppliers of loanable funds. His argument in many respects foreshadowed the approach to interest of the nineteenth-century classical economists, especially Nassau Senior.

The failure to distinguish between profit, interest and rent was by no means confined to Sir William Petty. Indeed, an important feature of mercantilism is the absence of any cogent theory of profit which linked it to the role of the entrepreneur. This absence is rendered all the more intriguing by the fact that many mercantilists were themselves merchant adventurers. An exception to this rule was Richard Cantillon, whose *Essai sur la nature du commerce en général* of 1755 contains the earliest and most perceptive observations on the role of enterprise and profit in mercantilist literature. It is worth considering Cantillon's contribution in some detail.

In his own personal dealings, Cantillon displayed all of the qualities of an entrepreneur including an ability to time deals to the maximum advantage. Much of his personal fortune arose from selling shares in the dubious Mississippi Company before speculative interest in the company collapsed in 1720. Cantillon divided the value of a product into payments to landlords, capitalists and labour. Like Petty, Cantillon made no clear distinction in the return to capitalists between interest and profit. Nevertheless, in his general treatment of enterprise it is apparent that he appreciated the importance of profit as an incentive for entrepreneurs (Cantillon was an early user of the term 'entrepreneur'). He also perceived that profit arose from entrepreneurs' adding value to products. To Cantillon, the entrepreneur was the central figure in the operation of a market economy, the risk-taker in trade and production who earned an uncertain residual between revenues and costs which could not be reduced simply to the 'wages of management'. The entrepreneur's return depended, as Cantillon saw it, upon his ability to seek out and exploit business opportunities.

In addition, Cantillon anticipated later discussion in classical and neoclassical economics of 'natural' or 'normal' profit when he argued that as entrepreneurs switched resources between different activities depending on the opportunities for profit-making, so profit would tend to reduce to an average, basic level. He appears, furthermore, to have perceived that this 'normal' profit would be included in long-run costs and thus in prices.

The relationship between the ownership of capital and the receipt of profit is a matter of long-standing debate in economics. Most Marxists and socialists prefer to link profit-making with the ownership of capital, while free market economists are more inclined to associate profit with a separate input called entrepreneurship. Cantillon was careful to distinguish the provision of capital from pure entrepreneurship as such. For example, he noted that in one sense beggars and robbers could be considered to be entrepreneurs in so far as they exploited the opportunities open to them! Though not well developed, Cantillon's ideas were close to those of the later Austrian economists (see Chapter 5). There are differences, in that the notion of normal profit implies that markets attain long-term equilibrium – an idea that not all modern Austrians would accept. Nevertheless, Cantillon's emphasis on the entrepreneur as a risk-taker makes his ideas of great interest in any study of profit and enterprise.

2.3 The physiocrats

The physiocrats, who preferred to call themselves *économistes*, flourished briefly in France during the third quarter of the eighteenth century. Their influence reached its zenith when Louis XVI appointed Turgot, (1721–81), a leading physiocrat, to the office of controller-general in 1774. The physiocrats were arguably the first real 'school' of economists in the sense that they shared a common set of ideas. They were also the first to make extensive use of deductive logic by which conclusions are drawn from basic premises. This method has become the standard approach in economics. For example, modern neoclassical economists start from the premiss that choices are made rationally and go on, by a process of deductive reasoning, to construct theories and hypotheses about employment, prices, output and other variables.

The term 'physiocrat' derives from a Greek word meaning the rule of nature, for the physiocrats believed in the overriding importance in economic affairs of nature and its laws. Impressed by the discovery of physical laws in science, the physiocrats contended that human societies were also subject to laws – the laws of nature. Since they held that nature owed its existence to God, natural laws were but a manifestation of divine law. Given the existence of these laws, they maintained that government policies should work in harmony with them. They thus argued that, left to itself, natural law would govern economic affairs to the benefit of all.

In this scheme of things private property arose out of natural law. The physiocrats accordingly opposed the system of state intervention in private property and market exchange in France which had grown up under the mercantilist era. As far as the physiocrats were concerned, the responsibility of the government was to maintain life, property and freedom of contract. Their maxim *laissez-faire, laissez-passer* – taken up by Adam Smith, who consorted with the physiocrats when he was in Paris in 1766 – remains a rallying cry of free market economists. The only exception to this opposition to state intervention was the physiocrats' support for controls on usury to protect debtors against creditors. This may perhaps be explained by the fact that their patrons, the French nobility, were heavy borrowers!

Besides their attack on regulation, the physiocrats also undertook pioneering work on the subject of economic surplus. The major contribution came from Quesnay (1694–1774), who produced in 1758 his *Tableau Economique* – the first input–output model in economics. This attempted to show the origin of what the physiocrats termed *produit net*. Quesnay defined *produit net* as production over and above supply costs. To investigate its source, he divided the economy into three classes – a method also used by the classical economists and by Karl Marx. Quesnay's classes were the cultivators, the landowners and, last, all other members of society. Only the first of these three, Quesnay argued, was able to produce more than it consumed and this was therefore the only productive class. Thus, whereas the mercantilists had broadly argued that exports were the source of additions to national wealth, Quesnay concluded that wealth originated in land or nature, i.e. agriculture, fishing and mining – the industries which we refer to today as the 'primary sectory'. In this model, landowners – the second class – made an indirect contribution to *produit net* by virtue of their improvements to their estates.

The third group Quesnay labelled the 'sterile' class. It was composed partly of artisans and manufacturers who transformed the raw materials of the primary producers into useful articles. These activities did not, in Quesnay's view, make them productive since the value of their output was matched by their costs of production: there was no contribution to *produit net*. Similarly the other members of the sterile class, the merchants and financiers, added nothing to output since, Quesnay reasoned, all trade (and borrowing and lending) involved the exchange of equal values. Although the physiocrats concluded that such activities were sterile, they did not argue that they should be abandoned since it was clearly necessary that goods should be manufactured and traded and that trade should be financed. Rather they held that, since the sterile class made no net contribution to economic surplus and hence to national wealth, its numbers should be kept to a minimum.

The physiocrats were nevertheless prepared to make one exception to their view that manufacture and trade were sterile. This was the case in which a manufacturer or trader succeeded in making a profit on the goods sold, since this indicated that the value of the goods had been enhanced. The physiocrats held, however, that making profit would be an exceptional event since – like Cantillon – they argued that profits would be swiftly eliminated as competition brought prices down. In so far as profits did exist, the physiocrats interpreted them as being a combination of payments to recover the cost of capital equipment and the salaries of management.

It is clear today that the physiocrats' view of the economic system was seriously flawed. Although it is true that sales revenues are matched by production costs (which then form the incomes of the factors of production), this equality does not mean that the processes of production and distribution are sterile. Indeed, the difficulty with the physiocrats' interpretation of production was that they saw only primary products as having value: the ability of other trades and services to add value to that produce was ignored. The root of the problem was the physiocrats' belief that nature was the sole source of net product. On the land, however, it is not nature alone which produces value but workers and machines working with or exploiting nature to produce commodities; value and net output are not gifts of nature but are created by the application of the human resources of labour, capital and of course enterprise. It is not surprising that the physiocrats' idiosyncratic views did not survive the 1770s.

Few physiocrats devoted much effort to the analysis of profit and enterprise or capital and interest. One who did was Turgot, who drew attention to the role of capital as a productive factor alongside nature. He recognised that in so far as capital was independently productive, a return to capital was justified and necessary. Without a return, he argued, capitalists would withdraw their money, disrupting agricultural production. Turgot portrayed the entrepreneur as essentially a rich person who advanced capital and, importantly, employed wage labour. This approach, which was carried forward by the later classical economists, obscured the distinction that Cantillon had laboured to make between enterprise and profit on the one hand and capital and interest on the other. By contrast, a late convert to physiocratic views, the Abbé Nicolas Baudeau (1730–92), depicted the entrepreneur as a risk-taker and an innovator. For the most part, however, the physiocrats added little to an understanding of enterprise.

The principal legacy of the physiocrats was their concern with the subject of net product. This exercised a powerful influence over the next generation of economists, the classical school. After studying physiocratic ideas, Adam Smith was to reject their central hypothesis that land was the sole source of surplus; yet the approach which Smith adopted in his analysis of wealth creation and his support for free trade owed much to the physiocrats.

2.4 Conclusion

Economic doctrines are invariably propounded within a social and political context. Adam Smith published his *The Wealth of Nations* (1776) when the commercial classes wanted to be free of governmental constraints; Karl Marx wrote *Capital* for an audience of socialists who needed a theory to explain the exploitation of labour in the new industrial cities; and John Maynard Keynes' *General Theory*, which attempted to explain high unemployment, was clearly designed to address the economic problems of the Depression of the 1930s. The economic ideas which achieve prominence at any particular time are those which match the needs and mood of the period. Economic ideas not only shape history, they are products of it.

In Britain and other nations medieval ideas such as the Just Price and the Just Wage and medieval practices such as usury laws and guild restraints on trade and production had, by the eighteenth century, been almost entirely swept away. They had been replaced by new ideas based around the individual and his right to contract freely in markets. Thus at the turn of the seventeenth century, de Boisguilbert (1646–1707) could assert that 'the desire of profit is the spirit of all markets' (quoted in Routh, 1975, p. 60). Similarly, in 1723 Bernard de Mandeville published *The Fable of the Bees*, an influential tract which argued that man's vices – particularly the quest for luxury and material gain – were conducive to the public well-being because they created the best climate for the generation of wealth and employment. Asceticism and puritanical self-denial would, he argued, bring no such benefits. Quite clearly, attitudes to profit-seeking had undergone some changes since the days of Chaucer and Dante.

Unresolved issues nevertheless remained. One was the origin of value, which the physiocrats had failed to explain adequately. Another was the nature and role of profit – which was often confounded with interest, rent and the wages of management in a general notion of 'economic surplus'. The distinctions made by Richard Cantillon were still to be refined. The next major contribution to the debate came from Adam Smith, whose work forms part of the next chapter – which is concerned with classical economics.

Further reading

For an exposition of traditional views on vocations, see Coomarawami (1977), *Traditional Art and Symbolism* (ed. Roger Lipsey), especially the essay 'The philosophy of mediaeval and oriental art', pp. 43–70; or Nasr (1976). Sahlins in his *Stone Age Economics* (1974) and Collis (1975), especially Book III, shed light on the economic practices of traditional societies. Gordon (1964), 'Aristotle and the development of value theory' (*Quarterly Journal of Economics*, vol. 78, February, pp. 115–28) is also useful.

For economic theory and practice in medieval Europe, see Ekelund and Hebert (1975, ch. 2), Schumpeter (1954, ch. 2) and de Roover (1988) 'The concept of the Just Price: theory and economic policy', *Journal of Economic History*, vol. 18, December, pp. 418–34. See Ekelund, Hebert and Tollison (1989) for a critical review of the medieval Church's position on usury. Weber (1976) and Tawney (1936) are again classics on the relationship between Protestantism and the development of a trading, capitalist mentality in late medieval Europe, while an overview is found in Kitch (1967). Kuhn (1962) provides an illuminating history of the changes in attitude to the nature of the world which occurred during the sixteenth and seventeenth centuries. Oser (1970), Ekelund and Hebert (1975), Rima (1978) and Routh (1975) contain informative chapters on mercantilism and the physiocrats. A classic text on mercantilism is Heckscher (1934). Also useful on physiocracy and its links with later classical theory is Niel (1949). Hoselitz (1951) contains a useful overview of early ideas on enterprise. For a good account of Cantillon's economics, see Spengler in Spengler and Allen (eds.) (1960), while Hebert (1985) is also interesting.

3
Classical economics in the age of enterprise

In the eighteenth century the balance of economic power in Britain shifted irreversibly from agriculture to commerce and industry. With major technical advances in steam power, iron smelting and the production of textiles, between 1700 and 1750 the output of industry rose by 7 per cent and exports of manufactures by 76 per cent. Between 1750 and 1770 the output of industry rose by a further 7 per cent and manufactured exports by a huge 80 per cent.

This Industrial Revolution was a product of capitalism and the pursuit of individual gain. New industries were not centrally planned but arose from the spontaneous efforts of individual entrepreneurs. Instead of the mercantilist belief that the state had an active role to play in trade and industry, these new capitalists favoured free markets, the abolition of regulations on commerce and low taxation.

Classical economics is broadly associated with theories and ideas which were in accord with this new spirit of *laissez-faire*. It was a school of thought developed mainly by British economists from the 1770s to the early 1870s. Leading contributors were Adam Smith (1723–90), recognised as the 'founding father' of free market economics, whose work *An Inquiry into the Nature and Causes of The Wealth of Nations* was first published in 1776; Thomas Robert Malthus (1776–1834), often regarded as the first professional economist and best remembered for the pessimistic views on population contained in his book *An Essay on the Principle of Population* which appeared in 1798; David Ricardo (1772–1823), a successful stockbroker turned economist whose *Principles of Political Economy and Taxation* was published in 1817; Jeremy Bentham (1748–1832), whose underlying philosophy that each person seeks his own greatest happiness influenced attitudes towards human nature in classical economics; Nassau Senior (1790–1864), professor of political economy at Oxford and a major contributor to economic and social policy in the first half of the nineteenth century; and John Stuart Mill (1806–73), economist, political scientist and leading logician, the last great economist of the classical school whose main work, *Principles of Political Economy*, was first published in 1848. Also worthy of specific mention is the Frenchman Jean Baptiste Say (1767–1832), who popularised Adam Smith's ideas on the Continent and who made an important contribution to classical economic theory in his own right.

The classical economists sought to explain the nature and workings of the rising commercial and industrial economies of northern Europe and more especially Britain. They were primarily concerned not with individual prices, costs and profits – the subjects of interest to later neoclassical economists – but with the determinants of long-run economic development and income distribution. The seminal thesis of classical economics is Adam Smith's *The Wealth of Nations*, which is primarily concerned with what Smith termed the 'progress of improvement' and what we today refer to as economic growth. Smith set out to determine the optimal conditions for growth through capital accumulation. In doing so he took up themes already introduced by the mercantilists and the physiocrats – the nature of value, income distribution and profit and the role of the state – thus setting the agenda for the subsequent debates of the classical school of economists.

3.1 The classical theory of value

The attitudes of the classical economists to profit were closely related to their views on the creation of value. What determines the value of goods and services had interested earlier writers such as the mercantilists. The classical economists were the first, however, to pursue the issue in a systematic fashion and in so doing they sowed the seeds of both later neoclassical theory and Marxist economics. The classical approach to value is set out in general terms in Smith's *The Wealth of Nations*, though it was subsequently developed and refined by Ricardo.

Smith differentiated between what he saw as the long-run value of a good or service or its 'natural price' and the current or market price. The natural price, he maintained, was the price around which the market price fluctuated. Short-term supply and demand movements would cause the market price to rise or fall but, in the absence of state intervention or other monopoly factors, this price would eventually move back to its natural level due to competition. If the price rose this would lead to an eventual increase in the quantity supplied so the price would decline.

If the price fell initially then some suppliers would leave the market and the price would recover.

Smith went on to reason that the price of a good or service needed to be clearly distinguished from its 'value in use'. While goods without a value in use would not be demanded in the market, it was not their value in use which determined their natural price. He arrived at this conclusion after pointing to what he believed was a paradox in value concerning the difference in the price and usefulness of water and diamonds: 'The things which have the greatest value in use (e.g. water) have frequently little or no value in exchange; and, on the contrary, those which have the greatest value in exchange (e.g. diamonds) have frequently little or no value in use' (Smith, 1979, pp. 131–2). Thus, he reasoned it could not be a good's utility which determined its natural price; it must be something else. Building upon an idea explored initially by mercantilist writers, Smith concluded that the primary determinant of the natural price of a good or service must be its cost of production.

The idea that the natural price is determined wholly or mainly by the cost of production in competitive markets became a central theme of classical theory. There could be exceptions: paintings and works of art fixed in supply clearly derived value from the demand for them in the market and not from their original costs. But in general, for reproducible goods the natural price reflected costs of production because changes in demand triggered changes in supply which restored the natural price. In effect the classical economists were implicitly assuming what we would today refer to as long-run constant cost production, for only when production can vary without causing changes in unit costs will the exchange value be unaffected by demand changes. This is illustrated in

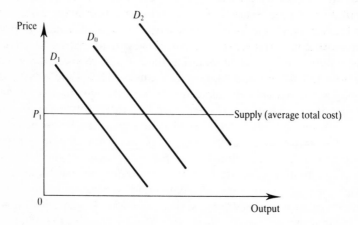

Figure 3.1   Prices and constant cost production

Figure 3.1, where the supply curve is horizontal; shifts in demand from D_0 to D_1 or to D_2 affect output but have no effect on price.

Once costs of production were identified as the primary source of differences in the relative long-run prices of goods and services, the classical economists were keen to discover what determined these costs. Smith and Ricardo looked to labour. Smith was influenced, it seems, by the physiocrats whom he had met in Paris in 1766 while acting as tutor to the son of the Duke of Buccleuch during his continental travels. But whereas the physiocrats argued that only 'nature' was the source of value, thus drawing attention to the importance of agriculture in the economy, Smith was more in tune with the spirit of the Industrial Revolution; a revolution more apparent in Britain than in France. He maintained that both agricultural and industrial labour could create an economic surplus – though he mistakenly believed that workers in services, especially in government, were essentially unproductive because they did not produce a physical product and hence could not create a net product. The idea that a physical product is necessary in the creation of economic surplus related to a labour theory of value and was most easily ditched once value was associated with utility in the neoclassical period – though it lives on in one form or another in Marxist theory and Soviet national income accounting.

Smith and later Ricardo developed a connection initially identified by the mercantilists, notably Petty, between the amount of labour time that went into the production of a commodity and its resultant value in exchange. This connection, Smith argued, was most obvious in 'early and rude' society where: 'It is natural that what is usually the produce of two days' or two hours' labour, should be worth double of what is usually the produce of one day's or one hour's labour' (Smith, 1979, p. 150). For example, he reasoned, if it takes a hunter twice the labour time to kill a beaver as to kill a deer, one beaver will exchange for two deer. Otherwise, it would make sense for the hunter to reallocate his time so as to spend more time hunting the relatively more valuable animal.

Both Smith and Ricardo were aware that this simple link between labour time and value in exchange could only apply in a primitive hunting economy where other factor inputs were negligible. They recognised that in more sophisticated economies land and capital both enter into production, in which case the relationship between labour time and value becomes more complex. Ricardo dismissed the role of land rents in value by reasoning that as land is fixed in supply its rent is 'price determined' and not 'price determining'. But this still left capital as well as labour as a contributor to value. As Ricardo explained, something that takes 100 men two years to produce has the same labour input as a good produced by 200 men in one year, but the former ties up capital for twice as long and therefore requires 'a just compensation for the time the profits were withheld' (Ricardo, 1971, p. 79). This can best be understood if we interpret investment as forgoing current consumption. Ricardo reconciled this with a labour theory of value by expressing capital in terms of the labour time that went into its creation (embodied labour).

In terms of his approach to profit, however, there remains an inconsistency. Like Smith, Ricardo recognised that through competition rates of profit would gravitate to equality across the whole economy. If profit rates are not equal then capital will move from activities with relatively low rates of profit to those where rates of return are relatively high, bringing about a movement to equality. As long as fixed and circulating capital are used in the same proportion in all activities (that is, as long as all industries have the same ratio of capital to labour), then a uniform profit rate is consistent with his labour theory of value. In each sector of the economy the embodied labour in capital has the same proportion to direct labour; thus long-run prices have equal ratios of embodied labour – profits are immaterial. But where there are differing capital structures the strict labour theory of value must be qualified since it implies that profits will vary between industries and firms.

Ricardo never satisfactorily solved this problem (nor did Marx, who built upon Ricardo's theory of value; see Chapter 6). Indeed towards the end of his life, Ricardo decided that an invariable measure of value where there are differing capital structures could not be derived. Yet he retained his faith in the labour theory of value as 'the foundation of value' or as a best approximation. For this reason his approach has been labelled a '93% labour theory of value' (Stigler, 1958). In Ricardo's analysis direct labour time and the labour time embodied in the production of capital are the supply costs which determine long-run exchange value. The long-run relative prices of goods reflect the quantities of direct and embodied labour required for their production. It also follows that profit in Ricardian economics is inversely related to the output produced by labour that is absorbed by wages. Thus in Ricardian economics value and economic surplus are explained together and profits and wages vary inversely.

Through this approach to value Ricardo unwittingly provided support for the notion that the capitalist's profit is the product of exploitation of labour and that high profits necessarily mean low wages. In Europe 'Ricardian socialists' and later Karl Marx capitalised on this argument. If labour determined value, they argued, then profits must be paid out of the product of labour and ultimately, therefore, did not all the economic product including profit belong, by right, to the workers? If this was so, then did it not follow that the capitalist's income was the result of exploiting labour?'

Certainly Ricardo did not see it this way. As far as he was concerned labour and capital cooperated in the act of production; his venom was saved for the landowners who, he argued, without any effort earned rents when food prices rose. Ricardo believed in and defended private property rights, profit-making and capital accumulation. Like Smith, who stressed that capital was directly productive, he never intended that his emphasis upon the role of labour in value should be interpreted as an argument for a radical redistribution of income and wealth in favour of the working class.

After Ricardo, while classical economists for the most part retained a cost-of-production approach to value, there was a perceptible movement towards explaining and defending the role of capital in wealth creation and towards placing capital and labour on an equal footing. This way the later classical economists were able to distance themselves from working-class agitation based around a labour theory of value. There was more emphasis both upon labour and capital as joint inputs in the process of production and upon capital as a factor of production in its own right rather than as embodied labour.

Two economists in particular set out to reduce the importance within classical economics of the Ricardian labour theory. In so doing they laid a path for later Austrian and neoclassical theories. One was the Frenchman Jean Baptiste Say and the other was the Englishman Nassau Senior. Say was not only an economist but a successful textile manufacturer and his ideas reflect practical experience as well as high theory. He set out to assure the public that, contrary to the views of the agitators, labour and capital had common interests. Through their joint efforts, he argued, value was created and in the process of wealth creation all ultimately benefited. Capital accumulation is necessary to make labour more productive and raise economic prosperity; therefore the continuation of capitalism is in the interests of the workers as well as the capitalists. It followed that it was in the interests of the poor as well as the rich that no barriers were placed in the way of profit-making.

Though costs of production continued to play a part in his approach to the determination of value, Say also stressed the relationship between utility and value: 'Where men attribute value to any thing, it is in consideration of its useful properties: what is good for nothing they set no price upon . . . utility of things is the ground-work of their value' (Say, 1821, vol. 1, p. 3). A similar principle, he reasoned, must apply to the demand for factor inputs. Whereas Smith and Ricardo emphasised the role of costs of production or labour time in the determination of exchange value, Say in effect reversed the reasoning (though he was not entirely consistent) and concluded that factors of production, including labour, derived their demand from the demand for or value of the goods they produced. Thus where the demand for a good is high there will be a large demand for the labour to produce it. The same applies to the capital input. Therefore in Say's economics, labour has no special or unique role in the creation of value and, by implication, the return to capital is not paid out of the product of labour and hence cannot be exploitive.

In Britain Nassau Senior also distanced himself from a strict Ricardian approach to value, notably through his treatment of demand and his insights into the role and nature of capital. He too believed that the market prices of goods were in some sense proportional to their utility (though like Say he missed the concept of diminishing marginal utility). But Senior's major contribution to economics lay in his work on capital and his treatment of 'abstinence'.

Smith and Say both argued that more frugality leads to faster capital accumulation and Ricardo recognised that capital investment necessitates 'waiting' for a return. But it was Senior who first successfully combined these ideas into a theory of capital. In so doing, he moved away from the suggestion that capital could be usefully treated as embodied labour time. Instead, in Senior's economics capital has a specific and separate identity of its own, and cooperates with labour in the production process. Thus, like Say, he was able to dismiss the notion that labour makes a unique contribution to the creation of value. Smith and Ricardo recognised that products incorporating more capital in their supply must have a value different to their labour value, reflecting the time the capital was invested. More 'roundabout' methods of production which necessitated larger amounts of capital investment were associated with more valuable production. But Senior was the first to develop a coherent theory to explain all of this in terms of compensating the capitalist for tying up his capital.

Senior reasoned that what he termed the 'primary productive powers' – human labour and nature or land – need a third instrument of production in modern economies, capital. Capital is created, he continued, by 'abstinence' from consumption: 'a term by which we express the conduct of a person who either abstains from the unproductive use of what he can command, or designedly prefers the production of remote to that of immediate results . . .' (Senior, 1938, pp. 58–9). The return to capital in the form of profit and interest is, he concluded, a necessary payment to reward people who sacrifice immediate consumption. It is a payment, in modern parlance, to overcome a 'time preference' that people have for consuming now rather than in the future: 'To abstain from the enjoyment which is in our power, or to seek distant rather than immediate results, are among the most painful exertions of the human will' (*ibid.*). Senior also stressed the general economic benefits that come from rising productivity when there is high capital investment. 'Roundabout' production methods involve the pain of waiting but provide the benefit of a larger output. Out of this higher output profit and interest can be paid without reducing the return to labour. Senior's message was clear: capital, which is now associated with abstinence rather than embodied labour, creates value.

By the end of the classical period in economics exchange value was determined by demand as well as supply factors and capital was identified as a separate and equal factor input alongside labour in production. Nevertheless, the influence of Smith and Ricardo was still evident in the writings of John Stuart Mill, the last of the great classical theorists. Mill synthesised and refined classical economics while adding the idea of the demand schedule and an understanding of demand and supply elasticities and their influences on prices. These concepts would be capitalised upon later by the neoclassical economists, notably Alfred Marshall.

Following the lead set by Say and Senior, Mill was aware that normally both demand and supply factors affect the relative values of goods and services and he recognised that only where costs of production were constant was demand irrelevant in determining market price. His approach to economics, however, was still heavily influenced by Ricardo. He continued to stress the important contribution of labour to the production of value while at the same time acknowledging the role of capital. Interest on capital, he argued (borrowing from Senior), is a 'remuneration for abstinence' and compensation for risk and speculation. At the end of the classical period in economics, therefore, the approach to value was still based heavily upon costs of production, the supply side of the market. Demand factors were recognised but relatively underexplored. This did not trouble Mill. He felt able to conclude optimistically: 'Happily, there is nothing in the laws of value which remains for the present or any future writer to clear up; the theory of the subject is complete . . .' (Mill, 1875, p. 265).

3.2   The entrepreneur in classical theory

The Industrial Revolution in Britain was a product of individual entrepreneurship. Industrialisation happened because some people recognised that by introducing new machinery and methods of working and by setting up factories and employing people they might earn a handsome profit for themselves. Adam Smith recognised where this was leading when he wrote:

> [the entrepreneur] . . . intends only his own gain, and he is in this, as in
> many other cases, led by an invisible hand to promote an end which was no
> part of his intention. Nor is it always the worse for the society that it was no
> part of it. By pursuing his own interest he frequently promotes that of
> society more effectually than when he really intends to promote it. I have
> never known much good done by those who affected to trade for the public
> good. (Smith, 1950, p. 421)

Given, therefore, that the spirit of private enterprise was crucial in
Britain's rise to economic power, we might have expected that the classical economists and especially Smith would have devoted considerable
time and energy to studying it. In fact, however, with the major exception of Say they not only failed to provide a theory of enterprise; they
also failed to add much of significance to our understanding of the
entrepreneurial role. This does not mean that Smith and Ricardo were
ambiguous about the importance of enterprise in economic development. Both recognised that the entrepreneur was crucial; but possibly
because this seemed axiomatic neither chose to dwell upon it. The
entrepreneur was taken for granted.

In *The Wealth of Nations* Smith discussed the role of the businessman
in bartering and exchange and he was aware of the importance of innovation and its connection to the division of labour and wealth creation
(Reekie, 1984). Also, Smith stressed the entrepreneur's role in combin-
ing the factors of production to produce output. Yet *The Wealth of
Nations* contains merely a series of observations on the entrepreneurial
process rather than a coherent explanation or theory of enterprise. Furthermore, although Smith had consorted with the physiocrats and may
well have known of Turgot's work on the entrepreneur, he often por-
trays the entrepreneur as essentially an unimaginative individual who
merely adjusts to market changes (Spengler, 1959, pp. 8–9). As Professor Samuel Hollander has commented in relation to innovation:

> Smithian 'innovation' should not, therefore, be identified with the
> Schumpeterian variety, which reflects the operations of a minority of
> creative leaders who undertake radical changes in process at substantial risk.
> The Smithian process of improvement is summarized in his discussion of the
> effects of demand expansion upon costs, where technical progress was seen
> to be an almost automatic and assured process engendered by competition.
> (Hollander, 1987, p. 167)

In Ricardo's economics the entrepreneur and the 'entrepreneurial
spirit' are even more neglected. Ricardo was concerned with exploring
the cause of relative values using a highly deductive method of reasoning (a methodological approach not dissimilar to that adopted by later
neoclassical theorists) based upon his labour theory of value. In this

exercise he provided no role for the entrepreneur – especially in relation to innovation which seems to occur automatically in response to market signals. The Ricardian economy operates as if on autopilot. Apart from labour, the other important input into Ricardo's market system is the provider of capital. Therefore the entrepreneur is a capitalist who seeks to maximise profit by investing and employing labour and providing ill-defined management skills.

Like earlier mercantilist writers, in general the classical economists failed to distinguish clearly between interest on capital and pure profit. Both were often subsumed in the terms profit or economic surplus (Redlich, 1966). Occasionally in *The Wealth of Nations* Smith is at pains to stress the difference between interest and profit, in particular when he comments that profit is the revenue derived from stock by the person who manages or employs it and interest is the revenue derived from stock 'by the person who does not employ it himself, but lends it to another'. But more often profit and interest are conflated so that profit became essentially little more than just compensation for the 'risk and trouble of employing the stock' (the term used at this time rather than capital). Profits are then related to the stock put at risk 'and are greater or smaller in proportion to the extent of this stock' (Smith, 1979, pp. 190ff). In other words, profit is essentially a yield on capital and the unique contribution of the businessman is to risk his capital. Smith refuted any suggestion that profits could be usefully related to the managerial function or to what he called the effort and skill in 'inspection and direction' of the business. Such functions, he reasoned, could be undertaken by salaried labour.

This approach to enterprise, with its emphasis upon investment, is more understandable if we bear in mind that prior to the major development of joint-stock companies and the general introduction of limited liability in the second half of the nineteenth century, as often as not the entrepreneur was indeed a capitalist who risked his own funds. Nevertheless, linking enterprise and profit to resources invested meant that the two separate inputs of enterprise and capital were merged, with important consequences for perceptions of the role of the entrepreneur. Socialist writers, for instance, were able to conclude that if entrepreneurs were simply capitalists then through a major redistribution of property it should be possible for capital to be commonly owned without any detriment to the production process.

Certain of the classical economists did endeavour to distinguish profit and interest but were not entirely successful. Malthus divided profit into 'net profits' or interest and 'the profits of industry, skill and enterprise'. This, however, begged the question of what type of industry, skill and enterprise is involved which is separate from normal management duties remunerated by wages. Later economists like Senior recognised interest to be the reward to investors for 'abstinence' from current consumption but this left the remainder of profit unexplained and, importantly, unjustified. Where attention was specifically drawn to the entrepreneur as an innovator and risk-taker, as in certain of Jeremy Bentham's writings, the treatment remained incomplete and was in any case neglected within classical economics.

Continued uncertainty about the nature of enterprise is evident in Mill's writings at the end of the classical period, where profit is associated with both an interest payment to compensate for risk and postponement of consumption and a payment for the provision of managerial skills. This mixture of explanations was not a great advance on Smith's observations seventy years earlier. Profit is not clearly distinguished from interest and it is unclear whether there is a difference between normal managerial duties and the provision of enterprise. Also, since Smith had separated profits from the payment of managerial wages, Mill's treatment of profit and enterprise may be viewed as being in some respects a step backwards. While Mill popularised the term 'entrepreneur' in British economics and was aware of the writings of Bentham and, more importantly in this context, Say, he added little to our understanding of entrepreneurship.

Outside of the mainstream classical tradition, however, more attention was paid to investigating the nature of enterprise. Certain German economists, though seemingly little known in Britain, provided early explanations of profits in terms of a specific entrepreneurial input. For example, Adolph Riedel (1809–72) linked the entrepreneurial function to uncertainty. As the outcome of any economic transaction, he observed, can rarely be predicted accurately, uncertainty is inevitable in market economies. Also, because not all individuals are willing to take risks, preferring an agreed and relatively stable income, the entrepreneur plays a vital role in the economy in being the person who pays contractual returns to others and who accepts the risk that his income may be high, low or negative.

Complementary to Riedel's insights are the writings of J. H. von Thunen (1783–1850) and Hans Karl Emil von Mangoldt (1824–58). Von Thunen developed his treatment of the entrepreneurial function by clearly distinguishing 'entrepreneurial gain' from interest on capital, compensation for risk of loss on capital and managerial payment. Entrepreneurial gain, he argued, is qualitatively different from the return on capital and payment to management and is a reward for ingenuity. Successful entrepreneurs are those who best seek out and exploit market opportunities. He also went on to argue that whereas many risks in life can be insured against, the entrepreneurial function involves risks which are inherently uninsurable because they are unpredictable. The likelihood of success in setting up a business, producing and selling cannot be easily predicted. A similar theme was developed by von Mangoldt, who stressed the role of risk in entrepreneurship, with this risk related to the length of time in producing and selling. The longer the period the greater the chance that the market will have changed so that a potentially profitable transaction ends up making a loss. For von Mangoldt the entrepreneur therefore provides a distinct contribution to production and one which not everyone would risk making. The entrepreneur accepts the risks of losses while receiving profits if a business venture is successful. Since profits are related to individual initiative and effort, von Mangoldt concluded that the most able entrepreneurs earn the highest profits.

The idea that profit and enterprise are associated with the uncertainty that exists in market economies had some similarities to the approach in Cantillon's earlier writings (Chapter 2, pp. 28–9), and it would be taken up in the twentieth century by Frank Knight, professor of economics at Chicago University, and by the Austrian economists (see Chapter 5). But in the meantime, although it cried out to be developed, it remained neglected – as did another important continental contribution provided by Say (Gide and Rist, 1915, pp. 113–14; Hoselitz, 1951/60). Say, having been a successful industrial entrepreneur before becoming the first European professor of economics, argued that the entrepreneurial function was the key to capitalism and to the success of Britain. Its industrial ascendancy he attributed in large part to 'the wonderful practical skill of her entrepreneurs' (Say, 1821, vol. 1, p. 53).

The nature of enterprise had already been explored in France by Turgot and Cantillon. Thus Say may well have been influenced by ideas on entrepreneurship current in France but neglected in Britain. Yet he pursued an independent line in his two major works *Traité d'économie politique* (first edition 1803) and *Cours complet d'économie politique pratique* (first edition 1828/9). In these works he described at length what contemporary entrepreneurs actually did; by this means he hoped to shed light on the role of the entrepreneur. Such descriptions, however, threw up a multitude of different characteristics; he therefore also provided generalised insights into entrepreneurship in an attempt to develop what might be called a general theory of enterprise.

Say concluded that entrepreneurship is not simply a matter of recognising the existence of uncertainty. Rather he argued that the key to entrepreneurship lies in exceptional 'judgment, perseverance, and a knowledge of the world, as well as of business'. The entrepreneur acts, he explained, as a 'broker' between sellers and buyers. Motivated by profit he uses his judgement to employ or buy factors of production in appropriate proportions; he then produces and prices the goods which he thinks the consumers will want, and as a consequence he takes the inevitable risks that go with business decisions: 'He is called upon to estimate, with tolerable accuracy, the importance of the specific product, the probable amount of the demand, and the means of its production' (*ibid.*, pp. 104–5). Say's entrepreneur is, therefore, an employer of labour, a purchaser of materials, an organiser of production and a person who discovers and reacts to market demands. Importantly, he is not necessarily a supplier of capital – the usual focus of classical economists. Although Say observed that in practice the entrepreneur often supplied the funds, it remained the case that the entrepreneur could always borrow to invest. Thus it was important, he maintained, to distinguish clearly between the supply of capital and the provision of enterprise and consequently the payment of interest and profit. Interest was the reward for 'frugality and forbearance . . . and self-denial' – an approach later independently developed by Senior. But profit he linked directly to the entrepreneurial role as an organiser, manager or decision-taker. Risk implies investment of capital but Say linked entrepreneurship to good commercial judgement:

> [the entrepreneur's] . . . principal quality is to have good judgment. He can lack personal knowledge of science, by judiciously employing that of others, he can avoid dirtying his own hands by using the hands of others, but he must not lack judgment; for then he might produce at great expense something which has no value.

Say's approach to enterprise can be illustrated as follows. Economic activity, he recognised, involves first a degree of knowledge. An example of this would be Abraham Darby's discovery some time after 1709 at Coalbrook Dale in Shropshire, England, that iron could be smelted using a local coal low in sulphur content. The next step, which is the real entrepreneurial input, was the decision to profit from this discovery by raising the capital and organising the production. Finally, the production stage involved capital, labour and management; but simple management of resources to produce given ends is different from the entrepreneurial function. The entrepreneur has to judge correctly the best way of organising production and sales to profit from the production. In return, Say concluded, the entrepreneur is rewarded by profit.

Smith had noted that people willing to take business risks were in short supply but this was highlighted by Say. Not everyone, Say explained, has either the requisite capital to invest in a good idea or the reputation which will attract lenders; nor has everyone got the necessary skills to judge market demand correctly and to undertake the type of 'superintendence and administration' of labour and capital required to make profits: 'Thus, the requisite capacity and talent limits the number of competitors for the business of entrepreneurs' (Say, 1821, vol. 2, p. 105). He reasoned that as in the case of the prices of other inputs the demand and supply of willing and able entrepreneurs must determine the level of profits earned in any venture. While aware that the return to enterprise was unique among payments to inputs, in the sense that no one could accurately predict which ventures would necessarily succeed and which would fail, Say believed that some trades were inherently riskier than others. He believed that there was more risk in being a manufacturer or trader than a farmer and more risk in being a retail trader rather than a wholesaler. In riskier trades there would be a smaller supply of willing entrepreneurs and hence higher profits would be earned. Also, since entrepreneurship involved more risk and effort than employment it followed that the entrepreneur needed to receive more income than the manual labourer. Thus not only did Say provide a detailed account of what he believed to be the entrepreneurial function, he established a rationale both for the existence of profit and for the fact that profits exceeded wage levels.

Say's contribution to our understanding of the entrepreneur stands out in classical economics. But in certain ways his approach was limited and recently some economists have interpreted his ideas as inferior to Cantillon's and Turgot's earlier insights (Hebert and Link, 1988, p. 34). In particular, Say's entrepreneur is nearest to a super-manager with good judgement who organises, coordinates and supervises the factors of production in return for a varying profit rather than a fixed salary. Say failed, in short, to distinguish clearly between management and entrepreneurship. In his writings, profit appears at times to be little more than a wage for a particular type of skilled labour. Profits earned by Say's entrepreneur are also reduced to the same level as the returns to other factor inputs and are related to the demand and supply of entrepreneurs. It is difficult to reconcile this view with dynamic markets subject to constant change for then the notion of a market-clearing profit loses meaning. Say's approach to risk and uncertainty and his treatment of profit stand uneasily together.

3.3   Profit in income distribution

Reference has already been made to the classical economists' approach to profit in the earlier discussions of value and the entrepreneur. Here, however, attention centres upon profit in income distribution. The classical economists' views on income distribution followed naturally from their approach to value; indeed their study of value was intended to shed light on the economic forces which determined incomes. Ricardo, for example, observed that: 'To determine the laws which regulate this distribution is the principal problem in Political Economy' (Ricardo, 1971, preface, p. 49). The classical economists, especially Ricardo, expended a great deal of time and energy in attempting to explain variations in the rate of profits and other incomes.

Central to the classical analysis of income distribution was the notion of a 'wages fund'. Long abandoned in mainstream economic theory, in classical economics this idea represented the circulating capital available to pay wages to labour. The argument went that during the production process labour was paid wages by the entrepreneur, who had to wait until the output was sold before receiving income and taking his profits. The total wages paid and the number employed, therefore, were limited by the size of the wages fund. Also, for a given labour force, the larger the wages fund potentially the higher the wages could be since it appeared that the average wage level depended upon the ratio of the size of the labour force to the size of the wages fund.

In fact, the wages fund cannot determine incomes to labour and capital without some statement as to the proportions of labour and capital employed and this requires information about labour and capital productivity and the costs of employing different inputs. Also, the notion of the wages fund makes most sense in relation to agriculture when labour has to be financed by the capitalist farmer until crops are gathered and sold. It makes less sense in other industries where production and the receipt of sales revenues are part of a continuous process. Nevertheless, despite such shortcomings, the wages fund played a leading role in the economics of income distribution down to the neoclassical era.

The classical economists chose to apply the idea of the wages fund to all economic activities with profound implications for their perception of the relationship between wages and population. Like certain mercantilist writers before them, the classical economists believed that once real wages rose above their subsistence level the population would tend to rise. A higher real income would relax an important constraint upon family size leading to a higher birth-rate, while the death-rate might temporarily fall due to a better diet. The rise in population would have two important effects. First, unless matched by a rise in the wages fund it would reduce the average real wage. Second, the larger number of mouths to feed would mean a rise in food prices and a fall in real purchasing power per head. This would induce a fall in population until real wages were back to their subsistence level. Food prices would rise because, as Ricardo explained in meticulous detail, currently the most productive lands were cultivated so that attempting to feed a larger population would mean bringing less productive land into cultivation.

Thus it appeared that real wages for labourers would tend towards the level necessary to provide a subsistence diet unless the population increase was kept in check. This general approach to wages was soon labelled, with good reason, 'the iron law of wages'.

It was left to Malthus, however, to provide the best remembered and most pessimistic predictions on food supplies and population. He concluded that because, in his view, agricultural production rose arithmetically – 2, 4, 6, 8, etc. – but population rose geometrically – 2, 4, 8, 16, 32, etc. – 'the power of population is indefinitely greater than the power in the earth to produce subsistence for man.' Therefore, the best chance of raising workers' real incomes permanently, he concluded, lay in 'moral restraint' among the working class coupled with fast capital accumulation to increase the wages fund. Otherwise disease, misery, war and famine would overtake the country (Malthus, 1960, pp. 12ff).

This Malthusian nightmare would haunt all of the classical economists to a greater or lesser degree and reinforced their belief in capital accumulation, for as they saw it capital accumulation offered the best chance of breaking out of a low wage economy. Fast economic growth would raise the demand for labour and, importantly, a greater stock of circulating capital would mean a larger wages fund thus permitting higher real wages. The prospect that capital accumulation might lead instead to more fixed capital rather than circulating capital, producing technological unemployment as some labour agitators argued, was generally dismissed. It was possible, they speculated, that capital accumulation might cause a rise in fixed capital leading to a substitution of machines for labour, but this they concluded was not a major threat to employment and wages since it was unlikely to reduce the overall size of the wages fund. In addition higher productivity would lead to higher wages and hence more demand in the economy. As Senior concluded, technological unemployment was not a major threat as long as labour was willing to move into new lines of work. Only Ricardo, who initially argued that more investment in fixed capital must benefit labour, later in life dissented, arguing that more fixed capital investment might reduce output and employment by depleting the wages fund.

The classical economists discussed the distribution of income in terms of classes – in Smith's words a distribution between 'the three great, original and constituent orders of every civilized society' – land, labour and capital (Smith, 1979, p. 151). This class approach to incomes, however, implied a conflict over the amount of income going to each 'constituent order' and this is certainly evident in parts of Ricardo's analysis of income distribution. For example, he reasoned that if food prices rose, labourers would demand higher wages to maintain a subsistence diet, landowners would earn economic rents, and profits and capital accumulation would be squeezed. Similarly, lower wages implied a higher profit since profits in classical economics are paid out of realised income when goods are sold. They are a residual after costs of supply have been met – something that Smith had stressed earlier: 'The value which the workmen add to the materials resolves itself . . . into two parts, of which one pays their wages, the other the profits of their employer' (Smith, 1979, p. 151). But though Ricardian socialists and Marx would couple this class approach to incomes with the labour theory of value to produce a theory of labour exploitation, Smith and Ricardo came to a very different conclusion. As far as they were concerned, although profit was a residual and in the short run there was a trade-off between wages and profits, over the longer term higher profits led to more savings which would be reinvested, leading to faster capital accumulation. This capital accumulation would expand the wages fund producing higher wages as long as population growth was restrained.

Therefore there is no conflict in classical economics between labour and capital for the prosperity of both is dependent upon a growth in capital. This is especially evident in *The Wealth of Nations*: 'It was Smith's great emphasis on the economic role of profit on capital and capital accumulation which more than anything else gave unity and strength to *The Wealth of Nations*' (Meek, 1954, p. 139). Similarly, Ricardo stressed the importance of profit-making:

> The farmer and the manufacturer can no more live without profit, than the labourer without wages. Their motive for accumulation will diminish with every diminution of profit, and will cease altogether when their profits are so low as not to afford them an adequate compensation for their trouble, and the risk which they must necessarily encounter in employing their capital productivity.

Both Smith and Ricardo warned that capital accumulation would stop if profitability fell to a very low level and both felt that as wealth increased eventually opportunities for profitable investment might disappear. Ricardo linked this to rising food prices as the population grew. A rise in the demand for food would lead to higher prices, triggering a rise in the subsistence wage and ultimately a transfer of income from capitalists to landowners. The outcome would be a 'stationary state' in which the rate of profit fell to zero or near to zero and capital accumulation ceased. The same idea crops up in certain later classical (and Marxist – see Chapter 6) writings, notably in Mill's *Principles* – although Mill contended that its event would mark the start of a new and more desirable millennium of cooperation and social reform: 'when minds cease to be engrossed by the art of getting on' (Mill, 1875, pp. 452–5). But the classical economists were agreed that this 'stationary state' would only occur, if at all, in the distant future. In the meantime, social well-being would be maximised through the individual pursuit of profit and maximum capital accumulation.

3.4 Capital accumulation and economic policy

The policy prescriptions of classical economics reflect the classical belief in both the common interests of labour and capital and the benefits of private profit-making in a free market economy. Only private property brings forward the capital which expands the wages fund: 'The consideration of his own private property is the sole motive which determines the owner of any capital to employ it' (Smith, 1979, p. 474). Thus state intervention in the forms of high taxation, state regulation of business and controls on trade which attenuate private profit-making were condemned. In addition, the classical economists believed that the competitive market economy was self-regulating, so there was no need for state intervention of the kind now referred to as 'macroeconomic management'. In their support for *laissez-faire* economic and social policies the classical economists built upon the 'late mercantilist' and physiocratic predilections for smaller government.

The classical position on the role of the state in the economy was set out clearly and dramatically by Adam Smith. Smith argued that government should be limited to providing the necessary services that the private sector might not adequately supply – such as national defence and 'public works' including roads and harbours – as well as protecting private property rights by establishing law and order and providing sound administration in such matters as the issuing of paper money. At the same time, conscious that it was often the extravagance of governments that ruined countries through high taxation, he advocated taxes that were cheap to collect and proportional in relation to income rather than progressive. Smith was not, however, an unconditional *laissez-faire* ideologist as is sometimes implied by his critics. For instance, he favoured the continuation of the usury laws and advocated some state responsibility for 'cultural activities'. In addition, he was cynical about the motives of capitalists whose interests he recognised to be at direct variance to those of the general public: businessmen, he argued, too often attempt to 'deceive and oppress the public'; while they 'seldom meet together, even for merriment and diversion, but the conversation ends in a conspiracy against the public, or in some contrivance to raise prices' (Smith, 1979, p. 232). But the economically harmful effects of the pursuit of self-interest, he felt, could be kept in check through competition. In *The Wealth of Nations* it is self-interest which guides and limits human actions, with competition providing the checks and balances which ensure that the pursuit of self-interest promotes the general good. Only with competition did capitalism, in Smith's schema, become 'the system of perfect liberty'. Thus Smith advocated maximum competition in trade precisely because it inhibited the creation of trade conspiracies against the public. It followed that no intervention in markets should be allowed which weakened the competitive process. In particular, Smith recognised that it was often state monopolies and firms protected by tariffs and quotas which exploited the public through high prices.

Like later classical economists, notably Senior, Smith was cynical of the notion of the state or for that matter anyone else purposefully pursuing the 'public good', for it was his sincere belief that rarely would the public good be so achieved. Instead, bureaucracy and waste would result. Far better, he concluded, for people to pursue their own self-interest in a competitive market, thus maximising personal wealth and incidentally achieving a general economic and social improvement: 'It is not from the benevolence of the butcher, the brewer, or the baker that we expect our dinner, but from their regard to their own interest' (Smith, 1979. p. 119). He was especially critical of what is today sometimes referred to as 'social engineering' because of what he felt were its damaging effects on the market process. For example, he attacked the British Poor Law, which made payments out of taxes to the destitute in their own parishes, on the grounds that it undermined the ability of labour to move in search of work.

Such attitudes to state intervention on economic and social grounds were echoed and developed by subsequent classical economists. Ricardo, Malthus, Say and Senior opposed high taxation because of its disincentive effects on profit-making, hard work and frugality. They were also highly criticial of poor relief (latter-day 'social security') for the able-bodied, which they felt must act as a disincentive to work and, by raising taxation, depress capital accumulation. Ricardo concluded that Poor Laws 'instead of making the poor rich, they are calculated to make the rich poor' (Ricardo, 1971, p. 126). At the same time, Say reasoned that state support must reduce the incentive to prepare and save for ill health, misfortune and old age; and Senior, as a member of the Royal Commission which preceded the 1834 Poor Law Reform, justified changes to the poor relief on the grounds that no one should rely on state hand-outs. The introduction in 1834 of the principle of 'less eligibility' in British social policy and the resultant harsh regime in the workhouses was necessary because, as a general principle: 'every man desires to obtain additional Wealth with as little sacrifice as possible' (Senior, 1938, p. v). At this time it was generally believed that labourers were by nature indolent.

It was not that Senior was indifferent to the plight of the poor. Rather he believed, as did the other classical economists, that in the longer term poverty would be eradicated only by economic growth, which in his view depended upon hard work, frugality, high profitability and, above all, capital accumulation. Only if we appreciate this can we understand why Senior favoured reform of the Poor Law, abolition of trade unions – which he considered a restraint on trade – and why later he opposed the passage through Parliament of the Ten Hour Day Bill in 1837, which limited working hours in the factories. Shorter working hours, he believed, would severely reduce profits, leading to economic decline. To Senior and the classical economists in general, social and economic inequalities were justified because they increased the pace of capital accumulation, which was ultimately in everyone's interests. Even Mill, who criticised the inequalities in income distribution which he saw around him and favoured some municipal ownership of public utilities to improve social conditions, in the final analysis was reluctant to countenance reforms which might impede private investment.

Besides welfare and taxation, a further issue in economic policy is the role of the state in regulating employment. During the twentieth century a major argument for state intervention in capitalist economies has centred upon the possibility that the free market will not produce a full employment level of national income. The seeds of this idea go back a long way. Certain of the mercantilists, notably Sir Douglas North, Richard Cantillon and Bernard de Mandeville, had speculated on whether the demand for commodities in an economy must always be sufficient to purchase the supplies available so as to avoid market gluts. Similarly, certain of the physiocrats had discussed whether there might sometimes be inadequate demand to absorb all of the output available for sale. Parsimony, they argued, might lead to underconsumption by depriving the market of necessary purchasing power. Neither the mercantilists nor the physiocrats, however, were able to provide a coherent argument to underpin their worries. Instead, the physiocrat Turgot provided an early version of the thesis that 'supply creates its own demand' to dismiss worries of a general oversupply in markets. Savings would be reinvested – resulting, he argued, in: 'this advance and this continual return of capitals which constitute . . . that useful and fruitful circulation which gives life to all the labours of society, which maintains movement and life in the body politic' (Turgot, 1898, pp. 62–3). Only in 1936, in *The General Theory of Employment, Interest and Money*, did the Cambridge economist John Maynard Keynes provide the economic theory of underconsumption which had eluded his eighteenth-century predecessors.

Smith echoed Turgot and thus shaped what became the dominant view of classical and later neoclassical economics: that there will not be inadequate consumption (excessive savings), except perhaps for short periods as markets adjust, because all income must ultimately be spent or invested. It was repeated by Ricardo, who concluded that 'demand is only limited by production' (1971, pp. 290ff). Also, whereas Smith allowed for the possibility that a rigidity of wage levels in recessions could prolong unemployment, Ricardo preferred to treat wages as being flexible like any other price in a competitive economy. Therefore, if there should be an excess supply of labour this would lead to a fall in real wage rates, a corresponding recovery in profits and the restoration of full employment.

Neither Turgot, Smith nor Ricardo, however, provided a detailed theoretical explanation of why supply might create its own demand. This appears to have been first set out formally by John Stuart Mill's father, James Mill, a close friend of Ricardo, though it is today more commonly associated with Say. In his 'law of markets', Say reasoned that the competitive market, free of state regulation or other interference, was self-adjusting to a full employment income level through the forces of demand and supply in both the product and capital markets. This was most obviously true, he recognised, in a barter economy, where products are given in exchange for products and there can be no excess supply of goods at the market rates of exchange. All those who wish to trade will find a consumer at some market-clearing exchange rate. The introduction of money, he continued, merely complicated the argument:

> It is worth while to remark, that a product is no sooner created, than it, from that instant, affords a market for other products to the full extent of its own value. When the producer has put the finishing hand to his product, he is most anxious to sell it immediately, lest its value should vanish in his hands. Nor is he less anxious to dispose of the money he may get for it; for the value of money is also perishable. But the only way of getting rid of money is in the purchase of some product or other. Thus, the mere circumstance of the creation of one product immediately opens a vent [demand] for other products. (Say, 1821, ch. 15)

Hoarding money, for instance under the floorboards, which prevented it from being borrowed and invested made no sense to Say and subsequent economists, since depositing savings with banks or lending directly to investors provided a reward in the form of interest.

As long as savings and investment were a function of interest rates then there had to be one rate at which what people were willing to save just equalled what businessmen wanted to invest. This is illustrated in Figure 3.2 where r_1 is the equilibrium interest rate. Here the supply of and demand for loanable funds are equal at q. Investment is assumed to fall as interest rates rise because it becomes more costly to borrow.

Savings are assumed to rise as interest rates increase since it is more beneficial to save rather than spend at higher interest rates. In Figure 3.2 suppose the preference to save rises. The savings function shifts to S_2 leading to an excess of savings over investment at the previous equilibrium interest rate, and threatening a general glut. The excess of savings in the capital market, however, will cause the interest rate to decline as potential lenders seek out borrowers. As the interest rate falls savings will decline along S_2 and investment will increase. The result is a new equilibrium interest rate at r_2. Similarly, if savings or investment intentions should change in such a way as to cause a shortage of savings in the capital market, then interest rates would rise. Thus savings and investments are brought into equilibrium through changes in interest rates. As long as the movement from one equilibrium interest rate to another occurs quickly and smoothly there cannot be a general surplus of consumer goods due to excess saving. All income is reabsorbed into the economy through consumption spending or investment.

To the next few generations of economists Say's Law suggested that there could be no general surpluses leading to a long-term economic depression. Occasional temporary surpluses might occur in some markets due to entrepreneurial miscalculation or unforeseen changes in market demand, but these would quickly lead in the free market to a reallocation of capital and labour and full employment would return. By so redistributing resources in response to price changes the entrepreneur was fulfilling an equilibrating role in the market economy. There could be 'trade cycles' involving recurrent trade booms and reces-

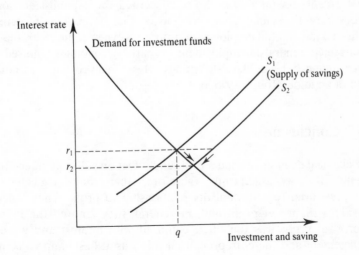

Figure 3.2 Equilibrium interest rate

sions as markets responded to changes in demand and supply but not persistent 'general gluts'. For example, Mill recognised that in trade recessions people might prefer to hold cash rather than buy commodities, delaying their purchases and thus denuding the market of purchasing power. Nevertheless, this did not lead him to abandon the view that 'every increase in production . . . creates, or rather constitutes, its own demand' (Mill, 1948, p. 73). Also, while periodic trade cycles occurred in the nineteenth century, Say's Law seemed to be confirmed by the absence of prolonged general unemployment.

Malthus was the only major classical economist to dissent completely from the view that 'supply creates its own demand'. With an eye to the unemployment following the end of the Napoleonic Wars in 1815, he argued that while the poor would spend all that they earned, a certain part of income, which he defined as expenditure on 'conveniences and luxuries', was susceptible to major downward shifts in demand. At certain times the richer sections of society, notably landowners, might choose not to spend all of their incomes on such commodities: 'A nation must certainly have the power of purchasing all that it produces, but I can easily conceive it not to have the will' (in Ricardo, vol. vi, 1955, pp. 131–2). Unfortunately, Malthus, like the mercantilists and the physiocrats before him, failed to formulate this idea in such a way as to place it on a par with the intellectual rigour of Say's Law. Thus, the possibility of general gluts of commodities was discounted in mainstream economic theory until well into the twentieth century. With the important exception of Malthus, the classical economists provided no rationale for macroeconomic demand management. As far as they were concerned the capitalist economies were inherently stable. There was no conflict between self-interested profit-making and full employment. Prior to Keynes in the 1930s the idea of sustained general unemployment in market economies featured as a major theme only in Marxist writings. Marx believed Say was nothing short of an idiot (Routh, 1975, p. 125).

3.5   Conclusion

The classical economists had a profound effect on subsequent economic debate. It was significant, therefore, that they neglected the entrepreneurial function and its relationship to profit. They failed to provide a theory of profit and, in general, they ignored the input of enterprise. Profit was too often confused with interest and wages to management and the entrepreneurial role was at best simply taken for granted. Only Say and a few German economists outside the mainstream of classical theory chose to emphasise and explore the role of entrepreneurship in the economy, but their ideas had little influence on classical economics, which remained firmly rooted in the Ricardian tradition.

This neglect had two major consequences, one profound in its effects on world politics, the other having important implications for the treatment of profit and enterprise in economics teaching today. First, although the classical theory of value is closest to a cost of production theory, by emphasising the role of labour in the creation of value, Ricardo in particular paved the way for the 'Ricardian socialists' and later Karl Marx to argue that profit comes out of the value created by labour and therefore belongs to labour. Senior attempted to legitimise capital as an independent input into the production process but by then the damage had been done and in any case there seemed no obvious reason to socialist writers why the workers or the state could not provide the capital. If the capitalist simply provided funds and some ill-defined 'administration or superintendence', which on the face of it could be undertaken by employed management or civil servants, it appeared that not only did he extract his profit from the product of labour, he was inessential to the production process. This argument had obvious appeal to a propertyless proletariat at the time and has left its mark on the economic policies of socialist parties down to the present day.

Second, the absence of an explanation of the entrepreneurial function separate from routine management or the provision of capital meant that the classical economists provided no basis for the neoclassical school to build a theory of profit and enterprise. The consequence of this was the continued neglect of the entrepreneur after neoclassical economics superseded classical theory from the 1870s.

Set against this criticism, however, the classical economists highlighted the importance of profit for investment and prosperity. Although their approach to income distribution might imply a trade-off in the short run between wages and profits, they recognised that in the longer term all incomes could only rise if there was fast capital accumulation and that this was related in a market economy to profitability. This idea shaped their attitudes towards the state and social and economic policy. Reforms were supported or opposed depending upon the predicted impact on profits and savings. In the late twentieth century the principles which guided the classical economists still have meaning and purpose.

Further reading

Classical economics is a branch of European liberalism. For an overview of the development of liberal values see Girvetz (1963) and Myers (1983).

No serious student of classical economics should avoid the original sources, notably Smith's *The Wealth of Nations*. Nevertheless, there are useful secondary sources on the major figures of classical theory: e.g. O'Brien (1975) and Hollander (1987), who discuss the contributions of the classical economists in general; while Campbell and Skinner (1982) study Adam Smith and his economics. Hollander (1979) provides an erudite but none the less enjoyable treatise on the economics of David Ricardo; and Wood (ed.) (1986) is a good starting-point for the debate on Malthus and classical economics. Also Hicks (1983, pp. 60–70) provides an important study of John Stuart Mill's economic ideas and how they straddle the classical and post-classical eras. For books on economic thought with good treatments of the theory of value, see in particular Blaug's (1978) lengthy review, and Oser (1970). For 'livelier', shorter and more idiosyncratic treatments of classical economics see Heilbroner (1980) and Routh (1975).

All of the above include some reference to classical ideas on profit and to a lesser degree enterprise. But for a more direct approach see Meek (1954) and Hebert and Link (1988). The latter gives particular attention to the ideas of Say but at the cost of skirting over Ricardian economics. For a complete contrast and a distinctly Ricardian approach to profit in classical theory, see Howard (1983). For balance, Hebert and Link and Howard are best read together! Other Ricardian approaches can be found in Dobb (1973) and Garegnani (1984). Also useful are the articles by Bowley on capital and Rosenberg on profit in Skinner and Wilson (eds.) (1975).

Finally, for an excellent introduction to the classical economists and economic policy see the collection of readings in Coates (ed.) (1971).

4

Enterprise sidelined: the neoclassical perspective

Neoclassical economics developed out of classical theory from the 1870s. Whereas the classical economists had been primarily interested in exploring the forces determining long-term wealth creation, the conditions of production and the long-run distribution of income, however, neoclassical economists were more concerned with studying the determination of equilibrium prices and outputs in individual product and factor markets and with developing the allied concept of a general equilibrium. Yet the change from classical to neoclassical economics should not be exaggerated; as the name suggests, 'neoclassical' assimilates many of the ideas and approaches of classical theory and it evolved gradually (Hollander, 1987). In addition, some of the chief theoretical concepts of neoclassical economics, notably the concepts of utility and marginal productivity, had already been introduced before the 1870s, although they had not come to prominence. Therefore, it is not the case that from the 1870s economics underwent a sudden and revolutionary change. Nevertheless, over time economists distanced themselves from the classical theory of value, with its emphasis upon the role of labour, and its approach to income distribution based upon the notion of a wages fund and subsistence wages. Consequently, many economists refer to the introduction of neoclassical economics as the 'marginalist revolution'.

This shift in the focus of economic theory cannot be divorced from economic and social changes. When Adam Smith wrote his *The Wealth of Nations* Britain was at an early stage of industrialisation. Hence, he was interested in the forces which determined capital accumulation and what impeded it, including restrictions upon trade and state regulation. At the tail-end of mercantilism the case for small government needed to be made. But by the 1870s Britain was a well-established industrial economy, the 'workshop of the world', and free trade with minimal state intervention was accepted by most economists. The 'cause' which had fired the imagination of Smith had triumphed in Britain and also, in large part, elsewhere in Europe and in the United States (a partial exception was Germany where *laissez-faire* economics was less securely rooted). Thus attention switched away from capital accumulation, that is the act of *increasing* resources, towards the distribution and use of *existing* resources. The neoclassical economists were primarily interested in exploring how markets distribute resources to achieve 'maximum welfare' for consumers.

There were many contributors to the development of neoclassical economics. Especially noteworthy in the early days were William Stanley Jevons (1835–82), professor of logic, philosophy and political economy at Manchester University and later at University College, London; Alfred Marshall (1842–1924), professor of political economy at the University of Cambridge from 1885 and often considered the true founder of neoclassical theory – his *Principles of Economics* (1890) went through eight editions in his lifetime and inspired generations of students; John Bates Clark (1847–1938) in the United States, who developed the concept of marginal productivity; and Leon Walras (1834–1910) in Switzerland, who provided a theory of 'general equilibrium'. A further major influence were the Austrian economists, notably Eugen Von Bohm-Bawerk (1851–1914), who developed capital theory, and Friedrich Von Wieser (1851–1926) and Carl Menger (1840–1921), who explored the significance of subjectivism in economics. In the twentieth century, however, Austrian economics has developed its own, independent tradition, which is discussed in Chapter 5. Although Austrian and neoclassical theories initially shared common ground, they spawned radically different traditions in economics, especially evident in their contrasting treatments of profit and enterprise.

Neoclassical economics has become the predominant paradigm of economics in the twentieth century. Therefore the way that profit and enterprise have been treated – or rather neglected – in neoclassical theory has had an important bearing upon the way that they are studied in economics texts and courses today. Neoclassical economics now encompasses a wide body of theorising. Inevitably, therefore, this chapter must adopt a broad-brush approach. We shall be concerned in the main with the general thrust of neoclassical theory as it is taught in introductory and intermediate economics courses rather than with more specialised studies of the theory, where indeed some of the more elementary aspects have in recent years been subjected to further development.

4.1 Price determination and the competitive equilibrium

As in the case of the other schools of economists discussed in this book, the views of the neoclassical economists on profit and enterprise cannot be divorced from their approach to value or what neoclassical economists prefer to call 'market price'. In neoclassical theory the market price represents value. If a commodity is bought for £10 in the market then that reflects its value to the purchaser. Value, therefore, is reflected in the individual's willingness to pay, with the market price being the outcome of demand and supply forces. This approach to value is premised on the belief that value is what people perceive something is worth to them or what they are willing to pay for it. This will vary from individual to individual and hence it is *subjective*.

The idea that value or price depends upon demand and supply in the market is evident in the classical economists' approach to exchange value and can be traced back to certain scholastic writers (Langholm, 1979) and later to Locke and North in the mercantilist period. The classical economists, however, highlighted the difference between current market price (exchange value) and the long-run 'natural price' which they related to costs of production and, in Ricardo's formulation, largely to labour time. In addition, the classical economists, being especially concerned with capital accumulation, stressed the forces affecting supply rather than demand; when demand featured it was mainly explored in terms of subsistence consumption or what was necessary to maintain the labour force. In contrast, in neoclassical theory no distinction is made between market price and the 'natural price'; indeed, the concept of natural price does not feature. Moreover, in neoclassical theory demand as well as supply affects price.

The source of value, which had exhausted the energies of a number of the classical theorists, now became simply a reflection of *subjective* evaluations in the market. Central to this was the concept of marginal utility, an approach to value which can be traced back through the writings of Bentham and Say to sixteenth- and seventeenth-century Italian and Spanish scholastic writers, but which was developed after 1870 by Jevons in England, Walras in Switzerland and Menger and Wieser in Austria. Also important was the notion that consumers 'act rationally' to maximise the utility or satisfaction from their given incomes. This requires that the marginal utility (the utility from the last unit consumed) for each good or service purchased, in relation to the price paid for each good, should be equal. If this is not the case then the consumer, by adjusting the level of purchases of goods and services, will be able to raise his or her total utility. To illustrate, suppose the choice is between two goods X and Y which have prices P_x and P_y, the consumer's utility will be maximised where:

$$MU_x/P_x = MU_y/P_y \text{ or } MU_x/MU_y = P_x/P_y$$

If $MU_x/MU_y > P_x/P_y$ then it would pay the rational consumer to spend more on X and, given a limited budget, this would imply spending less on Y. On the basis that the more we consume of anything at any given time the lower its marginal utility (that is the less the additional satisfaction we obtain), as more of X and less of Y are consumed eventually a new 'consumer's equilibrium' is achieved where $MU_x/MU_y = P_x/P_y$. Through this formal approach, neoclassical economics establishes the nexus between value in use and value in exchange which had foxed the classical economists. It is able to answer the question which had puzzled Adam Smith and led the classical school to reject utility as the basis of value – why are diamonds dear although they are inessential to life while water is cheap? Armed with the concept of marginal utility, neoclassical economists were able to demonstrate that the solution lay in water having a high *total* utility but, being abundant in supply in many countries, having a low *marginal* utility – the last unit of water consumed adds little to total utility and thus attracts a low price. In contrast, diamonds, being scarce and consequently having a high *marginal* utility, attract a high price.

The stress upon utility implies that to understand value we must begin by looking at the demands of individuals. Neoclassical theory therefore departs from the class-based approach to value central to Marxist and evident in much of classical theorising. Once consumers register their demands in the market-place and prices achieve market-clearing levels in competitive markets, the outcome is an 'efficient' allocation of resources. Labour inputs have no special role or importance because the value of goods is a subjective value unrelated to factor inputs. Thus Jevons prefaced his study of economics by specifically attacking Ricardo for 'shunting the car of economic science on to a wrong line': 'I feel sure that when, casting ourselves free from the wage-fund theory, the cost of production doctrine of value, the natural rate of wages, and other misleading or false Ricardian doctrines, we begin to trace out clearly and simply the results of a correct theory' (Jevons, 1970, pp. 68 and 72). Instead of labour or other inputs determining value, the value of inputs is *derived* from the value of the commodities which they produce. This principle of 'imputation' was developed in early Austrian writings, though it is also evident in the neoclassical approach to factor rewards and the concept of marginal productivity. Labour and capital will tend to earn high wages and interest if they are utilised in the supply of goods and services which have a high value in the market.

The idea that marginal utility – or individuals' subjective evaluations – is the source of value is evident in both the writings of Jevons and the Austrian economists from the early 1870s. But it was left to Marshall to develop the theory further by synthesising subjectivism and Ricardian economics, thus formulating neoclassical value theory as we know it today. Marshall believed that to concentrate upon subjective demands and to ignore supply factors entirely when explaining price was an over-reaction. He likened the debate over the relative contributions of demand and supply in determining price to the argument over which blade of a pair of scissors cuts a piece of paper. The debate was pointless since both blades are vital. Market price, Marshall concluded, is the product of both demand and supply. Only where supply could not be varied, such as for works of art or in the very short run before any factor inputs could be changed, would demand be the sole determining factor. In the long run it was possible that supply factors would be the dominant influence on price, as in classical theory, but this would turn on the nature of the supply curve. Thus Marshall's theory of price relates directly to time periods (Marshall, 1966, pp. 281–91).

The importance of time in Marshall's price theory can be illustrated by considering the price of strawberries. The price of fresh strawberries at any given time is demand- rather than supply-determined because supply is fixed once the strawberries are in the shops. In the short run, however, it may be possible to change the supply of strawberries by altering certain factor inputs or the so-called 'variable' factors of production. For example, more labour might be employed to harvest a larger strawberry crop. This will mean a rise in marginal supply costs and thus both demand and supply affect price. Finally, in the long run all factor inputs can be varied – more strawberries can be grown by switching land from other uses. In this case the relative roles of demand and supply on price depend upon the extent to which, as factor input combinations are altered, marginal or incremental costs of supply increase, decrease or stay constant. If costs rise or fall both demand and supply affect price, as in the short run. But if costs stay constant then changes in demand cannot affect price. These different effects of supply and demand on price are illustrated in Figure 4.1.

Thus through his use of time periods, Marshall was able to demonstrate that the classical argument that price is dependent upon supply costs is a special case of constant cost production. In other cases, either demand alone or more usually a combination of demand and supply factors determines market price. Post-Marshall neoclassical price theory was usually posed in terms of increasing costs of production or an upward-sloping supply curve so that both demand and supply were important (a quick perusal of any basic economics text will confirm this).

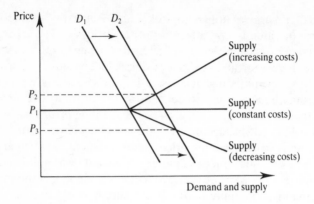

Figure 4.1   The effect of costs on price. As demand increases from D_1 to D_2 with constant cost production the price is unchanged at P_1, but with either increasing or decreasing cost production the price varies

Although Marshall, by emphasising the role of costs, did not suggest that value was purely subjective, his approach to price is well distanced from the early classical view that it is largely related to the labour input.

Another important contribution made by Marshall to neoclassical economics concerned his approach to competition. The classical economists had stressed the importance of competition in maximising economic well-being and had argued that through competition profits were reduced to the bare level necessary to sustain production. Marshall, through the means of what he called the 'representative firm' – a hypothetical firm with average access to markets, resources and information – formalised the discussion. With the assumptions of 'freedom of industry and enterprise' and a market with a large number of buyers and sellers of a homogeneous good or service, Marshall observed that firms would be price-takers, accepting the going price for their products in the market (Marshall, 1966, pp. 264ff).

This principle led subsequently to the development of the standard neoclassical market models found in textbooks today – perfect competition, monopolistic competition, oligopoly and monopoly. By introducing limiting assumptions about individual behaviour, notably that consumers act 'rationally' to maximise their utility and entrepreneurs act 'rationally' to maximise profits – and that both have perfect information about all possible prices, outputs and profits – predictions about prices and outputs under competition and varying degrees of 'imperfect competition' were derived. In particular, the perfect competition market model became a keystone of the neoclassical analysis of markets and the firm. Developed out of Marshall's analysis of competition, it is an especially intense form of market rivalry in which 'pure' or 'supernormal' profits are competed away so that only 'normal profits' are earned in the long run. Normal profits represent 'opportunity costs' or what the entrepreneur could earn in the next best alternative occupation and are included in the costs of production.

The perfect competition model is depicted in Figure 4.2. Given a sufficiently large number of firms in an industry all producing homogeneous products, each firm faces a horizontal demand curve for its output. This means that the firm must accept the going price in the industry – the firm is a 'price-taker'. With the further condition of rising marginal costs, the firm maximises profit where marginal cost equals marginal revenue at output Oq_1. If at this output the firm earns more than normal profit – in other words average cost (AC), including normal profit, is less than average revenue (AR) – there is an incentive for new firms to enter the industry. The resulting rise in the industry's output reduces the market price until only normal profit is earned (AC = AR) in the long run. If firms should earn less than normal profits (AC > AR) then the industry would contract as entrepreneurs left the industry seeking higher profits elsewhere. The market price would rise as the total supply shrank until normal profit was earned and there was no further incentive for entrepreneurs to move to other activities.

Since profits are competed down to a 'normal' level and as only those firms which minimise production costs can survive in highly competitive markets, the central message of neoclassical theory is that competition produces the lowest prices to the consumer and thus maximises consumer welfare. Only where there are significant economies of large-scale production or economies of scope might a single firm supply more cheaply than a number of competing firms (Parker, 1989). But such cases of 'natural monopoly' are considered rare.

While most economists sympathise with this conclusion, the

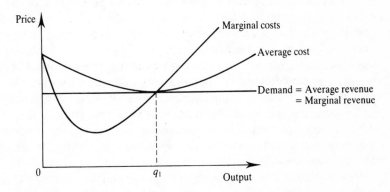

Figure 4.2 Long-run equilibrium in perfect competition

methodology adopted in neoclassical economics to arrive at it has been subject to considerable criticism, not least by Austrian economists (see Chapter 5, pp. 93–8 and Chapter 7). In particular the standard neoclassical competitive model is 'comparative static', that is to say it compares static or equilibrium positions. Once a market equilibrium is disturbed prices quickly, smoothly and predictably change until demand and supply are back in balance. In contrast, there is no attention to the actual *process* by which markets move between one equilibrium and another; thus interesting questions about *how* markets adjust are neglected. Neoclassical economists defend this approach on the grounds that it trades *descriptive reality* for a high degree of *predictive ability* (Friedman, 1953; Machlup, 1955). Competitive market prices and outputs tend to change in the way that the model predicts when subjected to exogeneous 'shocks', e.g. new taxes. None the less, although the methodology has proved valuable, it has meant that choice under conditions of uncertainty, which lies at the heart of business, has been treated as a special case. In standard neoclassical models all market participants are *assumed* to have perfect information about what is the most profitable price to charge, output to produce and factor input combination to employ. This applies both to the Marshallian treatment of demand and supply equilibria in separate markets (so-called 'partial equilibria') and to the complementary study of the 'general equilibrium' developed by Walras.

At the same time as Marshall was laying a path for the future development of neoclassical market models, in Lausanne, Switzerland Leon Walras was taking the evolving approach to price determination in individual markets and applying it to 'a hypothetical regime of perfectly free competition' across all markets (Walras, 1954). The product was a theory of 'general equilibrium' in which the market economy is brought into balance. Using mathematical techniques, Walras was able to reduce the demand and supply relationships in all output and input markets into a series of simultaneous equations. By this means he derived the important result that, in a perfectly competitive economy, a set of prices for goods and services and factor inputs can be derived which clears all markets, leaving no excess or deficiency of supply or demand at those prices. He was also able to demonstrate that an auctioneer shouting prices would eventually stumble upon this set of prices! In essence Walras confirmed mathematically Adam Smith's claim a century earlier that the divergent interests of producers and consumers can be reconciled in a competitive market and thus a competitive equilibrium for the whole economy can exist.

Under Walras' successor as professor of economics at Lausanne, Vilfredo Pareto (1848–1923), general equilibrium theory was extended to demonstrate formally that the competitive equilibrium maximises welfare. Like Marshall at the 'partial equilibrium' level, however, Walras and Pareto reached their conclusions by working with a highly stylised model of the economy. The Walrasian general equilibrium involves clearing all markets, including futures markets, simultaneously and therefore requires not only a current equilibrium across all markets but an 'intertemporal equilibrium' (Hicks, 1957; Debreu, 1959). Not surprisingly, to achieve this outcome the assumptions required are extensive. They include perfectly competitive markets, unchanging technology and consumer preferences, frictionless movements to equilibrium in markets and unchanged relationships between firms' inputs and outputs. Perfect information is also often assumed although it is not essential. In recent years a literature on 'uncertainty' within equilibrium theory has developed in which decision-taking by individuals centres upon a subjective assessment of the probability of a number of possible outcomes. This approach relies, however, upon certain restrictive assumptions. Also, it has had only a limited impact on the bulk of neoclassical theorising (for a review, see Gravelle and Rees, 1981, ch. 19).

Like Marshall in his discussion of the 'representative firm', Walras was not attempting to describe real markets nor did he wish to suggest that resources should be allocated by a grand 'auctioneer'. Rather he was providing an analytical device based upon what he recognised was a very artificial view of the economy. His method of analysis was typical of subsequent neoclassical methodology – by creating an abstract or stylised model, he wished to shed light on actual competitive markets. Also, as is the case of Marshallian partial equilibrium analysis, the approach is *comparative static*; that is, it is concerned with end states rather than with the process of adjustment. What happens in the *transition* from one market equilibrium to another is neglected. Like the theory of partial equilibrium, neoclassical general equilibrium theory ignores how markets *actually* adjust.

The above discussion of value and competition in neoclassical economics provides three conclusions crucial to an understanding of the neoclassical approach to profit and enterprise. First, the idea of value was distanced from labour inputs. Neoclassical economists could therefore abandon the Marxist notion, drawn from Ricardian economics, that labour or class is the ultimate source of value. Instead, in neoclassical theorising the source of value lies in consumers' marginal evaluations in the market alongside producer costs, of which labour is but one.

Second, the neoclassical treatment of competition centres upon perfectly defined markets and non-discretionary movements from one equilibrium to another. Prices and outputs alter in a manner fully determined in the model. The market moves automatically to a new equilibrium whenever conditions change. Although the concept of the equilibrium is intended by neoclassical economists merely as a methodological device to facilitate predictions about outcomes in actual competitive markets, it has had an important effect upon the way in which market economies are studied. Neoclassical economics has focused the attention of economists upon end states rather than on the *process* by which market economies move towards equilibrium.

Allied to this argument, the 'firm' in neoclassical theory is a 'black box'. Its internal organisation and the process by which decisions are reached are generally ignored. Given perfect information, the firm is reduced to a simple 'production function' in which the supply of a commodity is a function of given prices of inputs and the technical relationship between inputs and outputs. The optimal output, price and employment of inputs are perfectly determined; there are no choices to make. Business decision-taking is reduced to a mere routine.

Third, profit maximisation is a central *assumption* in standard neoclassical market models. This facilitates precise predictions about equilibrium prices and outputs and can therefore be defended. But as a consequence, the purpose and nature of profit are relatively neglected. In later neoclassical theorising various models of 'imperfect' competition have been developed in an attempt to reflect growing concentration of industry in capitalist economies (e.g. Sraffa, 1926; Robinson, 1933; Chamberlin, 1946). In these models assumptions about entrepreneurial behaviour other than profit maximisation have been introduced, for example sales maximisation, and occasionally the assumption of perfect information has been lifted (Baumol, 1959; Stiglitz, 1985). But the subject of profit, and more especially its relationship to enterprise, have remained relatively uninvestigated. These variations still, in the main, involve equilibrium models and in equilibrium models there is little or no scope for entrepreneurial action.

4.2   Factor prices

The marginal techniques developed to analyse product markets were gradually extended to the analysis of incomes. Income distribution was interpreted in neoclassical economics as the 'pricing' of factors of production, with the incomes of factors explained by their 'marginal productivities'. The marginal product is the addition to total production from employing an additional input and is normally expressed in value terms as the 'marginal revenue product'. In wage determination the idea of the marginal product of labour displaced the notion of the 'wages fund' central to classical economics.

The idea that incomes are related to outputs produced was not new in the 1870s – indeed, it dates back to at least the mercantilists; while in Germany Johann Heinrich von Thunen (1783–1850) had developed a marginal product theory for capital and labour well before the neoclassical period. But it was in the last quarter of the nineteenth century that a precise theory of incomes based on marginal productivity became popular. Jevons hit on the rudiments of a marginal product theory, but it was more fully developed, simultaneously and independently, by Knut Wicksell (1851–1926), Philip Henry Wicksteed (1844–1928), Alfred Marshall and especially the American economist John Bates Clark (1847–1938). Clark reasoned that in competitive markets a rational supplier would employ labour, land and capital (he tended to lump land and capital together) to the point where the marginal product of each was equal to its marginal cost.

Ricardo had suggested that as corn output was expanded each additional unit of land cultivated would have a lower productivity. As the margin of cultivation was extended less and less suitable land would be turned over to the production of corn. This concept of diminishing returns was now applied to *all* factors of production. Each input of any factor, applied to one or more fixed factors of production, would eventually result in a declining marginal productivity. From this principle neoclassical economists were able to conclude that eventually the marginal revenue product would decline to the point where it was equivalent to the marginal cost of employing the input. It would then not pay to increase inputs further because, with diminishing returns, the marginal revenue product would fall below the employment cost. As it paid an entrepreneur to employ inputs only to the point where the value of their marginal product equalled their marginal cost, it followed that variable inputs would be paid their marginal revenue product, with any fixed factor receiving the residual income.

Marginal product theory thus led to a unique and calculable level of employment which then produced a particular income distribution. All of the income is distributed to factor inputs according to their marginal products. This is illustrated in Figure 4.3. Assume two factor inputs labour and capital, with, in part (a) of the figure, capital as the fixed factor. The curve BC represents the marginal product of labour and is downward-sloping because of diminishing returns. If AD workers are employed then the total product is the area under the marginal product curve, area OBCD. Since each labourer receives the value of the last worker's marginal product as a wage (CD), the total wage bill is OACD and the residual of the total product, ABC, is a surplus which goes to capital in the form of interest. By the same method of reasoning, if capital were variable and labour fixed in supply, labour would receive

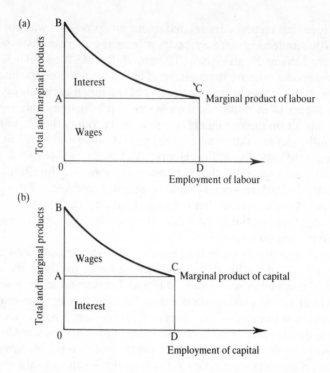

Figure 4.3   Marginal productivity theory (a) labour as the variable factor; (b) capital as the variable factor

the residual (as illustrated in part (b) of the figure). The approach appears to be neutral in its treatment of labour and capital – both are judged by the same marginal product mechanism.

As distributive shares are functional rewards, all factors of production appear to have an equally legitimate claim to their incomes. There seems to be no 'exploitation' or 'institutional robbery' as Marxists argue. This important conclusion was no accidental by-product of marginal product theory. As J. B. Clark explained in the preface to his book *The Distribution of Wealth*:

> It is the purpose of this work to show that the distribution of the income of society is controlled by a natural law, and that this law, if it worked without friction, would give to every agent of production the amount of wealth which that agent creates. (Clark, 1899)

Clark recognised that factor markets might not be highly competitive and that, for example, employers might consort together to force wages below the marginal product of labour; but equally well, he argued, through trade union pressure wages might be pushed above labour's marginal product so that capital received less than its due return. 'Institutional robbery', in so far as it occurred, was potentially a two-way problem and arose from a lack of competition rather than from any inherent tendency towards exploitation in the capitalist system. By the divorcing of value from labour and the relating of incomes to marginal products, rather than classes or the ownership of the means of production, the Marxist view of income was overturned.

Marginal product theory as developed by Wicksell, Wicksteed and Clark, however, stressed simply the role of demand for factor inputs in determining incomes. It was left to Marshall, just as in the case of the determination of product prices discussed earlier, to take fuller account of the supply of factor inputs. In particular, in relation to wages he argued that the idea that workers' wages are determined by their product at the margin is meaningless without consideration of the supply of labour. In looking at the supply of labour he emphasised that work involves disutility or is irksome – people, everything else being equal, prefer leisure. Hence the supply of labour is forthcoming only in return for wages; the supply curve of labour is positively related to the real wage level (as in Figure 4.4). This applies, he further reasoned, to other factors of production. Thus after Marshall, generally factor rewards in neoclassical theory became a product of both marginal productivity and the responsiveness of the supply of factor inputs to a change in their rewards. In Figure 4.4 the 'equilibrium' or market clearing wage is Ow_1.

Once the supply of labour was considered to be positively sloped, neoclassical economists were able to show that at the margin labour received a return in relation to its contribution to production, with intra-marginal units of labour earning a payment over and above what is necessary to bring forward their supply (in Figure 4.4 area Oaw_1). Hence, not only is labour not exploited by the market system, it is capable of earning surpluses or rents like the owners of capital in

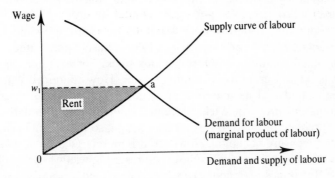

Figure 4.4 Neoclassical wage determination

Marxist theory and landowners in Ricardian economics. In other words, all factor inputs appear to be subject to the same laws of economics. Marshall, like Clark, concluded that production in capitalist economies is essentially a cooperative venture:

> It is not true that the spinning of yarn in a factory, after allowance has been made for wear-and-tear of the machinery, is the product of the labour of the operatives. It is the product of their labour, together with that of the employer and subordinate managers, and of the capital employed; and that capital itself is the product of labour and waiting; . . . (Marshall, 1966, p. 487)

The idea that the return to capital arises out of 'waiting', that is the postponement of current spending, was an extension of the approach adopted by the classical economist Nassau Senior (see pp. 40–1). In Marshall's writings the suppliers of capital receive interest which is justified as a reward for 'waiting'. He reasoned that people would always prefer to consume now rather than in the future; therefore they need to be induced to save by the receipt of interest from borrowers. The larger the amount that people want to borrow, the higher the level of savings and therefore the higher the interest rate must be. The supply curve of savings is thus a direct function of interest rates, just as the supply of labour is directly related to wages.

The relationship between interest and capital was further developed in terms of capital raising productivity. Thus it appeared that capital, like labour, had a marginal product for which interest or the return on capital was the reward. In subsequent neoclassical economics equilibrium interest rates were considered to be the result of the interaction of the demand for and supply of loanable funds in the capital market. The demand for loanable funds to invest was related to the marginal productivity of the resultant capital stock created; while supply was the supply of loanable funds by savers which was related to the thriftiness of society, itself a function of interest rates.

This approach to capital, however, had a number of possible flaws, as indeed some of the early neoclassical economists appreciated. In particular, fixed capital is a heterogeneous stock. For example, the steel-works is very different to a computer system. How, therefore, can capital be aggregated and its marginal product calculated? In an attempt to overcome this problem Wicksell treated capital as the cumulative *value* of resources committed to further production, so that value became the common measure of capital. However, this merely substituted one problem for another. To value capital requires a knowledge of equilibrium prices. But prices are themselves based partly upon the capital inputs into the economy (Sraffa, 1960; Napoleoni, 1972, pp. 26–9).

The problem of aggregation is not the only difficulty facing neoclassical capital theory. There is also the issue of identifying capital productivity. In particular, it is problematic to separate the contributions of capital and labour when both are complementary or joint inputs in the production process. In neoclassical economics fixed capital makes labour more productive and thus the productivity of capital is embodied in the output of labour. Furthermore, as Wicksell recognised, a higher marginal product of capital in a competitive market would lead to a higher demand for capital goods, which would in turn lead to higher payments to the factors of production which produced the capital. The product of capital would thus be embodied in the incomes of the factors of production which produced it.

Leaving capital to one side, marginal product theory also involves a degree of circularity as an explanation of wages – the use to which it is put in most textbooks today. In marginal product theory it is the value of the marginal product which determines the demand for the factors of production. But this value depends upon prices achieved for the outputs the factors produce, which depends in part upon the quantity of goods supplied to the market. The supply of goods, however, is itself related to the cost of the inputs employed: thus a certain amount of circularity. Moreover, the whole marginal product approach to incomes is typically neoclassical in its underlying assumption about information. If factor inputs are to be employed on the basis of their *actual* marginal revenue products, this requires perfect information about their marginal physical products and the relevant product prices. In the absence of perfect information, factors might be employed according to their *expected* rather than actual marginal products. But if this is so there may be no relation between incomes and actual marginal products.

Despite these serious shortcomings, marginal product theory remains central to the neoclassical theory of incomes and especially wages. Wicksell, Wicksteed and Clark were aware of a number of the above difficulties but were unwilling to let them stand in their way. All three appear to have believed that they had solved the problem of the determination of incomes which had dogged the classical economists. Wicksell concluded that:

> If for the moment we leave aside the question of the origin of the productivity (or value-creating power) of capital and regard it as an empirical fact, we may readily apply to capital the theory . . . that the share of the product going to any particular factor of production is determined by its marginal productivity. (Wicksell, 1935, p. 147)

Wicksteed similarly concluded that marginal productivity theory determined the returns to *all* factors of production and went on to reason that as a result there was no need to enumerate them separately (Wick-steed, 1894). The rules which determined the returns to capital also applied in determining wages. Moreover, Clark, confident of the predict-ive power of marginal productivity theory, concluded that incomes based on marginal product give 'to labour what labour creates, to the capitalist what capital creates, and to entrepreneurs what the co-ordinating function creates' (Clark, 1899, preface).

Marginal productivity reduced the determination of all incomes, in-cluding interest on capital and profit, to the same explanation, the pro-ductivity at the margin of the relevant inputs. Issues of class and the historical forces which produced capital and wage labour, central to Marxism and to a lesser degree to early classical theorising, were swept aside. Profit was thus a legitimate reward, but at the same time it did not need to be singled out for special treatment.

4.3 Profit and enterprise

Profit and enterprise are, as noted above, relatively neglected in neo-classical economics. This lack of concern relates to marginal productiv-ity theory. The idea of inputs being paid their marginal product, alongside the general neoclassical approach to markets, makes the role of the entrepreneur ambiguous, for two broad reasons. First, if markets move smoothly and predictably from one equilibrium to another and if in employing factors of production firms are assumed to know *in ad-vance* their marginal products, so that optimal input combinations are employed, entrepreneurship appears to be devoid of any rationale. Moreover, technical progress and innovation appear to fall 'like man-na from heaven' in neoclassical market models. There is rarely discus-sion of why and how technical progress and innovation occur. Consequently, there is in neoclassical economics no independent role for the entrepreneur in decisions about employment, production, in-vestment and innovation.

Second, and as we saw earlier, in a competitive equilibrium the in-come or total product is distributed between the factor inputs in accord-ance with their marginal products. This suggests that profit is associated with a specific factor input into the production process. Clark realised that there were severe problems in inputing a marginal product to entrepreneurship separate from the return to capital. Like Marshall he preferred to view profit as a windfall as markets moved towards their long-run equilibria. Disequilibrium profit was therefore strictly tem-porary while the forces of competition were played out – an idea that influenced Schumpeter (see pp. 90ff). When Clark did consider profit over the longer term, he associated it with a reward to management. In Clark's writings the entrepreneur appears to be a super-manager who 'coordinates capital and labour' in the face of risk (Clark, 1899, p. 46). But this begs an obvious question about the distinction, if any, between professional managers remunerated by salary and the entrepreneur who is rewarded by profit.

Clark was not alone in finding difficulty in identifying the role of the entrepreneur and its relationship with profit. Jevons, for example, considered that profit could be resolved into (1) the wages of superintendence, (2) insurance against risk and (3) interest. But as the wages of superintendence are a return to management, not enterprise (as Smith had explained a century earlier), and interest is a reward for providing capital, Jevons' justification of profit reduces to a return to risk-taking. This is no advance on the ideas of the later classical theorists, such as Mill, and leaves open the issue of what risk entrepreneurs take. Many commercial risks can be insured against, for example loss of stock by theft, fire or flooding, and in the final analysis it is investors who take most of the risks when they invest their capital in ventures, not the entrepreneur (unless the entrepreneur is also the supplier of capital). If the business fails it is the investors who lose their money. Moreover, the idea that profit is related to risk is in some logical difficulty in neoclassical competition theory when perfect information is assumed. If there is perfect information there can be no risk because all outcomes are known in advance.

Another contribution came from Walras. Despite the fact that the entrepreneur had no role in Walrasian general equilibrium theory, where markets and outcomes were perfectly defined, Walras provided elsewhere in his writings an approach to the entrepreneur and profit from which, it has been claimed, the Austrian economist Joseph Schumpeter derived inspiration (Walker, 1986, p. 18; for Schumpeter's views, see Chapter 5). Walras considered that the entrepreneur was an important fourth factor of production alongside land, labour and capital, 'whose role it is to lease land from the landowner, hire personal faculties from the labourer and borrow capital from the capitalist, in order to combine the three productive services in agriculture, industry and trade' (Walras, 1954, p. 222). By so arguing, he clearly separated the entrepreneurial function from the provision of capital – Walras's entrepreneur is not necessarily a capitalist – and highlighted the role of the entrepreneur as a coordinator of other inputs. Once the task of coordination is introduced, attention turns to the entrepreneur correctly judging the amounts and types of inputs and timing production to maximise profits. Balanced against this, however, he failed to clarify the distinction between enterprise and management. Why could salaried management as agents of, say, shareholders not undertake this coordinating role equally well?

Marshall similarly emphasised the role of organisation. Profit, he suggested, was a payment for entrepreneurial ability in reacting to market signals and organising production. Broadly, he divided entrepreneurs into two groups – the 'active' and the 'passive'. The active 'open out new and improved methods of business' and are imaginative business leaders or 'captains of industry', while the passive 'follow beaten tracks' (Marshall, 1966, p. 496). This approach could have started a fruitful discussion on the characteristics of 'active' entrepreneurship; however, Marshall failed to develop this train of thought. Instead, like Clark and Walras, in the final analysis he could only conceive of entrepreneurs as super-business-managers or super-organisers of existing resources. The business ability called for appeared to amount to more than the 'superintendence' suggested in Mill's economics, but it was not clearly delineated from management. Although he highlighted 'new and improved methods of business', Marshall gave little prominence to the role of entrepreneurship in invention and innovation. Moreover, unlike Walras, Marshall failed to separate interest, as a return to capital, from profit. In particular, at times he seems to associate normal profit with the long-term interest rate related to the reward for waiting.

One interesting observation by Marshall on entrepreneurs related to their supply and relative ability. The supply of entrepreneurs, like the supply of labour and capital, he argued, involved a cost – the cost of bringing forward the required supply of entrepreneurs. This he associated with the costs of obtaining the necessary skills to be a good entrepreneur. From this he reasoned that if entrepreneurs were to be forthcoming then they would have to expect to earn a profit at least equal to the costs they incurred in becoming entrepreneurs. Moreover, as business ability is unevenly distributed, through a kind of Darwinian process of 'natural selection' (Marshall was much taken with Charles Darwin's contemporary work on the evolution of the species), those entrepreneurs with unique skills would earn a surplus profit or economic rent. That is to say, with the supply of entrepreneurs not in perfectly elastic supply, 'intramarginal' entrepreneurs would earn a 'rent of ability'. This was not entirely an original idea, for the notion of profit as a rent of ability had already been implied in Mangoldt's writings (p. 45). Nevertheless, Marshall brought the idea to the attention of a much larger readership. In Marshall's analysis the implication is that the marginal entrepreneur earns a return equal to his or her supply cost, with especially talented 'captains of industry' earning profit representing additional ability. Thus at least a part of profit is an economic rent reflecting entrepreneurial ability (Marshall, 1966, pp. 503ff).

This idea raises two issues. One relates to the factors which determine the supply of enterprise; this has led to research into the possible economic, social, cultural and political factors which might influence this supply (Baumol, 1983; also Chapter 1 above). The second issue concerns the nature of profit. If profit is a payment representing exceptional entrepreneurial talent then continuing high profit appears justified in terms of the contribution such entrepreneurs make to the economy – though the precise nature of this contribution remains to be identified. Neoclassical economics, however, emphasises markets in which profits decline to 'normal', implying no rent of ability in the long run. Thus, as in the case of the ideas of Clark and Walras, Marshall's discussion of the entrepreneur stands awkwardly alongside the neoclassical approach to competition. In discussing the perfect competition model it is often assumed that all entrepreneurs are of equal ability and through competition prices fall until all profits, other than normal profits, are competed away. Thus long-run economic rents are ruled out.

Marshall noted that in practice the method by which competition would equalise profit rates would be through the effect of 'expected' profit on investment, and he recognised that the *ex post* profit could only equal the *ex ante* profit when expectations were completely fulfilled. But in the perfect competition model full information ensures that *ex ante* and *ex post* profits must be identical. If the entrepreneur earns an economic rent, due to some change in market conditions, the competitive market automatically adjusts until profits are reduced to 'normal'. If rents or 'supernormal' profits are still earned then this must be because competition is imperfect. In the inter-war and post-war years increasingly complex models were designed by neoclassical economists to show that where there is imperfect competition, including oligopoly and monopoly, rents can be earned. This drew attention to 'barriers to entry' into industries and competition-reducing strategies such as predatory pricing. In other words, long-run supernormal profits were rationalised in terms of defects in the competitive process which should be tackled through 'competition policy'. The possibility that continuing high profits are a feature of a healthy competitive process (implicit in Marshall's account of the 'rent of ability') was discounted.

As neoclassical economics has evolved the role of uncertainty in production and the relationship between uncertainty and entrepreneurship have been emphasised notably by Frank Knight, Frederick B. Hawley (1843–1929) and Frank W. Taussig (1859–1940). Taussig in particular stressed imagination and judgement as attributes of successful entrepreneurship (Hawley, 1893, p. 464; Taussig, 1915, pp. 159ff; Hebert and Link, 1988, pp. 83–5). Also, certain recent developments in economic theory move away from the idea that consumers successfully maximise utility and producers successfully maximise profits (see Hey and Lambert, 1987), but these developments are discussed only, if at all, on advanced economics courses. The exception is Harvey Leibenstein's work on 'x-inefficiency'. Leibenstein (1976) stresses that due, for instance, to human inertia, incomplete contracts and organisational entropy the normal state is that profits are not maximised and costs are not minimised within firms. Thus there are opportunities for entrepreneurial initiative to reduce 'slacking' and raise profits which are missing in the neoclassical competition model. The most successful entrepreneurs will be those who do this best, hence earning a kind of Marshallian rent of ability. Thus in Leibenstein's theory profits are related to entrepreneurs improving operating efficiency.

Another interesting development in recent years has involved the idea of the firm as a 'team' of inputs coordinated by a 'monitor' or entrepreneur (Alchian and Demsetz, 1972). In this theory the role of the entrepreneur (or what Alchian and Demsetz call 'the monitor') is to employ inputs to maximise the use of scarce resources given imperfect information about inputs and outputs. Walras, for example, had identified the entrepreneur as a 'combiner' of the other factor inputs. But in this approach the relationship is formalised in terms of the 'monitor' employing and utilising inputs to produce the largest profit. Drawing upon Ronald Coase's earlier work on transaction costs (Coase, 1937), this approach to entrepreneurship suggests that the entrepreneur must calculate the optimal combination of factor inputs to employ and the profit-maximising output to produce. Some might see in this emphasis upon calculation a distraction from the true function of entrepreneurship, which they relate not to calculation but to judgement (see Chapter 5). In addition, once again the distinction, if any, between an employed 'monitor' (a manager) and an entrepreneur is unclear. Nevertheless, the idea provides a rationale for entrepreneurship in terms of minimising the costs which arise from imperfect information in market economies – a problem which is, of course, absent in the neoclassical model of competition (cf. Casson, 1982).

These developments, however, have not been allowed to alter the major thrust of neoclassical economics, which essentially revolves around perfectly determined equilibria in which there is no judgement, 'monitoring' or other entrepreneurial duties to perform. Thus today economics textbooks often include a chapter on the entrepreneur or profit – in which risk-taking, coping with uncertainty and good judgement are emphasised – but such a chapter sits uneasily alongside a much lengthier discourse involving neoclassical market models in which such entrepreneurial attributes are redundant. Where economics involves no uncertainty there appears to be no business ability worth talking about to reward.

4.4 Neoclassical economists and the state

Like their classical predecessors, the founders of neoclassical economics were in general opposed to state intervention and believed in achieving economic harmony through the competitive market. The function of government was primarily to establish and defend private property rights. None the less, over time neoclassical economics has established the basis for wide-sweeping state intervention in the economy. The key to this paradox lies firstly in the idea of pricing with full information. If the allocation of resources is simply a matter of setting prices according to marginal costs, then on the face of it the state can achieve an optimal allocation by marginal cost pricing. In the inter-war years a number of economists speculated upon whether this was possible and concluded that a planned economy could rationally set prices and factor rewards so as to clear all markets. This conclusion has been attacked, especially by Austrian economists, partly on the grounds that it ignores the important issue of motivation. This debate is reviewed in the next chapter after a full discussion of Austrian economics.

A second key to the paradox lies in the concept of 'market failure'. Neoclassical economists have allowed for state intervention in markets where the free market might produce outputs and prices which do not maximise welfare. This is especially reflected in attitudes towards income distribution, externalities, monopoly and unemployment where some neoclassical economists have proposed extensive state involvement. In such cases the implications for profit and enterprise have been relatively ignored. The presumption has been that the state has the ability and motivation to identify market failure accurately and to undertake the necessary ameliorative intervention without damaging private enterprise.

Income distribution

Walras and later Pareto recognised that the outputs and prices determined in their general equilibria reflected a given income distribution. Each income distribution would produce a different set of prices and outputs. There was therefore no unique general equilibrium. Whereas Walras, however, believed that judgement on the merits of income distributions was outside the scope of economics, many other neoclassical economists were less detached. Marshall, for instance, while generally supportive of free market outcomes and opposed to 'socialism' – which he argued would 'deaden the energies of mankind, and arrest economic progress' – believed that economics should be a tool of social improvement (Marshall, 1966, p. 593). To ameliorate poverty, Marshall recognised a case for state intervention in income distribution and in the provision of goods which the market might undersupply to the poor, such as education. Developing an idea from Jevons, Marshall acknowledged that more equality might raise social well-being because of the diminishing marginal utility of money: 'The happiness which an additional shilling brings to a poor man is much greater than that which it brings to a rich one' (Marshall, 1966, p. 393). Although later neoclassical economists have questioned whether there can be any such simple intercomparability of utilities between individuals to arrive at this conclusion, the idea that the state may play a useful role through tax policies and provision of certain public services, such as education, has continued in neoclassical economics. It is reinforced by the neoclassical approach to externalities.

Externalities

Externalities are benefits and costs which do not accrue directly to the parties in a market exchange but to others in society, so that private costs and benefits diverge from social costs and benefits. For example, a factory producing chemicals might pollute the local environment. Also, education may have benefits beyond those to the individuals being educated through the creation of a better-qualified and more 'cultured' population. It is now a central feature of neoclassical welfare economics that there is a case for state interference in the market to reduce outputs where there are external costs and to increase outputs where there are social benefits (Millward, 1971; Samuelson, 1954; though cf. Coase, 1960). These objectives can be achieved through regulation and direct state provision; but generally neoclassical economists have tended to prefer the use of taxes and subsidies. As A. C. Pigou demonstrated in his *The Economics of Welfare* (1920), taxes could be placed on goods with external costs to reduce demand and output; and subsidies, by making goods cheaper, could be used to increase demand where there are external benefits.

Monopoly

Just as a case is made for state intervention in markets where there are externalities, many neoclassical economists favour state involvement where there is a monopoly – defined as market dominance or the adoption of practices by firms which act to restrict competition. Marshall recognised that economies of scale might give a large firm a continuous competitive advantage leading to monopoly, but concluded that after a phase of growth, firms would face eventual decline as management and control fell into the hands 'of people with less energy and less creative genius' (Marshall, 1966, p. 264). This suggested that despite an underlying tendency towards decreasing cost production, monopoly was unlikely to become a serious problem.

Other neoclassical economists were less sanguine. J. B. Clark, for instance, saw the growth of monopoly power as a major threat to economic progress and called for government intervention to keep it in check, while later the idea that elements of monopoly power were pervasive in many markets took hold (Sraffa, 1926). Imperfectly competitive markets came to be associated with wasteful advertising, excess capacity and long-term 'supernormal' profits. Thus many neoclassical economists became active proponents of state antimonopoly policies both in the United States and in Europe. In addition, neoclassical economists have generally accepted a need to regulate or nationalise the 'natural monopolies', such as water, gas and electricity, where competition raises supply costs.

Unemployment

Despite an undercurrent from North to Malthus to Marx that general trade depressions were possible, indeed likely, in capitalist economies, the prevailing view in the nineteenth century was based on Say's Law of markets, that 'supply creates its own demand'. Whenever goods and services are supplied the potential purchasing power to buy the goods and services is also created. This idea from classical economics carried over into neoclassical theory. If for some reason the purchasing power was not used to buy the available goods and services, then the solution lay primarily in wage cuts, which would enable the prices of the products to be reduced until demand was restored. Any notion that there could be inadequate demand due to excess savings was dismissed on the grounds that the interest rate would vary to bring savings and investment into equilibrium. Where unemployment and overproduction occurred this was merely the result of a temporary market disequilibrium. As long as markets remained competitive, full employment would be restored and markets would clear, as the Walrasian general equilibrium demonstrated. Jevons dismissed the idea of general depressions as 'evidently absurd and self-contradictory' (Jevons, 1970, p. 212).

The main challenge to this view came from the presence of high and continuing unemployment in the 1930s. A worldwide trade slump followed the Wall Street crash of 1929. In the United States industrial production by 1932 stood at only a little over half of its 1929 level, while in Britain unemployment reached 22.1 per cent and in Germany 25 per cent. In recent years this Depression has been attributed by the monetarist economist Professor Milton Friedman to a severe restriction of credit following the stock market crash (Friedman and Schwartz, 1963). Falling share prices and bank closures reduced liquidity in the economy, leading to a decline in output. In the 1930s, however, the Cambridge economist John Maynard Keynes (1883–1946) came to a very different conclusion. As he was reared in the neoclassical tradition, Keynes' ideas were quickly absorbed into neoclassical teaching after the War so that Keynesian macroeconomics was presented alongside neoclassical microeconomics in textbooks. (However, a separate Keynesian tradition lives on at Cambridge University and its followers dispute whether Keynes' insights can be easily reconciled with neoclassical precepts. Space precludes exploring this controversy.)

In *The General Theory of Employment, Interest and Money* (1936), Keynes attempted to explain continuing unemployment in terms of prices being 'sticky downwards', business expectations, and the failure of interest rates to equate savings and investment to prevent a shortfall in demand. Prices were sticky downwards, Keynes argued, because of the development of imperfect competition in product and labour markets. The growth of large companies restricted price competition for goods, while trade unions resisted major wage cuts even when high unemployment existed. This was not a novel idea; it was a main ingredient of the so-called 'Treasury view' of the 1930s which Keynes did much to undermine. But whereas the Treasury view relied upon a decline in resistance to wage and price cuts to restore employment, Keynes argued that 'sticky' prices and wages were a fact of modern life that economic theory needed to accommodate. Also, Keynes pointed out that if wages fell, and prices did not fall as quickly, there would be a loss of real purchasing power which would aggravate the economic depression. Thus Keynes' message was that directly reducing wages might not be possible and, even when possible, it was not an obvious cure for unemployment.

On the issue of business expectations, Keynes recognised the weakness of the neoclassical approach to uncertainty and business motivation. As we have seen, much of neoclassical theory had relatively little to say about these subjects. Keynes, however, placed them at the centre of his analysis. Keynes' entrepreneur operates in a world of uncertainty and in this respect his views are not too dissimilar to those of modern Austrian economists (see Chapter 5). However, Keynes' approach is distinguished by his pessimism about where individualism can take economies. In particular, he linked enterprise to 'animal spirits' rather than to profit calculations – especially in the financial markets where he appears to have viewed speculation in shares as little more than a game of roulette, which could have devastating effects on the economy as in 1929. Moreover, it was shifting expectations that could lead investment to contract even when interest rates declined. Even with lower interest rates, if expectations of future returns on investment deteriorated sufficiently, investment would not increase. Businessmen might not be motivated to invest by low interest rates in the depths of a trade recession. Thus a simple link between interest rates and investment in Say's Law of markets was broken by the introduction of business expectations.

Furthermore, Keynes was able to demonstrate that the interest rate was not simply a product of the demand for and supply of loanable funds (investment and savings), but was also affected by the demand to hold money (liquidity preference) and by the supply of money. In Keynes' analysis, interest was not a reward for 'waiting' or 'abstinence', as in classical and early neoclassical theory, but a reward for parting with liquidity. Keynes' major insight revolved around a tendency for people to hoard cash (remain highly liquid) in periods of economic depression, so that savings did not enter the financial markets driving interest rates down to a level necessary to revive the economy. With monetary policy thus impotent, Keynes emphasised the need for active fiscal policies, involving public expenditure and tax cuts, to restore full employment. For this reason Keynesian economics after the War became associated with high state spending.

Keynes also believed that a stationary economic state in the long term was a real possibility. The idea that there might come a time when capital accumulation slowed down and the economy stopped growing had interested a number of the classical economists and, although it was not assimilated into the mainstream of neoclassical economics, it was also acknowledged by Marshall, Walras and J. B. Clark. Marshall speculated that in the very long term as wealth rose savings might increase to the extent that there existed inadequate outlets for investment at any positive interest rate; Walras and J. B. Clark similarly concluded that over time the profit rate might fall. But it was Keynes who took a particularly pessimistic view of the ability of market economies to continuously generate opportunities for profit-making, associating the stationary state with declining returns on investment as investment opportunities were exhausted. Consequently, there would be a need for permanent state interference in the economy to overcome a growing gap between savings and investment at full employment (Hansen, 1939).

One product of this fear of a savings gap was a renewed interest in income redistribution. This led to the view that redistribution was not only socially desirable or justified in terms of an intercomparability of utilities, it was an economic *necessity* if recessions were to be avoided. A redistribution from rich to poor would help to reduce savings and boost consumption since the poor had a higher marginal propensity to consume than the rich. The message seemed clear: the survival of capitalism depended upon active state involvement in the economy to counter the problem of excessive thrift, to stabilise the economy and thus facilitate private investment and to offset inadequate private demand. For most post-war Keynesians 'pump-priming' was adequate whenever there was evidence of insufficient demand in the economy. But for others, governments had a continuous role to play in providing the conditions for full and stable employment and, later, in maintaining stable prices.

In the post-war period down to the mid-1970s economic policy on both sides of the Atlantic was heavily influenced by Keynesian precepts. Only with rising inflation and the revival of a monetarist theory to explain it, growing concern about the level of state spending and taxation, and fears that public sector borrowing was 'crowding out' private investment, did Keynesian economics lose its dominant position in macroeconomics. To its critics Keynesian demand management worsened economic fluctuations through badly timed intervention and in the final analysis was unnecessary (Buchanan *et al.*, 1978). Contrary to Keynes' argument and that of his followers, free market economists (including Austrian economists and non-Keynesian neoclassical theorists) maintained that market economies are essentially stable and that unemployment, in the absence of impediments to wage and price adjustments, is essentially a short-term problem. In so far as Keynesian techniques lead to high taxation, 'big government', bureaucracy and politically inspired economic policies, they create for business further disincentives and uncertainty and are therefore counterproductive in terms of stimulating investment. Thus whereas Keynes assumed that government intervention to stabilise a high level of demand would increase rather than diminish enterprise, his critics contended that Keynesian intervention undermined the entrepreneurial spirit.

4.5   Conclusion

In 1879 Cliffe Leslie (1827–82), professor of jurisprudence and political economy at Queen's College, Belfast, observed:

> The bane of political economy has been the haste of its students to possess themselves of a complete and symmetrical system, solving all the problems before it with mathematical certainty and exactness. The very attempt shows

an entire misconception of the nature of those problems, and of the means available for their solution. (Leslie, 1888)

This criticism is no less apposite now. Today neoclassical economics forms the core of mainstream economics teaching, especially at the micro level, and is primarily concerned with the optimal allocation of resources assuming the existence of complete information. It has provided a body of theory which has allowed a rigorous study of market-clearing prices – and this has been of considerable value. A major drawback, however, relates to the dynamics of a market economy. In neoclassical economics the *process* by which market economies adjust and change is neglected in favour of an analysis which focuses upon market equilibria. In particular, in the neoclassical system there is no real analysis of motivation – too often profit maximisation is an assumption 'plucked from the air', competition and innovation 'just happen' – nor is there much attention to the supply of entrepreneurship; where do entrepreneurs come from, what motivates them and what is the entrepreneurial function? Critics of neoclassical theory, especially modern Austrian economists (whose ideas are reviewed in the next chapter), attack it for overlooking the *essence* of a market economy. The notion of the economy in a state of constant change is missing in neoclassical analysis. In addition, with perfect information about optimal prices, outputs and factor input combinations there are no real entrepreneurial decisions to make.

Also, neoclassical economics has no theory of profit; rather there are a number of insights relating profit to the remuneration of abstinence, compensation for risk-taking and wages of superintendence, which leave unclear the difference, if any, between profit, managerial payments and interest on capital. Above all, profit maximisation is treated as an assumption about business behaviour with profits falling to a 'normal' return through the forces of competition. Where supernormal profits continue in the long run they do so because of 'market imperfections'. The possibility that high profit is an ongoing feature of a healthy market economy is discounted.

This neglect of profit and enterprise was reflected in the stance taken by many neoclassical economists towards state intervention. The emphasis was upon 'market failure' and the potential benefits from correcting it through state interference, whether the failure took the form of an inequitable income distribution, externalities, monopoly or unemployment. Much less attention was paid to the effects of 'state failure' upon the viability of a private enterprise economy, at least until the 1970s and the onset of economic 'stagflation'. The implications of this for economic policy are considered in more detail in Chapter 8.

Inevitably, the neoclassical economics reviewed in this chapter has been something of a 'straw man'. There are pockets of neoclassical theory which deal, for example, with imperfect information and the motivation of entrepreneurs. But the important point is that very little of this specialised study enters the textbooks used by the bulk of economics students, especially at the introductory level. Given that many students of economics do not study the subject beyond this level, for example those on business and management courses, it follows that they receive a particularly restricted view of the market economy. A market economy which appears to run on autopilot is no market economy.

Further reading

There are many volumes dealing with neoclassical economic thought. Particularly noteworthy for providing highly readable accounts are Blaug (1978, 1986a) and Ekelund and Hebert (1975). More critical but none the less interesting studies can be found in Routh (1975) and Wolff and Resnick (1987). The structure of neoclassical economics is summarised at a technical level in Hicks (1957) and Debreu (1959), and both are a good starting-point for anyone sceptical of the 'straw man' treatment adopted in this chapter. Alternatively, they can move directly to almost any introductory economics text, for example Begg, Fischer and Dornbusch (1987).

The classic defence of neoclassical methodology is Friedman (1953). For comments on the treatment of enterprise in neoclassical economics see Baumol (1968) and Loasby (1982). On the development of Keynesian economics, Stewart (1972) provides a highly readable account and Blaug (1986b) a more thorough and up-to-date study. For an especially penetrating attack upon neoclassical economics and state intervention see Littlechild (1986).

Once again, there is no substitute for reading the 'originals'. Readers are especially recommended to sample Alfred Marshall's *Principles of Economics* (1966).

5
The Austrian approach to profit and enterprise

At the same time as Leon Walras and Alfred Marshall were sowing the seeds of neoclassical theory, a different but parallel tradition in economics was taking shape in Austria. Both neoclassical and Austrian economics are rooted in a subjectivist approach to value, and early Austrian economists made a major contribution to what became neoclassical principles. Whereas, however, the adherents of the 'marginalist revolution' went on to determine efficient market equilibria in terms of *given* tastes and costs, the Austrian school progressed by arguing that because all economic knowledge is subjective there are no 'objective' solutions to the problem of equilibrium. In addition, neoclassical theory was primarily concerned with partial or general market equilibria often under conditions of complete or perfect information. But in Austrian economics the emphasis falls on the market as a *process* and on economic decisions made under conditions of uncertainty. As a consequence neoclassical economics struggles to provide a rationale for enterprise, while Austrian theory places the entrepreneur at the centre of its discussion of the market system, much in the way that he had featured in Cantillon's and Say's earlier but neglected analyses. In important respects Austrian economics can be seen as a further development of the continental European treatments of enterprise and profit, just as neoclassical economics continued the neglect of the subject in British classical theory. Today many aspects of the debates on enterprise and profit in economics derive from clashes between the Austrian and neoclassical perspectives on markets and economic decision-making.

5.1 The foundations of modern Austrian economics

The first landmark in the development of Austrian economics was the publication of the book *Principles of Economics* in 1871 by the professor of political economy at the University of Vienna, Carl Menger (1840–1921). In this work Menger set out to replace both the classical theory of value (pp. 35ff) and German historicism (pp. 126ff) with economic principles based on subjectivism. At the heart of subjectivism lies the principle that consumers demand products and services according to the marginal utility they receive from them. Hence value results from personal evaluations of products or the subjective decisions of consumers in the market. It does not arise from 'objective' considerations such as long-run production costs or the 'labour theory of value' as in classical and Marxist theories. In pursuing this line of reasoning, Menger maintained that decisions to buy and sell in market economies are essentially decisions which are taken by individuals solely on the basis of the information available to them.

In addition, Menger introduced the principle of 'imputation' in which, broadly, factor rewards (salaries, interest and rent) are the *consequence* of consumer demand for the products they produce. By contrast, in classical and Marxist theories the emphasis was upon the costs of factors *determining* final selling prices – with the major exception of land rents which, Ricardo explained, were dependent upon the price of food. Menger reversed the causation (as Say had also done some decades earlier). Factor costs do not determine the value of goods; rather the demand for and hence the price of inputs is derived from consumers' demands for the products the inputs produce.

Menger's economics was developed further by two disciples, Friedrich von Wieser (1851–1926) and Eugen von Bohm-Bawerk (1851–1914). Von Wieser argued that economic costs, like utility, are essentially subjective since they depend upon alternatives forgone or what is termed 'opportunity costs'. Opportunity costs (what the resources could have produced if used in a different way) can only be determined, he reasoned, by the individuals involved in making the choices. Only they can know what the alternative uses would be. Von Wieser therefore helped to ditch the idea that value is derived from inputs or costs, that is to say the 'objective' factors in classical and Marxist theories such as labour time or subsistence wages.

Von Bohm-Bawerk, who took over the chair of economics at Vienna from von Wieser, made his major contribution to modern Austrian economics through his study of capital and more specifically the relationship between interest and postponing consumption (for details see p. 102). By highlighting the relationship as he saw it between interest, time and capital and by treating capital as merely a feature of production over time, he clashed head-on with Marxist economics. This conflict with Marxism was by no means accidental; from the outset one of von Bohm-Bawerk's chief objectives was to undermine Marxist economics which, he contended, was 'low theory' and 'fallacies – wanton, unproved assumption, self-contradiction, and blindness to facts' (Bohm-Bawerk, 1949). In Marxism the returns to capital and the existence of capital can only be truly understood through an analysis of class and the historical developments that produced capitalism. Von Bohm-Bawerk argued that capital was not related to the economics of 'class' but rather it was a feature of intertemporal production at *all times* and in *all types* of economies. Thus economic principles could be detached from history and capital could be detached from a process of exploitation. Capital was politically neutralised.

Menger, von Wieser and von Bohm-Bawerk laid the foundations of Austrian economics, which were built upon in the twentieth century by three highly influential Austrians – Ludwig von Mises (1881–1973), his student Friedrich von Hayek (b. 1889) and Joseph Schumpeter (1883–1950) – as well as by a 'non-Austrian', the American Frank H. Knight (1885–1972). Knight's work on uncertainty and risk and the connection between uncertainty and entrepreneurship had a major influence on subsequent Austrian thinking.

Today Austrian economics has established a small but influential following in the United States and to a lesser extent in British universities. One consequence is that the term 'Austrian' no longer has any geographical significance but instead describes a method of economic analysis. The major proponents of current Austrian or neo-Austrian views in the United States include Ludwig M. Lachmann (b. 1906), Israel Kirzner (b. 1930), a student of von Mises, and the libertarian Murray N. Rothbard (b. 1926); and in Britain G. L. S. Shackle (b. 1903) and Stephen Littlechild (b. 1943). The ideas of these economists differ in emphasis and detail, but they broadly share an approach to economics which is critical of the predominant paradigm of twentieth-century economics, neoclassical theory.

5.2 Von Mises, von Hayek, Schumpeter and Knight

Von Mises emigrated to the United States in 1940, where he became professor of economics at New York University. His major contribution to Austrian economics lay in his concept of *praxeology* (the study of human action), which he set out in his book *Human Action* (first English edition, 1949). Mises' starting-point was his belief that people, at least when freely allowed to, pursue their own self-interest and thus act purposefully or intentionally to achieve their chosen ends. Building upon Menger's and von Wieser's work on subjectivism, von Mises went on to argue that no ethical judgement should be made about whether individuals' actions are wise, for the private experience of the individual must be the sole foundation of knowledge. This approach, today known as 'methodological subjectivism', leads to the conclusion that normally no other person or institution, such as the state, should attempt to override the decisions of individuals when they are freely arrived at, since individuals have the best information about how to maximise their own well-being. Von Mises was able to conclude from this that the competitive market system, where people are free to make their own choices, is the best economic system.

That individuals should be given the maximum freedom possible to pursue their own ends and that this is best served by a free market economy is also a central theme in the prolific writings of the Nobel prize-winning economist Friedrich von Hayek. In the post-war period, von Hayek has been a most important propagator of the Austrian view of the world, both to fellow economists and to policy-makers.

The competitive market exists, in von Hayek's view, to solve what he calls the 'central theoretical problem of all social science' (von Hayek, 1982, p. 88):

> The really central problem of economics as a social science . . . is how the
> spontaneous interaction of a number of people, each possessing only bits of
> knowledge, brings about a state of affairs . . . which could be brought about
> by deliberate direction only by somebody who possesses the combined
> knowledge of all these individuals. (von Hayek, 1948, p. 79)

In von Hayek's view the decentralised price system is undoubtedly the best supplier of information about individual wants and supply costs and is thus the most efficient 'kind of machinery for registering change' (von Hayek, 1948, p. 87). As von Hayek points out, the price system is a means of passing information between a multitude of individual consumers and producers. It follows, therefore, that any interference with prices, for example by the state, will distort this information flow leading inevitably to a serious misallocation of resources and a decline in economic well-being.

An important influence upon von Hayek and other post-war Austrian economists was Joseph Schumpeter. Schumpeter, who was influenced by the German historical school as well as by his teacher von Bohm-Bawerk at the University of Vienna, held certain views especially about the long-term development of capitalist economies which are at variance with modern Austrian thinking. Yet Austrian economics owes a great debt to Schumpeter, most particularly because of his study of the inter-relationship between competition, innovation and the market process.

Schumpeter argued that the true nature of competition could not be fully appreciated using the comparative static models of neoclassical theory. In particular, he took issue with the Marshallian and Walrasian competitive markets in which small firms with identical products compete on an equal footing. Rather, he argued, competition is essentially a dynamic and ongoing process of change in which innovating firms competing against the rest produce different, not identical, products and use different, not identical, production techniques. Profit is then earned precisely because the competing firms are not equal in terms of outputs and costs of production.

Viewing competition in this way, Schumpeter was able to conclude that profit is the consequence of being one step ahead of the competition and is therefore a temporary monopoly rent until such time as other firms introduce even superior products or production methods (Schumpeter, 1950, pp. 123–41). Furthermore, he reasoned that competition in market economies involves 'a perennial gale of creative destruction' in which dominant firms and production methods are eventually undermined by new discoveries in production or sources of supply, or by new techniques in the management of resources, marketing or distribution. Thus profits are likely to be eroded in the long run but not in the frictionless and seemingly automatic way implied in the neoclassical competition model. Competition in this analysis is not about working within existing structures as in neoclassical theory – the 'perfectly competitive market' – but instead it is a process, inherent in capitalism, in which market structures are perpetually created and then destroyed.

Given this emphasis upon the role of innovation in the competitive market system, not surprisingly Schumpeter also highlighted the role of entrepreneurship. In Schumpeterian economics it is the entrepreneur constantly striving for market advantage who is able, through *creating* disequilibria in markets, to cash in on profit opportunities before competitors have time to react. The 'first in the field' earns a monopoly profit until such time as competitors respond. If perfect knowledge was instantaneous or given, as in the neoclassical competitive model, pure profit (an economic rent) would immediately decline since everyone would know where to invest to obtain the best return. Indeed logically, as Schumpeter noted, if everyone was able to anticipate correctly the future state of the market, decisions would become 'routinised' and profits would fall to zero. Schumpeter stressed that it was precisely *because* of the absence of perfect knowledge that an entrepreneur was able to steal an advantage on competitors and earn pure profit for a time.

Schumpeter's argument is therefore that pure profit arises out of imperfect information in market economies. Although this linking of imperfect information to profit in economic transacting was not really new – a similar line of argument, for example, can be found in von Mises' writings and much earlier in Cantillon's and Say's economics – Schumpeter was mainly responsible for exploring the linkage in the context of a ceaseless competitive process. As a result he broke with the idea, endorsed by his teacher von Bohm-Bawerk and which goes back at least to Cantillon, that profit is linked to risk. Risk, Schumpeter claimed, is borne by the supplier of the capital, who might lose his investment if the enterprise fails – i.e. the capitalist. What the entrepreneur faces is not risk but *uncertainty* and the two concepts are quite different. Schumpeter's entrepreneur is someone who, lacking complete information and perhaps using others' funds, seeks out new products, markets and innovations. The input of enterprise is therefore carefully distinguished from the input of capital – a distinction which remains of central importance in the thinking of later 'Austrians' such as Kirzner.

Consistent with his focus on knowledge in economies, Schumpeter justifies pure profit as the reward to enterprise for successful innovation or endeavour in the face of uncertainty: 'Without development there is no profit, without profit no development' (Schumpeter, 1934, p. 154). Schumpeter's entrepreneur is someone who is willing to face the uncertainty of innovation rather than collect a fixed salary or invest in fixed-interest securities. As such Schumpeter recognised that entrepreneurs will always be in scarce supply (an argument not dissimilar to that put forward much earlier by Say). But in Schumpeter's writings profit is not a differential rent of ability as Marshall suggested; indeed as far as Schumpeter was concerned profit was unlike any other payment to factors of production. It is not a wage of enterprise in some kind of managerial context, nor is it simply a residual when other costs are met. Schumpeter's profit is not always well defined, but it is clearly linked in some way to what the entrepreneur contributes to production in terms of innovating in the face of uncertainty, without in any sense being linked like wages to a marginal product. There is no marginal product of enterprise. At the same time, while discounting the idea that profit is simply some sort of fortunate residual over supply costs, Schumpeter maintained that profit 'does not enter into the price of products' (1934, p. 153). Schumpeter believed that the American J. B. Clark's approach to profit was the nearest to his own, in the sense that both believed that profit arose out of a market disequilibrium.

As far as Schumpeter was concerned it was precisely the failure of the neoclassical economists to understand the peculiar nature of enterprise which led them, erroneously in his view, to argue that profits tend towards equalisation at some 'normal' level. According to Schumpeter, given imperfect information about optimal price and output configurations in markets, at best equilibria in economies can emerge only through a sequential process of change and adjustment. But during that process innovations are likely to change the market environment so that equilibria are not achieved. In Schumpeter's economics the entrepreneur is an innovator who both *causes* and cashes in on disequilibria in markets. From this he was able to develop an impressive theory of trade cycles in which, when innovations crowd together, market prices and outputs fluctuate leading to economic booms and slumps. Thus he could conclude (like Marx!) that capitalism is inherently unstable (Schumpeter, 1939).

In his writings Schumpeter separated risk and uncertainty; but it was Frank Knight at the University of Chicago who explored the difference between the two to greatest effect and in terms of what he believed was a crucial distinction between insurable and non-insurable risk. In his *Risk, Uncertainty and Profit* (1921), Knight explained that risk could normally have a probability attached to it and thus through actuarial procedures could be insured against. For example, the risk of a particular 30-year-old woman having a car accident or a coronary can be statistically estimated from past evidence of similar women having car accidents or heart attacks. Uncertainty, however, implies that past experience is not a reliable guide to future events and therefore there is a lack of knowledge from which to estimate probability. In other words, no probability function can be constructed.

Knight concluded that economic decisions – and especially investment and production – involve uncertainty rather than simple risk. In his words: 'The uncertainties which persist as causes of profit are those which are uninsurable because there is no objective measure of the probability of gain or loss' (1951, p. 120). Each entrepreneurial decision is unique; that is to say, it is specific to each circumstance and cannot be aggregated and actuarially assessed. There is, Knight argued, no way of calculating the probability of entrepreneurial success.

In practice the probability of an individual succeeding in, say, a new business venture might be statistically estimated from the success rate of others recently entering the same field of business. To a degree, therefore, Knight probably exaggerated the uniqueness of entrepreneurial decisions. None the less, his argument draws attention to the difficulty of estimation. Entrepreneurial success depends, for example, on constantly changing consumer tastes, the timing of production and investment, personal ability and the reaction of existing suppliers to a new competitor. Even where success is theoretically predictable, wide scope for error must remain.

Given the existence of uncertainty in market economies Knight stressed, like Schumpeter, that the competitive process could not be simply a matter of smooth transitions from one static equilibrium to another, as implied in neoclassical theory. Knight judged that neoclassical theory emphasised calculation over choice or judgement, whereas markets involved a dynamic process of change in the face of uncertainty about outcomes. He therefore associated profit not with temporary market disequilibria, as in the neoclassical treatment of competition, but with entrepreneurial judgement in the face of uncertainty. Uncertainty, he concluded, transformed society into an 'enterprise organisation' in which 'The receipt of profit in a particular case may be argued to be the result of superior judgement' (1921, p. 311). Unlike wages, rent and interest, which are contractually fixed, he reasoned that profit was an uncertain residual reflecting the degree of success or failure in making entrepreneurial decisions in the face of uncertainty. He also analysed the relationship between enterprise, management and capital, separating the act of entrepreneurship from simple management of resources which could be rewarded by salary, and from the provision of capital which could be supplied to the entrepreneur by investors or lenders. Always he returned to the fundamental distinction between insurable and non-insurable risk:

> The essential point for profit theory is that insofar as it is possible to insure by any method against risk, the cost of carrying it out is converted into a constant element of expense, and it ceases to be a cause of profit or loss. The uncertainties which persist as causes of profit are those which are uninsurable because there is no objective measure of the probability of gain or loss. . . . Situations in regard to which business judgement must be exercised do not repeat themselves with sufficient conformity to type to make possible a computation of probability. (Knight, 1951, pp. 119–20)

5.3 The importance of information

Certain differences between neoclassical and Austrian theorising are already very apparent from the above review of the contributions of leading founders of modern Austrian economics. They can be summarised as follows: first, Austrian economists stress that economic decisions are made in the face of imperfect information about alternatives and outcomes – the market exists as a means of maximising information about consumer demands and supply costs; and second, Austrians are conscious of the role of time in production and supply and how the time between investment and sale adds to uncertainty. By contrast, the characteristic assumption of neoclassical theorising is perfect information and on those occasions when time features in neoclassical models it does so typically only in terms of stylised production periods, notably the Marshallian 'short run' and 'long run' which are related to the existence of fixed factors of production. Study begins by examining a given equilibrium position in the market – say for a particular commodity or factor input – which is then disturbed by a change in one of the determinants of this equilibrium, for instance consumers' incomes. The market then moves smoothly to a new equilibrium based upon the new set of market conditions and with supply varying according to the technical relationship between inputs and outputs and the ability of firms to alter their combinations of factors of production. The 'short run' and 'long run' differ in that only in the long run can all factor inputs be changed. The new market equilibrium is then compared with the old one in terms of price and output.

This method of analysis based upon comparing static positions pre- and post-market changes has no built-in process of time-related change. By contrast, in Austrian analysis the theoretical framework is one of the market as a *process* involving a dynamic and ceaseless flux in which the notion of an equilibrium has only very limited usefulness. Constantly individuals' tastes change and new technologies develop, raw material and energy prices fluctuate and labour becomes more or less scarce. While Austrian economists do not dispute the value of neoclassical reasoning in highlighting the *direction* in which markets react to changes in demand and supply (an exception is Shackle who rejects the whole equilibrium paradigm), they oppose the neoclassical 'general preoccupation with final equilibrium positions' (Kirzner in Dolan (ed.), 1976, p. 117). In particular, they stress that because of ceaseless change, markets will rarely reach stable equilibria. At best, equilibrium will be a fleeting event.

Furthermore, because of uncertainty it is generally impossible to forecast an equilibrium price and output in the manner implied in neoclassical market models; thus how can we know when a market is in equilibrium? Related to this, Austrians see little merit in assuming, as in much of neoclassical theory, that all consumers will be successful utility maximisers and that all firms will produce at maximum efficiency, choosing the mix of factor inputs which minimises the costs of producing any given output. To specify demand and supply functions fully in advance of trade would require a degree of knowledge of utility and costs that consumers and producers clearly lack in the real world.

Austrian economists stress that in practice economic agents have to make decisions over time based only on limited information and, importantly, that each individual interprets information differently. Uncertainty is, therefore: 'of the greatest practical significance in human economy' (Menger, 1950, p. 71). This attention to time and knowledge leads Austrian economists to view the seeking out and reaction to information as of prime importance in economic decision-making. In von Hayek's and Kirzner's writings (von Hayek, 1978a; Kirzner *et al.*, 1980, p. 114) the market is viewed as a subtle 'discovery procedure' of ends and means in which information is channelled between potential consumers and potential suppliers through prices. Prices reflect consumer demands and supply costs. Consumers and producers lack perfect information on which to base their economic decisions but they will react to prices. At the same time, price discrepancies reveal new opportunities for profit-making – for example, the possibility of buying cheap and subsequently selling at a higher price. Austrian economists therefore see in the competitive market and the price system the means by which new information is constantly generated about consumer wants and supply costs.

In this 'discovery procedure', competition is a continuous process of searching out profit opportunities and not simply a matter of movements to predetermined equilibria. This leads Austrians to argue that economic analysis is not reducible to using *given* resources in the most efficient manner to achieve *given* ends, as implied in much of neoclassical theory. They criticise the neoclassical approach to economic transactions for being concerned with end-state solutions in which the effects of uncertainty have been expunged or reduced to a well-defined probability distribution, and thus for missing the whole point of the competitive process. As von Hayek has commented:

> What the theory of perfect competition discusses has little claim to be called 'competition' at all . . . its conclusions are of little use as guides to policy. The reason for this seems to me to be that this theory throughout assumes the state of affairs already to exist which . . . the process of competition tends to bring about. (von Hayek, 1948, p. 92)

Von Hayek argues that to assume that sellers know the best outputs to produce, the correct inputs to purchase and the price to charge to maximise profit and move to equilibrium is to assume away the essence of markets.

For this reason, Austrian economists are especially critical of the neoclassical predilection for the concept of a general equilibrium in economies. In the Walrasian model of general equilibrium no trade is permitted by the 'auctioneer' until all intertemporal markets are in equilibrium. This requires full information on market-clearing prices (pp. 66ff) which, they rightly contend, requires as a prerequisite precisely what the competitive process sets out to achieve. Also, since market-clearing price and output configurations are set through a system of simultaneous equations there is no room for individual actions or choices. As von Mises succinctly commented, an economy in full equilibrium 'is not a human society, it is an ant hill' (von Mises, 1949, p. 249).

Austrian and neoclassical economists differ fundamentally in their approach to decision-making. In neoclassical economics, decisions are portrayed as reactions to circumstances, involving little or no real choice (Lachmann in Dolan (ed.), 1976, p. 217). For example, in the neoclassical model of perfect competition, when demand falls firms have no option but to reduce output and, in the long run, to leave the industry if they are failing to secure 'normal' profits. From an Austrian perspective this approach trivialises decision-making: in the real world, a range of responses to falling demand is possible, from producing a new product to slashing costs or developing new markets. All, moreover, are associated with uncertainty – and all give scope for entrepreneurial creativity which neoclassical models ignore. Nor are Austrians impressed by the attempts of neoclassical theorists to add 'more realism'. From an Austrian perspective, the development of models of imperfect competition and models where information is introduced as a further 'constraint' in a 'constrained optimisation' problem misses the point. The approach is still based on the idea that human behaviour is amenable to objective assessment. In accordance with methodological subjectivism, Austrians stress that people differ in both the amount of information available to them and also in their ability to react to it. As economic knowledge is subjective there is no objective solution to determine a market equilibrium.

These different approaches to information and equilibrium are reflected in the Austrian and neoclassical treatments of profit. In the neoclassical model of perfect competition with, *inter alia*, the assumption of perfect information about prices, costs and outputs, the market moves automatically and predictably in the long run to a new equilibrium where only 'normal' profits are earned. In Austrian analysis, however, in the competitive process pure profit is usually eaten away by competition but there is no determinate model of this process comparable to perfect competition in neoclassical theory. Instead, the emphasis is upon entrepreneurial initiative in 'discovering' profit opportunities and in overcoming a rival's competitive advantage. In the place of a mechanical model of competition, Austrians substitute the notion of entrepreneurial action. The Austrian view of the market process therefore draws attention to the pivotal role in the market economy of the profit-motivated entrepreneur.

The contrast between the Austrian and neoclassical perspectives on competition can be illustrated by recent changes in the computer industry. Dominated since the 1950s by IBM, this industry has seen rapid technological change from the initial huge and slow valve-based machines to the current desktop PC. Viewed from a neoclassical position, IBM's high market share could be interpreted as a sign of market dominance which is not in the interests of consumers. Austrian economists, however, would argue that the industry – leaving aside the discriminatory purchasing practices of several governments – is essentially competitive. IBM's market position has always been, and remains, vulnerable to competition from existing and new suppliers – i.e. the market for computers is highly contestable. The company's past market strength has rested not on legal protection but upon technological prowess coupled with a continuing ability to satisfy consumers' wants. Finally, while neoclassical economists might attempt to analyse the computer market in terms of a series of equilibrium positions, Austrian economists would see the technological and marketing changes in the post-war years as evidence of a never-ending process of exploration, as entrepreneurs – including those in IBM – have exploited new market opportunities.

5.4   The 'prime mover'

Whereas in the neoclassical model of competition all actions are fully determined within the model, in the Austrian approach to competition there is scope for independent entrepreneurial decision-making. It is entrepreneurship – the searching for new products or production methods – which in Austrian economics 'converts the theory of market equilibrium into a theory of market process' (Kirzner in Dolan (ed.), 1976, p. 120). To modern Austrian economists the entrepreneur is the vital 'prime mover' in economies.

Menger once described entrepreneurial activity in terms of: '(a) obtaining *information* about the economic situation; (b) economic *calculation* – all the various computations that must be made if a production process is to be efficient; (c) the *act of will* by which goods of higher order [the term he used to refer to those goods which become inputs into the final product] are assigned to a particular production process; and finally (d) *supervision* of the execution of the production plan so that it may be carried through as economically as possible' (Menger, 1950, p. 160).

Such a comprehensive approach to the entrepreneurial function, however, does not clearly distinguish enterprise from management – a common failing in nineteenth-century economics, as we have seen. Clearly, many aspects of the above tasks, but especially of (b) and (d), can be delegated to employees. This is particularly important from a modern Austrian perspective where it is usually argued that civil servants and other public sector managers cannot act entrepreneurially. If enterprise can be equated with management, then the idea of the enterprising civil servant cannot be easily dismissed. The modern Austrian perspective on enterprise can be traced especially to von Wieser, who introduced the ideas of entrepreneurial leadership and alertness, and von Mises, who emphasised uncertainty: 'The term entrepreneur . . . means . . . acting man exclusively seen from the aspect of uncertainty inherent in every action' (von Mises, 1949, p. 254). Von Mises went on to differentiate his approach to the entrepreneur from Schumpeter's on the grounds that the entrepreneur not only experiments with the new techniques and products but has to *decide* what techniques to use and products to supply. It is this decision-making which is peculiar to entrepreneurship according to von Mises – an idea which is close to that of Knight. Such an approach is echoed in the Austrian analysis of enterprise today. Shackle, for example, refers to entrepreneurial 'imagination':

> We are in the nature of things in some respects blind. The entrepreneur is a man whose characteristic act is a gamble on his imagination. Of course, the business man uses reason and knowledge. He sees principles in the natural universe, he has insights into human powers and propensities. He can form judgements of what can come about, he cannot know what *will* come about. . . . Let us then define enterprise. It is action in pursuit of the imagined, deemed possible. . . . The entrepreneur is a maker of history, but his guide in making it is his judgement of possibilities and not a calculation of certainties. (Shackle's introduction in Hebert and Link, 1988, pp. x–xi)

Kirzner, however, prefers to talk about entrepreneurial 'alertness' to profit opportunities. Today a leading proponent of the Austrian view of enterprise, Kirzner sees the entrepreneur as someone who through decision-making moves markets towards their equilibria (Kirzner, 1963, 1973, 1979). Once again entrepreneurship is a scarce resource; Kirzner's entrepreneur needs to be nurtured by economic policies and social attitudes which encourage enterprise.

In the past Kirzner, like von Mises, interpreted enterprise broadly in terms of taking advantage of existing opportunities in markets to make profits. Thus Kirzner frequently illustrated the idea of 'alertness' by reference to the case of arbitrageurs, people who discover opportunities in markets to buy cheap and sell dear because of intertemporal or interspatial differences in demand. But the arbitrageur faces only limited uncertainty – in terms of assessing the potential for resale at a profit and in terms of facing the possibility that market conditions might change between purchase and resale. More recently, however, Kirzner has moved nearer to the mainstream of the Austrian tradition. He now highlights the role of the entrepreneur in *creating* market opportunities in the face of uncertainty. The entrepreneur is 'alert' not only to existing opportunities but also to *potential* opportunities. This view of 'alertness' is now the generally accepted view among modern Austrian economists and distinguishes mere management from entrepreneurship (e.g. Littlechild, 1986).

Potential opportunities will exist to make profits, Kirzner goes on to argue, when there are disequilibrium situations in markets. For example, it is the existence of an excess demand for a commodity at the going price which raises the possibility of undertaking a profitable arbitrage operation. But also if there is an excess demand, for instance for homes, there is scope for an entrepreneurial individual to buy up large properties, divide them into separate homes and in so doing increase the housing stock, as well as earn a profit. An entrepreneur sooner or later will spot this opportunity. This entrepreneurial action moves demand and supply closer to equilibrium, though Kirzner acknowledges that equilibrium may not be achieved. The demand and supply of housing may be brought closer together through entrepreneurial action but it cannot guarantee an equilibrium in the housing market.

Kirzner chooses to concentrate upon the entrepreneur as someone who responds to a market disequilibrium and in so doing moves the market nearer equilibrium. By contrast, Schumpeter had claimed that the entrepreneur *through innovation* causes market disequilibria. This is an important distinction since in Schumpeter's approach the free market system is consequently plagued with periodic trade cycles. This implies a possible role for government in economic management to smooth out economic fluctuations. Kirzner, however, argues that while the free market cannot guarantee full employment it remains the best means of achieving the optimal use of economic resources. He therefore opposes most state intervention and especially demand-management. Yet the two different approaches to market equilibrium need not be viewed as inconsistent or contradictory for it is quite possible to view entrepreneurs as people who both *capitalise* on an existing disequilibrium in a market and *cause* the disequilibrium through Schumpeterian innovation. Creating and reacting to profit opportunities are not mutually exclusive: from an Austrian perspective both can be seen as part of the art of successful entrepreneurship.

5.5 Modern Austrian economics and profit

In Austrian economics, profits arise from the fact that everyone has limited information. It follows that there is no necessary connection between entrepreneurial effort at the margin and the profit earned, for example as there might be between the value of the marginal product of labour and wages. Austrian economists do not link the return to the entrepreneur to *realised* marginal product and it is especially wrong from an Austrian viewpoint to talk about a marginal product of enterprise. To Austrians profits are an incentive or signal to be entrepreneurial or 'alert' – to set up businesses, innovate, invest or redirect resources. It follows that profit cannot be in any sense the *price* of entrepreneurship. Similarly, it is erroneous to think in terms of profit compensating for entrepreneurial effort because there is no necessary connection between effort and the resultant profit. One bright idea gained in an instant may earn millions, while another idea in which great time and effort are invested may fail to make a profit at all. As von Mises concluded: 'Profit is a product of the mind, of success in anticipating the future state of the market' (von Mises, 1951, p. 21). The product of the mind is independent of physical effort.

By linking profit to entrepreneurial 'alertness' to market opportunities or 'imagination', Austrian economists dispute the neoclassical view that continued high profits necessarily imply market power or monopoly. In neoclassical theory higher than normal profit can only continue in the long run if there are barriers of entry to markets which protect incumbent suppliers from competition. Such barriers to entry might include patent rights, sole ownership of a mineral resource or 'know-how' in production. By contrast, in Austrian theory high profits may continue to exist because of dynamic changes in markets, such as continuous innovations, which mean that a firm stays ahead of the competition.

At the same time, high profits serve as a signal to potential competitors. Returning to the case of the computer industry, IBM has suffered in the 1980s from the introduction of 'compatible' models to its own PC which have eroded its market position. IBM's profits were a signal to entrepreneurs that there were profits to be gained from manufacturing PCs at prices which undercut IBM's. Through such competition the consumer has gained from lower prices and more choice. Influenced by Schumpeter's notion of 'the perennial gale of creative destruction', modern Austrian economists argue that a firm's dominance, like IBM's, in a market will be overcome in time by new producers using even more efficient production methods than the incumbent supplier or by producing new products. Only if the existing supplier remains more efficient in keeping costs of production down and meeting consumers' fickle wants can profits remain high. In this case, however, the high profit is justified. It is not a consequence of monopoly but quite the reverse: it is a product of market efficiency.

Austrian economists also directly challenge the Marxist view of profit (Chapter 6), i.e. that profit is the product of exploitation of labour by the owners of capital. In Austrian theory capital is a necessary factor of production and exists in any type of economy, capitalist or Communist, and the providers of capital must in all economic systems be compensated for investing and thus postponing current consumption. Without interest as an incentive savings would decline, thus reducing investment. Also, whereas the distinction between the provision of capital and the input enterprise was sometimes blurred in early Austrian writings, Schumpeter, von Mises and later Austrians have stressed the difference. The entrepreneur is the person who gets the 'good idea' to make profits, and whether he risks his own or another's capital is irrelevant to the getting of this idea (Kirzner, 1973, p. 19). If the idea is good then there will be no shortage of lenders or investors. In competitive economies entrepreneurs can borrow from lenders to finance schemes even when they lack their own resources. Lenders will receive an interest payment and the entrepreneur the residual profit. In modern Austrian economics an individual does not have to be rich to become an entrepreneur.

Not surprisingly this argument arouses controversy, even among non-Marxists, on the grounds that it underestimates the difficulty that someone with a good idea but no money to invest may have in finding backers (Casson, 1982, p. 92). At the very least the rich self-financed entrepreneur does not have to worry about convincing someone else of the merits of his proposed venture. This might prove difficult if, as Austrians argue, the entrepreneur is gifted with some peculiar means of identifying a profit-making opportunity. Alternatively, the entrepreneur who has to search out financial backers runs the risk that they might steal his idea. Various game theoretic models can be developed which suggest that fewer entrepreneurial schemes will get off the ground where capital has to be raised externally and the possibility of 'theft' arises.

If there is substance in such arguments then the ownership of capital may be an important factor in determining who becomes an entrepreneur and it should not be neglected. Austrian economics has never been interested in the 'morality' of profit or the history of property rights – Menger thought morality and ethics were no part of economics and von Bohm-Bawerk considered historical processes irrelevant to an understanding of the nature of capital. If individual wealth matters, however, then arguably it is not legitimate to ignore ethical issues relating to the 'justice' of the distribution of resources or the historical process which led to that distribution. This, of course, is the starting-point of the Marxist critique of capitalism.

5.6   Austrian economists and the corporation

In Austrian economics, it is the *individual* as an entrepreneur who seeks out new products or production methods with a view to making profits. Undoubtedly individual entrepreneurs were the driving force of the British and American industrial revolutions in the eighteenth and nineteenth centuries, but the question arises, does the Austrian view of the entrepreneur have any relevance to the capitalist economies of the late twentieth century which appear to be dominated by large, often multinational, corporations? For example, by 1979 firms with a thousand or more employees accounted for 63 per cent of total manufacturing employment and 67 per cent of manufacturing net output in the United Kingdom (Binks and Coyne, 1983, Tables III to VI, pp. 25–8). In the United States aggregate concentration, as measured by the share of manufacturing assets held by the largest 200 corporations, increased from around 48 per cent in 1948 to 60 per cent by the 1970s, by which time the largest 100 companies accounted for around 45 per cent of corporate net income (Scherer, 1980, p. 126; White, 1981).

These large firms, with assets in billions of dollars, professional management and thousands of employees, appear to be a far cry from the archetypal entrepreneurial business – the proprietor firm. Shareholders have the residual rights to the assets and to any profits generated through their shareholdings, while management directs the use of these assets and is often remunerated mainly by salary. Thus the relationship between the receipt of profit and the provision of enterprise can be blurred in the modern corporation.

Furthermore, individualism may be inconsistent with 'organisation', which by its very nature implies conforming to corporate or joint goals. Careers may be best promoted in large corporations by following rules and procedures rather than by showing entrepreneurial flair. Also, management in such organisations tends to be hierarchical and job functions are well defined (Dunsire *et al.*, 1988). This form of organisation might constrain enterprise or, at the very least, it is difficult to define precisely where it occurs. Austrian economists talk about the entrepreneur – not a firm or some subset of the firm, such as a department – but in large corporations decisions are rarely taken by individuals alone. More often, they are reached by committees or boards.

For this reason a number of economists argue that the growth of the large firm has changed the nature of business so that the idea of a firm headed by an entrepreneur is no longer especially relevant. John Kenneth Galbraith (b. 1908), in particular, is associated with the idea that twentieth-century corporate capitalism is qualitatively different from nineteenth-century capitalism (Galbraith, 1969). In what amounts to an extension of Veblen's work on 'technocrats' substituting for entrepreneurs (see pp. 128ff), Galbraith argues that the entrepreneur has been replaced by a 'technostructure'. This 'technostructure' is made up of an educated élite of salaried managers, scientists, financiers, administrators and so on who have in general common goals which have become those of the corporate state. In particular, the technostructure is motivated primarily by a desire to remain secure and to expand the corporation rather than to maximise profits. In addition, Galbraith observes that in the large firm decisions are usually made by a process of managerial consensus-building and this implies that they cannot be entrepreneurial decisions in an Austrian sense. That is to say, they cannot be ideas that *only the entrepreneur perceives*.

Another economist who thought that capitalism was changing in a way that raised questions about the future of the entrepreneurial function was Schumpeter, who, as described above, developed the idea that competition proceeds by way of a 'gale of creative destruction'. Schumpeter believed, however, that the growth of large corporations threatened this mechanism. As large corporations developed, the rejuvenation of capitalism through the introduction of new entrepreneurs would slow down. At the same time, he concluded, existing entrepreneurs would become less dynamic because 'everyone is an entrepreneur when he actually "carries out new combinations", and loses that character as soon as he has built up his business, when he settles down to running it as other people run their business' (Schumpeter, 1961, p. 78). Instead of decision-making by entrepreneurs motivated by profit, there would be decisions made by company bureaucracies motivated by the pursuit of non-profit goals. One consequence would be a reduction in technical progress and innovation. More generally, if capitalism was denuded of entrepreneurial flair and if the allocation of resources became increasingly bureaucratic, the pace of economic growth would inevitably slow down. Eventually Schumpeter predicted that capitalism as we know it could cease (Schumpeter, 1934). He therefore went much further than Galbraith and concluded that the growth of large firms threatened the whole existence of entrepreneurial capitalism.

Not surprisingly modern Austrians distance themselves from both Schumpeter's deep pessimism about the future of capitalism and Galbraith's notion of the 'technostructure'. While acknowledging that the scale of production in the developed economies has risen they deny that this has undermined the entrepreneurial function (Kirzner *et al.*, 1980). First, they maintain that concentration upon a relatively small number of large corporations draws attention away from the tens of thousands of small firms in which the entrepreneurial function is still clearly visible. Second, they point to evidence that large corporations are not a static collection of bodies. Many of the top 100 firms today in the United Kingdom and the United States were not in the top 100 firms even as little as 10 years ago and this implies considerable competition in the corporate sector. They further point out that many large corporations are dynamic in innovation and compete successfully against both large and small firms. In Japan, of course, large firms are notably entrepreneurial. Therefore, Austrian economists conclude that Schumpeter's fears are unfounded: there is no evidence that large firms are inherently less dynamic, competitive and enterprising.

Third, they dispute the importance of the separation of ownership and control in companies, pointing to the way the pay of managers is often related to their company's profit performance – through bonuses, stock option schemes and the like – and the ability of shareholders to force management to pursue profits. Shareholders can always sell their shareholdings if dissatisfied with the profits earned, and by deflating its stock price this makes a company vulnerable to takeover by new management. Thus, Austrians conclude, corporate management cannot ignore the need to act entrepreneurially (Parker, 1987).

Although the identification of 'the entrepreneur' may be more complex than it was in the nineteenth century, according to Austrian economists there is still a definite entrepreneurial function in modern capitalist economies (Rothbard 1982, p. 463; Lachmann, 1977, p. 316; Kirzner *et al.*, 1980). Kirzner maintains that as long as individuals can seek personal advantage from their actions enterprise can still exist:

> Entrepreneurship consists of finding opportunities to make profit for oneself. To the extent that an employee in a corporation is able to make profit for himself, entrepreneurship can and does exist within the corporation. The extent to which such profit is legitimate, or the particular legitimate forms such profit-making may take, may be quite subtle. There may be, for example, opportunities for advancement, for promotion, for attracting attention in the market at large – these are all more subtle concepts of entrepreneurial profit than the simple pecuniary profit we usually identify with entrepreneurship. There are thus somewhat conflicting elements of entrepreneurship in the corporation. (Kirzner *et al.*, 1980, p. 56)

At the same time, however, Kirzner concludes that enterprise cannot exist in the complete absence of the pecuniary profit motive. Therefore, the public sector can never act entrepreneurially – it can never be as dynamic, alert and enterprising as the private sector. Critics might argue that in this respect Austrians want it both ways, acknowledging 'subtle concepts of entrepreneurial profit' in the private corporation but denying their existence in the public sector. Surely civil servants also seek 'advancement and promotion'?

5.7 Austrian economists and the state

Austrian economists oppose the neoclassical prescription of piecemeal state intervention in the market mechanism to solve 'market failure'. In their view state intervention reduces rather than increases national well-being; in particular government policies increase uncertainty, therefore making the task of entrepreneurs more difficult (Cordato, 1980; Kirzner, 1981).

In particular, Austrian economists totally oppose the idea of planning economies. They believe that any attempt to plan will inevitably end in failure since civil servants lack the necessary information about costs and consumer wants to establish optimal prices. Consistent with their belief that economic costs are subjective, they argue that economics cannot be a predictive science lending itself readily to precise quantitative analysis. There are no statistical regularities in economics to expedite the production of reliable forecasts of demand and costs or input–output models which planners can use. Similarly, there are no 'laws' in economics regarding relationships between macroeconomic variables which facilitate planning. The 'laws' which do exist relate to the fundamentals of demand and supply, such as the 'law of diminishing marginal utility' and the law of 'rent', and arise out of the actions of individuals. Economics can therefore point, for example, to excess demand as the likely outcome of rent controls which lower the price of accommodation. Low rents reduce the rented accommodation offered in the market by landlords and increase the number who wish to rent. But from an Austrian viewpoint there is no similar relationship between, for instance, the money supply and price levels. Austrians argue that the impact of the money supply on inflation is difficult to predict accurately in the absence of full information about the reaction of individuals to a monetary expansion.

The idea that economies might be successfully planned from the centre arose out of the Walrasian general equilibrium. It was taken up initially by the Italian economist Enrico Barone in 1908. Barone pointed out that a general equilibrium required the planner to solve a large number of simultaneous equations relating to demand and supply in the product and factor markets. While he was sceptical of the ability of any planning body to undertake this task successfully, first Fred M. Taylor in his presidential address to the American Economic Association in 1928, and later Oscar Lange and A. P. Lerner in the 1930s, offered 'solutions'. Taylor suggested that the planner could adjust demand and supply to find optimal market-clearing prices by 'trial and error', while Lange and Lerner pointed out that the equations which faced the planner were the same as those which had to be solved under capitalism. Thus, they reasoned, relative prices in a planned economy could be determined by a mechanism which was an exact replica of the competitive market, with prices related to marginal costs (Lange, 1936; Lange and Taylor, 1938; Napoleoni, 1972, pp. 133–44). In so far as private industry was becoming less competitive, this suggested that publicly owned firms could in principle achieve a superior allocation of resources by marginal cost pricing. Private monopolies could be expected to price in excess of marginal costs.

From an Austrian perspective the reason that some economists fell into the trap of believing that the decentralised decision-making of the market could be replicated through planning lies in neoclassical economics robbing economic agents of their ability to make decisions:

> In this sense it can be said that the perfect competition model is not an approximation to capitalism but is a model of central planning. When all decision making is reduced to routine there is indeed little difference between so-called socialist and capitalist institutions, but the relevance of this model of mechanical agents to anything in the real world is highly questionable. (Lavoie, 1986, p. 5)

The notion of introducing marginal cost pricing in state enterprises was ridiculed in the inter-war years by von Mises, especially on the grounds that planners cannot know costs; they are only known to the individual transactors (von Mises in von Hayek, 1935). A similar argument has been repeatedly made by von Hayek throughout the post-war period. In von Hayek's view a planned economy is quite conceivable in theory, in that what is required is the solution to a general equilibrium system of equations, but it is equally inconceivable that it could work in practice. Even if the planner attempts (at great cost) to obtain the necessary information on prices and outputs, by the time this information is collected and analysed, inevitably it will be out of date and of little or no use (von Hayek, 1935 and 1976). In this sense the competitive market cannot be replicated. Only the competitive market provides continuous and contemporaneous information.

In addition to criticising planning on information grounds, Austrians also argue that under socialism there is no rational criterion for choosing between the various forms of resource allocation for there is no profit motive or comparable incentive system. In general, Austrians are sceptical of the idea of giving power to government to pursue the 'public good' through planning, public sector pricing or any other economic and social engineering. They maintain that the state inevitably falls victim to short-term political pressures arising out of the need to win votes or the need to buy off important interest groups. In addition, government managers, lacking the profit motive to hold down costs of production, will be prone to waste resources. As von Hayek has commented, echoing Adam Smith almost two centuries earlier: 'Men are, in fact, not likely to give their best for long periods unless their own interests are directly involved. . . . The problem of incentives in this sense is a very real one' (von Hayek, 1976, p. 93).

Some Marxists, such as the Englishman Maurice Dobb (1955), have attempted to rebut Austrian criticisms of planning by accepting that it introduces a problem of economic calculation and incentive, while arguing that this is of secondary importance to what they perceive to be the main economic problem, the act of accumulation. Capital accumulation (and, of course, the subsequent distribution of the product) is considered to be the important issue in economic well-being and, so the argument goes, planned economies are best equipped to achieve high investment by adopting a longer time perspective and taking risks that private markets would shun. Soviet planning from the late 1920s followed this principle, achieving high levels of investment, if sometimes at great social cost, while worrying less about the precise returns on the investment. Input–output models were developed to equate resources with needs in the absence of market prices but such models could only guarantee the internal consistency of each growth alternative; they could not choose between them. Choice about what to produce had to be left to the political system, but from an Austrian perspective this was a fundamental defect because Russian governments lacked the means and incentives to make such economic choices efficiently. Thus Austrians are not surprised by the identified failings of Soviet planning.

Austrian economists are also cynical about the ability of governments to manage the economy using Keynesian techniques. In addition to their rejection of the idea of predictable relationships between macroeconomic variables, they argue that government demand-management distorts price signals leading to an inefficient allocation of resources. They also believe that demand-management is unnecessary since left alone the market economy will be self-correcting; they thus reject Keynes' view that business expectations and financial speculation might trigger a long-term trade depression. Resources, including labour, reallocate in response to new sets of prices including real wage levels. Capitalist economies do not require 'pump-priming' or any of the other Keynesian tampering with aggregate demand. In the absence of government meddling, they naturally tend towards full employment – just as Say had demonstrated early in the nineteenth century. Moreover, Austrians are unsympathetic towards the view that investment funds might outgrow investment opportunities, leading to a fall in the rate of profit and the advent of a 'stationary state' – an idea that can be traced from the mercantilists to Keynes. Austrians believe that markets will always throw up new demands and entrepreneurs will invent new means to meet these demands efficiently and profitably.

Austrian economists conclude that trade cycles are often the *consequence* of state intervention, especially the resulting monetary disequilibrium. A government-promoted expansion of the money supply that lowers interest rates below the market or natural rate sends out a misleading signal to entrepreneurs, who undertake long-term investments that cannot be sustained given the level of savings. The result is eventual unemployment and recession. To prevent governments introducing destabilising monetary policies, Austrians advocate a return to commodity-based monies (e.g. the gold standard) or, von Hayek's preference, the introduction of a free market in currencies (von Hayek, 1978b). In a competitive market for money weak currencies would be driven out and this would place a strict limit on monetary expansion.

More generally, Austrian economists are opposed to concentrations of economic power including the state. Rather they place their faith in the competitive process to best allocate resources. To this end, they are leading advocates not only of competitive currencies but also of opening up economies to more competition through supply-side policies, including deregulation, privatisation, reduced taxation, lower state spending and the sweeping away of impediments to competition in the labour market – Austrians are especially distrustful of the monopoly powers of trade unions. The economic powers of the state, they argue, should be limited to providing the legal and political infrastructure in which private competitive enterprise can flourish – notably protecting private property rights and the provision of sound defence. Not surprisingly, on the issue of the role of the state modern Austrians see themselves as being the economists who follow most closely in the footsteps of the classical school.

5.8 Conclusion

Whereas in neoclassical economics the role of the entrepreneur and the profit motive are neglected, modern Austrian economists place enterprise and profit at the centre of their analysis. The attention Austrians give to the entrepreneur follows from their approach to economics. In Austrian economics the fundamental economic problem is information, especially about consumer wants and how they can best be met. It is the entrepreneur, interacting with the market and reacting to price signals, who solves this fundamental problem. The notion of decision-taking in the presence of imperfect information or uncertainty is part of a long tradition back to Cantillon and introduces a rationale for the entrepreneur.

In Austrian theory the entrepreneur is a heroic figure alert to market opportunities. The entrepreneur pursues his own interest and yet by reallocating resources from low to higher valued uses in the market he incidentally promotes the public good. It follows that Austrian economists are especially critical of state intervention in market economies, whether in the form of taxation, spending, regulation or public ownership, because state intervention reduces the potential for profit-making and thus for private entrepreneurship. Whereas neoclassical economists were inclined to recognise 'market failure' and prescribe state interference as a solution, Austrians remained, even during the high tide of Keynesian economics in the 1950s and 1960s, deeply sceptical of the benefits of state interference in the market. Until the 1970s, however, Austrian economics was relatively neglected by academic economists and policy-makers. Since then, the 1970s 'stagflation' and the subsequent election of governments in the United Kingdom and the United States interested in reviving entrepreneurial initiative and restoring free markets have led to a new interest in Austrian policy prescriptions.

Further reading

There is a growing body of literature on Austrian and neo-Austrian economics. For an overview of the subject see Dolan (ed.) (1976), Reekie (1984) or Shand (1984).

Another obvious source are the works of major contributors to Austrian theory. Of early contributions, particularly useful are von Bohm-Bawerk's *Capital and Interest* (1959), Menger's *Principles of Economics* (1950) and von Mises' *Human Action* (1949). In addition, Moss (ed.) (1976) includes a number of interesting contributions on the economics of von Mises. For the ideas of more recent 'Austrians': from von Hayek's prolific writings try *Individualism and Economic Order* (1948) and *New Studies in Philosophy, Politics and Economics* (1978a). Kirzner's *Competition and Entrepreneurship* (1973), Lachmann's *Capital, Expectations and Market Process* (1977) and Shackle's *Imagination and the Nature of Choice* (1979) provide different nuances in modern Austrian theory.

For a good discussion of Austrian methodology see Buchanan, 'General implications of subjectivism in economics', in Buchanan (ed.) (1976). On the Austrian view of the role of government see Cordato (1980) and Littlechild (1986). Specifically on the entrepreneurial role and Schumpeter's impact, see Blaug, 'Entrepreneurship before and after Schumpeter', in Blaug (ed.) (1986a). Finally, for a stimulating comment on the contrasts between Austrian and neoclassical theories see Streissler (1972).

6
Critics, radicals and revolutionaries

Although the theories of profit and enterprise examined in the preceding chapters differ in many respects, all have accepted the idea that profit is a useful incentive for business. There are, however, schools of economic thought which do not share this view. Some economists indeed have been openly hostile to profit. One view widespread among these critics is the belief that competition leads to wasteful duplication, while another is the idea that profit-seeking, with its emphasis on short-term results, can act as a brake upon technical progress. A more extreme position was adopted by socialists, pre-eminently Karl Marx, who argued that profit derives from the exploitation of the working class rather than from enterprise *per se*. Partly because of these attitudes, fierce political controversy has often followed the theories of profit examined in this chapter – Utopian socialism, Marxist economics, the German historical school and American institutionalism.

6.1 Utopian socialism

Modern socialist ideas first appeared in the early nineteenth century. This was a period of rapid intellectual, political and economic change in Europe. In England, new factories and mines were being created in which men, women and children laboured for long hours under harsh conditions. There were sporadic riots against the new machines and agitation for political and social reform was rife, influenced by the American and French Revolutions in which the rights of man and the ideals of liberty and equality before the law had been proclaimed. Small, feudal princedoms were being supplanted by modern nation-states like Germany and Italy. At the same time, established doctrines were being questioned by critical philosophers like Hegel and Feuerbach.

In many ways, the changes of the early nineteenth century were the birthpangs of a new society. Feudal Europe had been largely brought to an end as market relationships encroached upon traditional forms of economic organisation. In its place, industrial capitalism was developing, bringing into existence two new social groups. One was the middle class of merchants and mill-owners whose wealth lay not in land but in business: these were the capitalists or the 'bourgeoisie'. The other group was the workers who owned no property and were therefore compelled to earn a living by selling their labour to the capitalists.

There were marked disparities between the capitalists and their employees. Besides living in comparative opulence, the former (in conjunction with the nobility) exercised great political power, having the right to vote and to stand for election. The workers, by contrast, often lived in squalid conditions, worked long hours for low pay and had few political and social rights – labour unions, for example, were restricted in Great Britain and other countries and censorship was often used to control radical newspapers.

These conditions led many to suggest that society should be redesigned on what they held to be more egalitarian lines. One of the first to argue this point was Henri, Comte de Saint-Simon (1760–1825). Having lived through the French Revolution, Saint-Simon saw the period as one of transition from an authoritarian society buttressed by religion to a scientific–industrial world based on reason. Rejecting competition, Saint-Simon argued that in an ideal world, power and responsibility ought to lie not with businessmen and property-owners but with engineers and scientists. Their role ought to be to organise the nation like one huge factory with a view to ensuring maximum output. A second figure in this tradition was Charles Fourier (1772–1837) who, like Saint-Simon, also rejected competition. For Fourier, competition meant wasteful duplication, swindling and corruption. Whereas Saint-Simon had looked with favour upon the prowess of new technology, Fourier by contrast sought to abolish the evils of competition by establishing self-sufficient rural communes called 'phalanxes' in which work was to be organised collectively. Although Fourier did not participate in such a commune, around forty were set up in the United States, most lasting but a few years.

A further Utopian socialist was the Welshman Robert Owen (1771–1858). An entrepreneur who had made his fortune in the cotton industry by the age of 28, Owen believed that the new mills could be run profitably without reducing the workers to proverty. To demonstrate his ideas, he bought a mill and its houses at New Lanark in Scotland and ran the community there as an enlightened despot, arranging for the children to be educated, housing his workers decently and setting relatively short working hours. The experiment succeeded: New Lanark turned in a good profit. He proceeded in 1826 to establish a larger community at New Harmony in Indiana. This community, however, broke up within three years.

A characteristic of the Utopian socialists is that markets play little or no role in the ideal societies which they designed. For Saint-Simon, the economy was to be planned by a scientific–industrial élite; in Fourier's communes, goods were destined for consumption by the producers themselves rather than for sale upon the open market; and at New Lanark, business decisions were made not by the community's members, i.e. the workers, but by Robert Owen and his partners. Thus both the theories and the practice of the Utopian socialists neglected the question of whether or not there would be a demand for the goods produced. The consequence of this approach was that the Utopian socialists gave scant attention to the role of enterprise. The implication of their thinking seems to be that economies can be organised without reliance upon entrepreneurship.

For Owen, Saint-Simon and Fourier, the problems of contemporary capitalism were basically moral and political. Later radical thinkers, however, attempted to incorporate economic theories into their work. These were the so-called 'Ricardian socialists' like Pierre-Joseph Proudhon (1809–65), whose *Philosophy of Poverty* appeared in 1847. Drawing on the political economy of Smith and more particularly of Ricardo, he argued that goods and services ought to exchange at prices which reflected the labour time expended in their production. This suggested to Proudhon that the workers were entitled by right to the entire value of all the goods they produced. He went on to argue that the discrepancy between the wages paid and the value of output amounted to exploitation; the capitalists, he asserted, failed to pay labour its full value. In effect, Proudhon accused the capitalists of acting unjustly by failing to comply with the laws of economics.

6.2   Karl Marx – revolutionary economist

The economist who attempted to ground the case for socialism not on calls for justice but upon scientific logic – particularly the logic of economics – was Karl Marx. Marx was born of a German-Jewish lawyer in 1818 in the German Rhineland. He read law, history and philosophy at the universities of Cologne and Berlin, where he became interested in radical ideas. Debarred from a university career because of his views, Marx entered journalism, editing the opposition newspaper *Rheinische Zeitung* from 1841 to 1842 and his own *Neue Rheinische Zeitung* from 1848 to 1849. Both papers were suppressed by the Prussian government and Marx was exiled from Germany. In 1842 he met Frederick Engels (1820–95), who became his lifelong collaborator. Marx eventually moved to London, which he made his home until his death in 1883.

Marx's time in England was largely devoted to writing. His best-known work on economics is *Capital*, the first volume of which was published in 1863, but mention should also be made of his *Theories of Surplus Value* and *Grundrisse*, which were written in parallel with *Capital*. Since Marx believed that critical analysis and political action are necessarily linked, one of his major preoccupations was the International Workingmen's Association, a revolutionary organisation based in London.

The intellectual task which Marx set himself was of sizeable proportions. He attempted to prove that capitalism, besides being unjust, is fated to be overthrown. In his work, profit and enterprise play crucial roles. First, he endeavoured to prove, like Proudhon, that profit is extracted from the working class by their employers: that the owners of capital exploit their workers. Second, he sought to explain the process by which societies move through stages (or 'modes of production' as Marx termed them) such as classical antiquity, feudalism and capitalism. His purpose here was to demonstrate that the process would necessarily continue with capitalism inevitably being superseded by a further mode of production, Communism. His theory of enterprise – that capitalists are forced by competition to reinvest continually in larger, more advanced capital equipment – is critical for his prognostication that capitalism will eventually be overthrown.

The origin of profit

The point of departure for Marx's economic thinking was his disagreement with Proudhon. Whereas the latter had argued that profit arises from capitalists' deviating from economic laws, Marx tried to show that profit is created precisely by the untrammelled operation of those laws. Exploitation, for Marx, is no mere act of injustice but is intrinsic to capitalism. To demonstrate this point, Marx was obliged to construct a theory which could simultaneously explain wages, prices and profits. For Marx, just as for the classical and neoclassical economists, profit is inextricably bound up with prices. Marx's theory of profit can therefore be understood only by examining his theory of prices or 'law of value'.

Borrowing from the classical economists, Marx made a basic distinction between the 'use value' of any article and its 'exchange value'. By the latter Marx denoted the underlying, 'natural' price of an article rather than its day-to-day price. To explain prices, Marx adapted the labour theory of value which had first been expounded by Petty, Smith and Ricardo to create his law of value. For Marx the fundamental, universal input into all production is human effort, measured in time expended: products are simply crystallised labour time. Although raw materials are indispensable, the only cost of obtaining them is the labour of winning them from the mine, the field or the forest. For instance, the value of a wooden table comprises the sum of the work of (a) the forester who supplies the wood; (b) the carpenter; and (c) the blacksmith who made the metal tools for the other two workers. If these were, respectively, two hours, four hours and one hour, the value of the table would be seven hours (Q = value):

$$Q = 2\text{hrs} + 4\text{hrs} + 1\text{hr} = 7\text{hrs} \tag{1a}$$

If, at the same time, the production of a shirt absorbs three and a half hours, then a shirt would be half as valuable as a table. The law of value, according to Marx, thus determines the *relative* prices of all goods and services.

Marx was well aware that values do not necessarily reflect the actual time taken to produce a particular article. If that were the case, the tailor could increase the value of his shirt by using too much material (representing the time of the cotton-pickers, spinners and weavers) or by simply dawdling over his work. This would clearly be an absurd result, as Marx recognised. He therefore argued that values were determined by the *average socially necessary* labour time taken for production:

> In saying that the value of a commodity is determined by the *quantity of labour* worked up or crystallised in it, we mean *the quantity of labour necessary* for its production in a given state of society, under certain social average conditions of production, with a given social average intensity and average skill of the labour employed. (Marx, 1968, p. 205, emphasis in original)

Marx's law of value suggests, therefore, that the exchange ratio of one table to two shirts is determined by the average production time in the two industries concerned. By extension, precious metals could also be included: if seven hours' labour in the silver mines were to yield 100 g of silver, then a table would be worth 100 g and a shirt 50 g. Currencies in Marx's day were of course based on gold and silver so that 100 g of silver might have a nominal value of perhaps £1. If this were the case, a table would be worth £1 and a shirt £0.50. Equation (1a) can therefore be extended to read:

$$Q = 2\text{hrs} + 4\text{hrs} + 1\text{hr} = £1 \tag{1b}$$

The next step in Marx's argument is to introduce labour itself into the range of products bought and sold in the market. Since workers are compelled to sell their labour, Marx argued, labour is a commodity itself. More precisely, workers sell not themselves but their capacity to labour. This Marx termed their 'labour power'. The exchange value of labour power, Marx held, is determined in the same way as that of any other item, i.e. by the law of value. Wages therefore reflect the costs (in terms of time) of sustaining a worker. Thus to keep a worker fit and healthy may require that he consume every week goods and services which have taken fifteen hours to produce. In consequence, the exchange value of a week's labour power (the capacity to work) would be fifteen hours, and wages should therefore be sufficient to purchase fifteen hours' worth of products. (This standard of living would include an allowance for spouses and children because it is clearly necessary that workers be allowed to raise a new generation to replace themselves. In other words, fifteen hours' worth of goods should be thought of as a wage to sustain a whole family.)

The final stage in Marx's account concerned the bargain between the worker and the capitalist over the terms of employment. Although workers and their families might need to consume fifteen hours' worth of products per week, there is no need for a worker's weekly hours to be limited to fifteen. Since workers are forced to find employment in order to live, Marx reasoned, employers can dictate the terms of the bargain and force workers to labour for, say, forty hours per week. In effect, the capitalist can extract twenty-five hours of unpaid, forced labour from the worker. Denoting the value of the worker's output as Q, wage costs (which Marx terms 'variable capital') as V and surplus as S, this may be expressed as:

$$Q = 15_V + 25_S = 40\text{hrs} \tag{2}$$

(It may be noted that, like equation (1a), these numbers could be re-expressed in pounds, dollars or any other currency.)

The result is that the expenditure of fifteen hours' value on wages secures for the capitalist an output with a value of forty hours; the capitalist has thus obtained a surplus which Marx termed 'surplus value'. By this argument, Marx provided the economic theory to sustain the contention of Proudhon and other early socialists that the origin of profit lies in the exploitation of labour.

It can be seen that for Marx, profits do not arise simply from any underpayment of labour. Although workers can never be paid for the full value of their efforts, their exploitation does not arise in the 'wage bargain' itself. Rather, as far as Marx was concerned, exploitation arises from the very fact that a bargain has of necessity to be struck in the first place. Marx saw the ultimate origin of surplus value and profit in the workers' necessity to sell their labour power to a capitalist. This relationship he termed the 'relations of production'. Whatever terms and conditions of employment are set, they must always involve exploitation because that is the nature of the relationship between capital and labour. At root, Marx argued, profits arise from the fact that the means of production are owned by one class while the other class owns nothing.

It is plain that the magnitude of the capitalist's surplus must depend upon the way in which the working day is divided between the time devoted to workers' wages and the unpaid, surplus time, i.e. the relative sizes of S and V. Marx called the ratio between these two the 'rate of exploitation' or the 'rate of surplus value'; in the example above it is 25:15 or 167 per cent but, in principle, any ratio could obtain. If, at one extreme, workers were to consume forty hours' worth of produce a week, the capitalists would not obtain any surplus at all. Naturally, capitalists would respond to such a development by driving wages down or increasing the hours of work. Conversely, if workers' living standards were to fall to five hours' worth of production, the surplus would rise substantially. Marx eliminated the possibility of such wide variations by affirming the classical view that wages would gravitate towards subsistence level. Under capitalism, he concluded, there would always be a certain degree of unemployment which would produce intense competition between workers for the jobs available, thus defeating any attempts to raise wages. For Marx, as for Ricardo and Malthus, there was an 'iron law' of wages.

Although Marx held that wages would tend to be stable, he did not rule out the possibility that capitalists might still manage to extract more surplus value from their workers by altering the rate of surplus value. One way to do this might be to make workers put in longer hours (that is, more unpaid time) but in a competitive labour market such a move would not be easy. In any case from 1847 in Britain hours of work for adults in factories were restricted by law. A more fruitful approach was to raise productivity, so that more was produced in a given time and for a given expenditure of variable capital. This tactic Marx termed 'increasing the relative rate of surplus value' and it plays a vital role in his analysis of the dynamics of capitalism, as discussed in section 6.3

Although dynamic processes play an important part in Marx's theories of the development of capitalism, his fundamental proposition that profit is the result of exploitation is based upon an essentially static analysis of prices. The law of value for Marx determines the relative prices of all commodities including labour itself. Since the price of labour is less than the value of the goods which it produces, surplus accrues to the capitalist. For Marx, profit arises from equilibrium prices determined by the law of value.

Surplus value and profit

The purpose of the law of value was to demonstrate that profit was surplus value in monetary form. To do this, Marx was obliged to take the argument a few steps further. First, account had to be taken of the fact that production invariably needs raw materials and equipment as well as labour. Marx termed these items 'constant capital' on the grounds that, unlike labour, they generate no surplus value for the capitalist who buys and uses them. Rather, their value is simply transferred to the final output. For example, let us assume that production in equation (2) requires items of constant capital with a value of ten hours. Let us also assume that these are used up entirely in the production period (say a week). The value of the goods produced during the week would be as follows (expressed in hours of labour, where C = constant capital):

$$Q = 15_V + 25_S + 10_C = 50\text{hrs} \tag{3}$$

Typically, of course, production equipment is not used up entirely in one production cycle but lasts for many years. Marx accommodated this by allowing the value of such plant and buildings to be transferred gradually over their lifetimes to the products made. Marx's phrase for the ratio of labour to investment goods (that is, the ratio of 'variable' to 'constant' capital) was 'the organic composition of capital'.

Marx believed that it was, in principle, straightforward to use the above reasoning to calculate the rate of profit of any capitalist. The information in equation (3) cannot, of course, be used directly since this describes the components of the value of a single week's work. Rather, the computation would express the total surplus obtained during the accounting period – generally a year – as a percentage of the total value of capital goods and raw materials (constant capital – C) and labour (variable capital – V) used during the year. Denoting the rate of profit as π, the equation is (in hours of labour or their monetary equivalent):

$$\pi = S/(C + V) \tag{4}$$

For the economy as a whole, the average rate of profit could be calculated analogously by finding the total surplus value obtained by all capitalists and expressing this in relation to the total variable capital plus total constant capital employed.

It was clear to Marx that his analysis in this form was open to quite a serious objection, as Ricardo had found when he had worked with his own labour theory of value. The theory implies that profits would differ from industry to industry. To illustrate the point in terms of Marx's own economics, let us imagine two corporations with differing organic compositions of capital – perhaps an oil company and a garment manufacturer. Let us further assume that the rate of exploitation is the same in both industries at 167 per cent. Finally let us assume that the two labour forces are of equal size. Naturally, the amount of surplus value produced per year in the two corporations is the same. The oil company, however, has a production cycle which is far longer than the garment-maker's, besides using much more plant and equipment. While S and V are the same for the two businesses, C differs considerably. The result is that the oil company's rate of profit would be lower than the garment-maker's. As a general rule, moreover, capital-intensive industries would – by this formula – always earn lower rates of profit than labour-intensive ones. The origin of this result is not hard to see. If it is enunciated at the outset that labour is the source of all value, it follows naturally that firms employing relatively more labour (*ceteris paribus*) earn greater profits. The problem, of course, is that no such tendency has ever been discerned in the real economy.

To reconcile the law of value with empirical reality, Marx was forced to extend the argument yet again. He recognised that capitalists would naturally tend to quit low-profit industries for those offering better returns. The effect of this movement, Marx argued, would be that prices in the former industries would tend to rise while prices in the latter would fall. This process of price adjustment would end only when all capitalists are earning the same rate of profit. This argument, however, carries the implication that products do not exchange at prices which directly reflect labour values. Rather, they sell at prices ('prices of production') which are determined by marking up the cost of each product by a given percentage such that all capitalists earn similar rates of profit. 'Hence, the price of a commodity is equal to its cost-price plus the profit, allocated to it in per cent, in accordance with the general rate of profit, or, in other words, to its cost-price plus the average rate of profit' (Marx, 1960, p. 155). There is, in other words, no simple correlation between labour times and observable prices.

The advantage of this extension to the law of value was that it removed the embarrassing prediction of unequal rates of profit. It did, however, entail the concession that observed prices are not direct reflections of labour values. This is, in effect, a world (which everyone can see) of prices and profits, and a second world – which remains invisible – of labour-determined values. Nevertheless, Marx argued that the two worlds are connected because prices are related systematically to labour values. Moreover, for the system as a whole, Marx could claim that the total profit obtained by all capitalists was equal to the total surplus value extracted from the working class. Indeed for Lenin, writing in 1913, 'the doctrine of surplus-value is the corner-stone of Marx's economic theory' (Marx and Engels, 1968, p. 25).

Much controversy has attended Marx's device of prices of production. The debate has centred on whether or not labour values can logically be transformed into prices: the so-called 'transformation problem'. Some critics have questioned whether there is sufficient information in the theory to calculate the desired results (that is, whether the number of equations equals the number of unknowns). The internal consistency of the theory has likewise been questioned. Professor Ian Steedman, for example, has noted that Marx 'assumes that $S/(C + V)$ is the rate of profit, but then derives the result that prices diverge from values, which means precisely that $S/(C + V)$ is not the rate of profit' (Steedman, 1977 p. 31). Professor Steedman has gone on to argue that there is no necessary connection between surplus value and profit, so that the existence of profit is no proof that workers are being exploited. The importance of this criticism for Marxist economics is difficult to overestimate. It amounts to a complete rejection of one of Marx's central ideas.

While many Marxist economists have accepted Steedman's line of argument (Howard and King, 1985, pp. 166–77), others reject his reasoning. One argument put forward (Shaikh, 1981) has been that while surplus value and profit may well differ in magnitude, the deviation is nevertheless small and, more importantly, the ultimate basis of profit remains the exploitation of workers by capitalists.

6.3 Marx on enterprise: competition and change

Marx's second purpose, after proving that capitalism involves exploitation, was to demonstrate that it is bound to be superseded by a new social and economic system. He thus built on to his theory of value and profit a theory of change. In this branch of Marx's work, the business decisions of capitalists play the central role. In other words, in the Marxist perspective (as in others), change under capitalism comes about because of enterprise.

For Marx, the immediate cause of economic change in capitalism is the pressure of competition. In Marx's view, competition places imperative demands upon capitalists. If a capitalist is to remain in business, he has no option but to reinvest continually in new capital goods, new locations or new technology – activities which other economists would describe as 'enterprise'. Entrepreneurship, in Marx's view, is not an option but a necessity for the businessman. So powerful are the pressures for change that, for Marx, economic dynamism was the hallmark of capitalism. 'The bourgeoisie', declares the Manifesto of the Communist Party, 'cannot exist without constantly revolutionising the instruments of production' (Marx and Engels, 1968, p. 38).

Like the classical economists, Marx believed there to be a strong relationship between capital accumulation and the growth of output, both for the whole economy and for individual firms. For Marx, profit – the source of funds for investment – is not to be frittered on luxury consumption; the motto of capitalism is 'Accumulate, accumulate! That is Moses and the prophets!' (Marx, 1965, p. 595).

A capitalist who installed new machinery would naturally reduce the time taken to produce his goods. It might at first appear that their values would fall, with the result that he would derive no extra profit. There is, however, no contradiction between competition and the idea that the value of a product is set by the average socially necessary labour time used in its production. The key lies in the word 'average'. As long as the use of the new machines is not general, the value of the product is determined by the labour time taken by the firms using the older equipment. It therefore stays at its initial level, allowing the lower-cost firm to earn excess profits. As the new machinery becomes more widespread, the average labour time taken in the production of the commodity falls, thus reducing its value. The excess profits of the pioneering firm therefore dwindle. Firms which fail to adopt the new machinery, of course, find themselves taking more time to produce the item than is socially necessary: their costs become too high and their profits fall. Ultimately, such producers are forced to close. Far from overturning the law of value, competition can be seen as the means whereby the law of value is enforced: 'Competition carries into effect the law according to which the relative value of a product is determined by the labour time necessary to produce it' (Marx, 1963, p. 65).

From the point of view of the individual capitalist, competition is a scramble for profit. In classical, neoclassical and Austrian economics, competitive success is the source of profits. Marx, however, argued that this is an illusion, for competition cannot generate profit. Profit, for Marx, originates in the relationship between worker and capitalist. All that competition can do is to reallocate this surplus from one capitalist to another. An important caveat must, however, be entered here. The above conclusion holds only if technology and other conditions of production remain constant. If competition forces capitalists to raise productivity ('increase the rate of surplus value') then competition can indeed be a source of profit in Marx's economics, if at one remove.

For Marx, the significant result of competition is its cumulative effect upon the capitalist system. Marx saw the primary method of cost reduction as the exploitation of economies of scale. He accordingly saw the future in terms of the development of larger-scale production technologies. This, Marx believed, would lead to the accumulation of bigger stocks of capital which would in turn tend to depress the rate of profit: thus Marx's 'law of the tendency of the rate of profit to fall'. The logic of Marx's argument was that the ratio of investment goods to labour in every firm would tend to rise as all capitalists invested in larger-scale equipment. In equation (4), C rises and, *ceteris paribus*, π must fall. Although Marx foresaw several factors which could delay or mitigate this trend, such as attempts to prolong the working day or reductions in the cost of raw materials and machinery, he held that 'the general average rate of surplus value must express itself in a falling general rate of profit' (Marx, 1960, p. 209). (This clearly resembles predictions of falling profits in classical economics, though Marx arrived at his conclusion by a rather different route.)

These tendencies – larger plant and a falling rate of profit – have several effects. First, Marx predicted that firms would grow bigger, so that family firms would be supplanted by joint-stock companies. In such firms, the role of organising production would fall not to capitalists but to paid managers. Capitalists would thus degenerate into mere coupon-clipping investors. Second, a falling rate of profit would, Marx felt, drive the economy into semi-permanent depression. Capitalism would therefore lose its dynamism and unemployment would creep inexorably upward. Marx described this as a deepening of the contradictions between the 'forces of production' – technology and the skills of the workforce – and the 'relations of production' – the fact that wealth is owned privately, which means that it cannot be used in production if profits are too low.

The falling rate of profit was, for Marx, not merely an economic trend but the symptom of a deeper malaise. Capitalism, whose characteristic is dynamism, was expected to cease to fulfil its role of developing technology. In effect, Marx predicted that the capitalist system would fall into decline. While similar if more tentative prognostications are found in the works of Ricardo and Mill in relation to profit (see Chapter 3) and more especially Joseph Schumpeter in respect of enterprise (Chapter 5), the conclusions which Marx drew were more radical. For Marx, the deepening crises of capitalism would make it ripe for replacement. Thus while

Marx used his theory of the origin of profit – the law of value – to demonstrate that capitalism exploited the working class, he used his conception of enterprise to show that the system must eventually collapse.

Marx's approach to profit and enterprise stands in marked contrast to the views of Austrian economists. As noted in Chapter 5, these economists take pains to separate the factor services of capital and enterprise, arguing that each receives its respective reward – interest and profit. Moreover, whereas Marx saw the origin of profit in the exploitation of the employees, Austrians see profit arising from the inventiveness and alertness of the entrepreneur.

In conclusion, it is a feature of Marx's economic theories that profit is the income accruing to capital. Marx declined to distinguish sharply between profit and imputed interest. Neither did he distinguish enterprise from capital. For Marx, the running of a business – entrepreneurship – the provision of capital and the exploitation of labour were but different facets of the same role. Thus enterprise, because it was not separable from capital, did not merit a distinct return.

6.4 Marxist economics post-Marx: imperialism and unequal exchange

The capitalist system which Marx had attempted to analyse continued to evolve. One development of the late nineteenth century was the amalgamation of many companies in the United States, the United Kingdom and Germany into monopolistic trusts. Another was 'imperialism' – the industrial nations of Europe and America extending their power to all parts of the globe. Followers of Marx responded to these and other changes by developing Marx's analysis. The focus of interest of these later writers tended to fall upon the extraction of surplus value or profit; enterprise, however, played a much-diminished role compared with Marx's original analysis.

Although they held no brief for capitalism, Marx and Engels acknowledged the positive aspects of imperialism. They saw it as a means whereby traditional societies were forced into the modern epoch and were therefore brought closer to Communism. 'England has a double mission to fulfil in India', wrote Marx, 'the annihilation of old Asiatic society, and the laying of the material foundations of Western society in Asia' (quoted in Warren, 1981). Later Marxist writers like the German Socialist leader Rosa Luxembourg (1870–1919) were not so convinced of the 'advantages' of imperialism, seeing the colonies as being exploited by the capitalists of the metropolitan countries. The decisive shift in Marxist thinking occurred, however, in 1916 with the publication of *Imperialism – the Highest Stage of Capitalism* by Lenin (1870–1924), leader of the Russian Bolshevik Party. The pamphlet contained an important – and, in many respects, an innovative – analysis of capitalism from a Marxist perspective.

Noting the growth of the monopolistic trusts, Lenin argued that this was no passing phase but a necessary stage in the development of capitalism. Competition, indeed, was a temporary state in that the play of competitive forces was leading to the extinction of competition itself. Capitalism, according to Lenin, was becoming 'monopoly capitalism'. The new, monopolistic industrial concerns, Lenin argued, generated super-profits which needed to be reinvested. Given the relative abundance of capital already invested in Europe, the natural location for new investment was overseas. The role of providing safe locations for overseas investment fell to the state, and the governments of Europe were therefore drawn into the annexation of colonial territories. By such reasoning Lenin was able to conclude that imperialism was not caused by a quest for national grandeur as many believed but was fundamentally an economic phenomenon arising out of monopoly capitalism – capitalism's 'highest stage'.

Lenin's view of capitalism and, in particular, of the origin of profit differed from that of Marx in at least two significant respects. Marx saw profit as deriving solely from the exploitation of labour by capital. This exploitation arises from the ordinary workings of competitive markets: it is policed, as it were, by the forces of competition which ensure that products (and labour) sell at their 'natural' values. Lenin's first modification of this analysis was to assert that competition had been displaced, with the effect that many products sold at monopoly prices. Second, Lenin departed from Marx in his view of the generation of profit. Whereas Marx had seen profit as deriving from the exploitation of the working class, Lenin shifted attention to the extraction of profit from the colonies. These modifications of Marx's analysis of profit have been amplified by subsequent Marxist writers.

Although the empires of Lenin's day have largely been dissolved, Marxists have continued to argue that the exploitation of the Third World by the West still goes on. Amin and Emmanuel (Brewer, 1980, chs. 9, 10) have gone further and argued that profit is extracted from the Third World through the medium of international trade. The argument of these 'unequal exchange' theorists is that the commodities exported by the Third World sell below their values, while the goods which they buy are overpriced. This approach clearly differs from Marx's view that exploitation occurs through the mechanism of products exchanging precisely for their natural values. The common ground between these writers and Proudhon is plain.

Other Marxists (Frank, 1975) have argued that capitalism has tended to retard the economic development of the Third World. This 'under-development' school of thought holds that Third World economies have tended to be restricted to the role of producing primary products by a lack of investment funds (which have been siphoned off by unequal exchange) and by the control exercised by Western-owned multi-national corporations which has smothered local enterprise. These views have, however, been hotly contested by other Marxist economists who have written strongly in support of Marx's original view of capitalist imperialism as a force for the modernisation of Third World economies (Warren, 1981).

Other Marxist analyses of profit and enterprise have been concerned with features of Western economies themselves. One theme here has been state expenditure. The general thrust of Marxist analysis has been to try to relate public expenditure programmes to the needs of capital. Thus Marxian economists (O'Connor, 1973; Campbell, 1981, ch. 7) have tended to see public revenues essentially as part of the total surplus which has been diverted from the private profits of individual capitalists in order to fund their collective needs for trained workers, defence and law enforcement. Second, it has been argued that capitalists benefit from the public provision of health care and social security because these programmes make the system acceptable to the workers. These deductions mean that post-tax company profits are lower than the total surplus value which is extracted from the working class.

A strand which runs through these various extensions of Marx's economics is the idea that, fundamentally, profit is the result of exploitation. Whether that exploitation occurs through the medium of economic laws or through non-economic coercion or whether the exploited are the workers of the West or the subsistence farmers of the Third World are questions on which Marxist writers have differed, but the basis of profit in exploitation has not been in question. Enterprise, by contrast, has not endured so well. Although Marx saw capitalism as having a mission to develop the means of production both in the industrial countries and in the Third World, this notion has been progressively undermined in later Marxist writings.

6.5 German historicism and American institutionalism

Other economists standing apart from the mainstream of economic theory have contributed to the development of ideas on enterprise. One group was the 'historical' school, which dominated economic thinking in Germany for much of the nineteenth century.

The origins of the German historical school lay in the controversies over economic policy in Germany after the Napoleonic Wars. The German economy was then relatively backward, and many felt that its industry would develop only if its markets were protected from outside competition by tariffs. It was also argued that the state could assist in the process of development by, for example, building railways. Although both of these interventionist policies were subsequently adopted. they ran directly counter to the dominant school of contemporary economic thought – classical economics – which taught that economic growth would be best promoted by relying on the efforts of private, profit-minded entrepreneurs.

The processes of development of national economies occupied the focus of attention of the German historical school. The economists of this school thus rejected the idea that any principles of economics could have universal validity. In particular, they argued that policies such as free trade which drew upon classical economics were not absolute truths but simply reflections of the benefits which British industry was able to gain from these policies. In particular they rejected Ricardo's method of constructing theories by making abstract *deductions* from first principles without making reference to the social or political context within which markets or national economies operated. In place of deduction, the German historical school favoured an *inductive* approach involving the collection of historical data, anticipating that generalisations about the processes of development could be derived from this material. In 1883 this commitment to inductivism drew the then leader of the school, Gustav Schmoller (1838–1917), into a conflict (the so-called *Methodenstreit* or 'battle of methods') with Carl Menger of the Austrian school, in which Menger defended deductivism against Schmoller's attacks.

Their concern with processes of change led the historicists to examine the contribution of the entrepreneur. Schmoller drew attention to the *Unternehmer* or enterprising spirit, which he saw as 'a creative organiser . . . whose role was innovation'. Similarly the school's last member of note, Werner Sombart (1863–1941), saw the 'enterpriser' as the decisive force in history from the fifteenth century onwards. Sombart viewed the entrepreneur both as an initiator of new projects and as a leader of men able to stimulate his workforce to new efforts. In a similar vein to Marx and Schumpeter, however, Sombart saw the forces of enterprise gradually falling away in the epoch of 'late capitalism' which he dated from 1914 onwards. Sombart thus expected an increasing role in the economy to be taken by the state.

Some of the themes of the German historical school re-emerged in the ideas of the dissentient American economists of the institutionalist school, which began around the turn of the twentieth century. At that time it was argued that American industry was falling under the control of the 'robber barons', the millionaires whose already large business empires were forming into huge monopolistic trusts. In such a context, the lessons of mainstream economics about the benefits of competition seemed to be of little relevance.

Like the German historical school, the institutionalists rejected abstract deductivism in favour of induction and an evolutionary approach to economic analysis. In this approach the idea of change – as distinct from equilibrium – held pride of place. Economic matters, the institutionalists felt, could be examined meaningfully only by placing them within their political, social and psychological contexts – again, a view shared by the German historical school.

The first major institutionalist work was *The Theory of the Leisure Class* by Thorstein Veblen (1857–1929). In it, Veblen questioned the motivation behind many aspects of consumption by suggesting that many articles were consumed not for their intrinsic enjoyment but because they were a method of displaying the wealth of the consumer. For example the ankle-length dresses which women wore at that time were, Veblen argued, really (if unwittingly) intended – like the overgrown fingernails of Chinese mandarins – to indicate to the world that the wearers did not work and that their husbands were wealthy enough to support them.

Such behaviour was, Veblen considered, an example of customs or psychological needs which he termed 'institutions'. Veblen felt that compulsions like these were the true controllers of economic life rather than the rational, conscious decisions portrayed in neoclassical economics. Veblen thus rejected the notion of 'rational economic man'.

For Veblen, institutions could be divided into those, like ostentatious display, which do nothing to further mankind's progress (these Veblen held up to ridicule) and those which could be commended as progressive. Among the latter Veblen noted the 'instinct of workmanship' which led people to create new inventions. He argued that this instinct was, however, often thwarted by big business, which subordinated the making of goods to the making of money. Veblen had a simplistic belief in the future as a machine age and was convinced that scientists and technicians would rise up against the business class that prevented a continuous increase in production. A further aspect of Veblen's iconoclasm was therefore his rejection of the established idea that entrepreneurs were essential for economic progress.

Followers of Veblen included John Commons (1862–1945) and Wesley Mitchell (1874–1948). Besides teaching, Commons advised his state governor on employment legislation and became involved in trade union affairs, working closely with the American Federation of Labor. In his book *Institutional Economics* (1934) he drew a distinction between wealth and assets. From the point of view of society, Commons argued, wealth consists of a superabundance of resources like, for example, a large number of oilfields. Such superabundance would naturally imply low prices for (in this example) oil. Low prices would not, however, serve the interests of the individual oilfield owner, who would be better off if oil were not superabundant but scarce. In other words, the value of the assets of individuals rests not upon superabundance but upon scarcity. Commons concluded that the interests of individuals and of society could often diverge.

Mitchell was a researcher who founded the National Bureau of Economic Research in 1920 as a means of carrying forward the inductive and evolutionary programme of institutional economics. Much of his work was devoted to the analysis of business cycles. He became increasingly struck by the contrast between the conscious planning which was undertaken within business concerns and the more or less accidental consequences of firms' actions in terms of booms and slumps. This led him to favour a measure of national planning to coordinate business plans.

These ideas are echoed today in the work of the Harvard economist J. K. Galbraith. Galbraith is arguably the most important post-war institutionalist. He has built upon the work of Veblen, Commons and Mitchell a comprehensive critique of neoclassical economics. In a number of best-selling books, notably *The Affluent Society* (1961) and *The New Industrial State* (1969), Galbraith criticises the idea of consumer sovereignty, pointing to the power of advertising. He draws attention to the growing importance of large corporations, arguing that the demand-management policies of post-war governments can be seen largely as attempts to meet the needs of such firms for stable markets. Furthermore, like Schumpeter, Galbraith has questioned whether entrepreneurship can survive in an age of large corporations, by developing the idea that the real decisions in large corporations are taken not by their titular heads, the chairmen (who are usually concerned largely with public relations), but by committees of technical experts in marketing, production management and the other disciplines of management. These corporate bureaucracies of experts Galbraith terms the 'technostructure'.

6.6 Conclusion

The perspectives on profit and enterprise presented in this chapter differ as much from each other as they do from the more orthodox positions. There is nevertheless a theme which distinguishes many radical and socialist economists from those of the more orthodox schools of thought. It concerns the role of the entrepreneur. Whatever their differences, economists of the classical, neoclassical and Austrian schools see entrepreneurs as risk-taking innovators whose function is to take strategic decisions about production, namely what goods and services to supply to the market. While this role is relatively undeveloped in neoclassical economics it is, as Chapter 5 showed, central to Austrian theory. Joseph Schumpeter, for example, argued that technological advance, while resting upon the work of engineers and technologists, only occurs through the intervention of the entrepreneur who translates a technical possibility into a commercial proposition.

Many radical and socialist economists have taken a rather different view. Frequently they have perceived a separation – often an antagonism – between business and enterprise on the one hand and science and technology on the other. A conflict between the two is clear in the views of Saint-Simon, who saw the owners of capital as idle parasites, and of Fourier, for whom capitalist competition was wasteful. Marx also was explicit about the contradiction between the forces of production and the relations of production which he believed would deepen as capitalism evolved. The economists of the German historical school, by contrast, took the view that entrepreneurs were the agents of economic and technical change although, as we have seen, Sombart questioned whether this would continue. The theme re-emerges with the institutionalists. Veblen saw a conflict between the making of money and the instinct of workmanship while Commons perceived a similar conflict between assets and wealth. Finally Galbraith's theory of the way businesses are dominated by the 'technostructure' can also be seen as a variation on this theme. At bottom it is perhaps possible to discern in the works of these writers a tendency to identify the activity of resource conversion (transforming inputs into outputs) with the wider function of deciding what lines of production should be initiated and on what scale.

A strong implication of the arguments deployed by these writers is that, far from being an essential agent of technical and economic advance, the entrepreneur is of little or no importance. The development of industry and technology can often, these ideas suggest, be furthered by government intervention just as effectively as by private enterprise. In providing a basis for this line of reasoning, radical and socialist economists are clearly some way apart from the economists of other schools of thought discussed in this book: many of these radical ideas constitute a major departure from the general view of the economic function of enterprise.

Further reading

Useful accounts of the Utopian socialists' work can be found in Hardach and Karras (1979) or in Heilbronner (1980). With regard to Marx, the range of sources is enormous. Of Marx's own writing, *Wages, Price and Profit* is a short and unsophisticated exposition of his theory of value while *The Manifesto of the Communist Party* (written with Engels) sets out the Marxist view on both the history and the future of the capitalist system, again in a form designed primarily for political agitation rather than scholarly disputation. For those who wish to probe more deeply, *Capital* (vols. I–III) is the basic text. Between these extremes lies a multitude of works explaining (and inevitably modifying) Marx's work; examples include Howard and King (1985), Campbell (1981) and Resnick and Wolff (1987). For information on Marx's life, McClelland (1973) is very readable. The transformation problem is surveyed in, for example, Steedman *et al.* (1981) and Fine (ed.) (1986). Lenin's *Imperialism – the Highest Stage of Capitalism* (1970) – again a piece of agitational literature – sets the terms for much of modern Marxist thinking on international economic relationships. The various strands of Marxist thought on this question are surveyed in Edwards (1985), especially Chapters 4 and 5. Amin (1978), Frank (1975, 1979), Emmanuel (1972) and Warren (1981) are important works here. For Marxist analyses of the modern Western economies, see Mandell (1978), O'Connor (1973), Campbell (1981) and Burden and Campbell (1985).

The German historical school are well described in Oser (1970, ch. 11) and Ekelund and Hebert (1975), while a good analysis of Veblen is to be found in Seckler (1975). Dietz and Street (1987) apply institutionalism to the development of Latin America. Among the numerous and well-written works of Galbraith, the outstanding are perhaps *The Affluent Society* (1961) and *The New Industrial State* (1969).

7

The persistence of disagreement on profit and enterprise

The purpose of this chapter is to explain why the multiplicity of theories about profit and enterprise have persisted. Why is it, in other words, that economists have not been able to come to a clear judgement about which theory of profit comes closest to the truth? This chapter explains why the various economic theories of profit and enterprise – many of which are wholly incompatible – continue to exist.

It may appear that the matter could be easily settled by a systematic review of the evidence. In practice, however, the selection and interpretation of data are far from straightforward. The task is rendered complex by the fact that the various schools of thought employ different definitions of the knowledge. On the one hand, many Austrian economists hold that knowledge of economic matters is subjective. They argue, in brief, that no two persons' views of economic reality coincide and that there is, furthermore, no means of establishing the superiority of one person's view. Other economists take the view that theories ought to be capable of being tested in an objective manner, and they favour the testing of theories by means of empirical data. This latter method is of course the method favoured in the natural sciences. Its great advantage is that it allows rational discussion to take place over the merits of theories – theories are open to criticism since the evidence which supports them is, as it were, on the table for all to see. As the chapter shows, the disadvantage with empirical testing is that, despite high expectations, it cannot be used to establish the truth or falsity of a theory beyond all doubt.

7.1 Empirical proof and disproof in economics

The use of empirical data to establish the truth of different theories in economics is the method which, according to Professor Mark Blaug, has gained the widest acceptance (Blaug, 1980, p. 260). To undertake such testing, several steps have to be followed. First, the theory has to be formulated as a mathematical model which sets out precisely the relationships between the different variables such as price or profit. Second, 'conditional predictions' (alternatively known as 'conjectures' or 'hypotheses') have to be drawn from the model. These are statements about the consequences which would be expected if certain conditions were fulfilled. It is normal to highlight the effects of some conditions by holding others constant through the assumption of *ceteris paribus*.

An example to illustrate the above procedure might run as follows. The neoclassical theory of perfect competition begins with assumptions about the number of producers and consumers, the product and the conditions of entry into the market. It is also conventional to assume that consumers and producers are fully informed. From such assumptions, deductions are made about the equilibrium condition of the industry and the path by which it adjusts to changes in circumstances. Thus the model might produce the conditional prediction that if there were a decrease in business taxation then, *ceteris paribus*, there would be a rise in investment in the long run. The 'laws' of economics are examples of conditional predictions. The importance of these conditional predictions is that they – unlike the theories from which they derive – can be tested by comparing them with empirical data. Analogous deductions can be made from the theories of other schools of thought: Austrian theories, for example, link expectations of profit to the adoption of new ventures, while Marxist economics suggests hypotheses relating prices to labour inputs.

The next question is how such conjectures can be compared with the empirical evidence. The view common in the nineteenth century was that economic laws such as Ricardo's prediction that profits would fall were 'tendency laws'. These laws were not expected to operate in every circumstance but would hold true in some vague, probabilistic manner. This approach allowed the classical economists like Mill to point to instances of their predictions holding good as proof of the underlying truth of their theories. At the same time, it permitted them to discount any evidence which failed to confirm their thinking on the grounds that the laws were only 'tendencies' in the first place. This practice has been termed 'verificationism' since it places the emphasis upon finding confirming evidence (Blaug, 1980, ch. 3).

Since the days of the classical economists, it has become clear that verificationism cannot be a way of testing theories since it does not discriminate finely between the true and the false. The basic proposition of modern thinking (Blaug, 1980, p. 12) on proof and disproof is simply stated. It is that theories can *never* be proved to be true. On the other hand, it is perfectly possible to *disprove* a theory. There is, in short, an asymmetry between proof and disproof, which arises from the nature of conditional predictions or laws. Laws are 'universal' statements which attempt to describe events that always occur under specified circumstances, like the conjectured relationship between cuts in profit taxes and investment levels (*ceteris paribus*). To prove this hypothesis it would be necessary, following a tax cut, to survey every business unit in the economy. In practice this work could never be completed since new businesses spring up as fast as the research teams can trace them. Sample surveys could be used and the statistical significance of the results assessed, but these conclusions would be undermined as the population of firms changed. Repeated inquiries into business investment plans would not, moreover, serve to increase the likelihood of the conjecture being true. Since the hypothesis relates to all business units, and since the numbers of units – both those in being now and those which can potentially come into existence in the future – is infinite, there is no means of covering them all. The inescapable implication is that the theory could therefore never be proved beyond all doubt. On the other hand, to disprove the theory is, in principle, simplicity itself. All that is required is one firm with a reduced investment plan.

It would naturally be possible to escape from this difficulty by framing narrower hypotheses, such as one relating profit taxes to investment by firms trading in New York in August 1990. The problem with doing this is that the result – whether true or false – would be of uncertain relevance to other cities and other times.

This proposition – that confirming examples, however numerous, cannot prove a theory to be true – was first discussed in modern times by David Hume (1711–76), an associate of Adam Smith. Hume termed it the 'problem of induction'. As he demonstrated, the problem of induction is insoluble.

Sir Karl Popper, who held the chair of Logic at the University of London from 1949 to 1969, has taken Hume's ideas further. Accepting that ideas can never be proved to be true, Popper concludes that human knowledge about the world must always be conjectural. Even theories which have come to be regarded as true should really be described more tentatively as theories which *have not, as yet, been disproved*. While conjectures which have not in fact been disproved over the years may, in the eyes of some economists, assume the guise of truth, the conclusion remains that the acceptance of any hypothesis can only be provisional.

In the example above, it may well be the case that lower profit taxes increase investment, but the demonstration of the truth of that hypothesis lies beyond the powers of human beings. It must remain a conjecture.

While Popper, like Hume, denies the possibility of proving theories true, this does not mean that he sees theories as having no purpose. Indeed, for Popper, the formulation of new conjectures is critical to the process of discovering more about the world. Learning, for Popper, occurs through the falsification of hypotheses. Although ideas can never be proved true, the disproving of an idea serves to advance knowledge by eliminating misconceptions. Thus Popper argues that the key to all advances in knowledge lies in *disproof*.

In order for learning to occur, Popper argues, hypotheses have to be framed in particular ways. First, hypotheses must relate to phenomena which can be observed. For example, the hypothesis that 'managers work harder when they face competition' is impossible to disprove unless it is accompanied by some indication of how to detect both greater managerial effort and competition. By contrast, the hypothesis 'managers work longer hours in the textile industry than in government departments' *is* capable of being tested. Moreover, Popper stresses, only ideas about observable phenomena are open to rational and critical debate; disagreements about unobservable phenomena cannot easily be resolved through discussion.

Second, Popper argues that hypotheses should be open to the possibility of being falsified. Hence the term for Popper's approach to the evaluation of theories is 'falsificationism'. For example, the hypothesis 'if there is a cut in profit tax, then there will either be a rise in investment or there will not' could never be falsified since any change in investment would be taken as being consistent with the hypothesis. Being invulnerable to disproof, it cannot tell us anything about the economy – we can learn nothing from it. In other words, irrefutable hypotheses are incapable of generating knowledge.

For Popper, knowledge can be produced only by refutable hypotheses. For example, the hypothesis that a cut in profit tax from 50 per cent to 25 per cent will lead to a 30 per cent increase in business investment within two years is capable of advancing our knowledge since, if disproved, it would tell us what tax cuts do not achieve. In Popper's view, mankind in its scientific endeavours resembles a blind man finding his way across a field full of piles of stones with the help of various probes. Rigid probes (vulnerable conjectures) provide clear indications of the proximity of a pile; strips of newspaper (unfalsifiable conjectures), by contrast, are useless. Popper's ideas have gained widespread acceptance in science and philosophy. In economics, his ideas have found champions in such writers as Professors Richard Lipsey in Canada and Mark Blaug in the United Kingdom. Blaug, writing in 1980, commented that 'For the most part, the battle for falsificationism has been won in modern economics. . . .' (Blaug, 1980, p. 260).

7.2 Immunising stratagems

Despite widespread approval, falsificationism is not easy to carry into practice. More precisely, economists can all too easily evade the damning consequences of evidence which fails to conform to the conditional predictions that their theories have produced. In other words, they can often keep theories alive even when evidence is found against them.

The ability to defend theories which appear to have been falsified arises from the fact that testing in economics rarely involves merely comparing one condition ('if there were a cut in profit tax') with the evidence (data on investment plans). It is more usual for several conditions to be involved simultaneously, such as: 'If firms are seeking to maximise their profits, if entrepreneurs are aware of tax rates and if investment is related to perceived post-tax rates of profit, then a cut in profit tax will lead to a rise in investment by firms.' Furthermore, making the conjecture operational would require the addition of even more 'if' clauses specifying the evidence which would be needed, such as 'if the change in taxation announced on a given date had the net effect of reducing profit tax', or 'if the information in the Dept of Commerce survey of business sentiment is an accurate representation of business investment plans'. There is also of course a large range of conditions implicit in the phrase *ceteris paribus*: 'if there is no change in interest rates / demand / price expectations / exchange rates' and so on. The problem with these 'auxiliary hypotheses', as they are termed, is that when a conjecture with many conditional clauses fails to match the empirical evidence it may not be possible to tell which 'if' clause has been violated. A downturn in investment after a tax cut could therefore be explained by, say, the publication of gloomy predictions about future interest rate changes. In the minds of supporters, the main hypothesis – that lower taxes raise investment – could live on.

Such defences of falsified theories have come to be termed 'immunising stratagems'. It is clear that the more auxiliary hypotheses are involved, the more scope there is for the use of immunising stratagems. Indeed, the presence of large numbers of auxiliary hypotheses can have the effect of rendering a conditional prediction completely immune to disproof. Auxiliary hypotheses and immunising stratagems thus threaten to render unworkable Popper's idea of falsificationism; not surprisingly,

Popper argues strongly that auxiliary hypotheses (including *ceteris paribus* assumptions) should be kept to a minimum in order to preserve the possibility of falsifying a main hypothesis.

In many natural sciences, the problems posed by immunising stratagems can be reduced by the employment of controlled experiments which allow the defences of a falsified theory to be probed systematically. In fields in which controlled experiments are either difficult or impossible, such as astronomy and, of course, economics, there is naturally greater scope for the use of immunising stratagems.

Immunising stratagems can explain in part the persistence of rival schools of thought in economics: even when confronted with evidence which runs counter to their hypotheses, adherents of every school can claim that their chosen theory is not disproved but rather that some auxiliary hypothesis has been violated. Indeed, each school of economic thought is generally organised around a central idea which is taken by its adherents to be *incapable* of being tested against empirical evidence. In effect, central ideas are treated as being both self-evident and above empirical investigation. These central ideas are then used to generate lower-level hypotheses relating to specific questions. The lower-level hypotheses can, upon disproof, be discarded without necessarily undermining the central idea. For example, the central idea of neoclassical economics is that economic agents make rational, fully informed, maximising decisions. This can be used to generate lower-level conjectures like that linking lower profit taxes with higher investment. Disproof of this specific hypothesis would not lead to the rejection of the notion that firms made rational, profit-maximising decisions because neoclassical economists would be able to use immunising stratagems to defend it. Similarly, Marxist economists argue that in general products exchange at prices which reflect labour times. If confronted with an example of an article such as an old master which sold for a price far in excess of such a value, Marxists would argue that special conditions applied in such an instance, and their central idea – the law of value – would not, at least in their own estimation, be disproved. Again, the central idea of Austrian economics may be taken as the notion that profit acts as an incentive to enterprise in markets characterised by uncertainty, and any evidence which threatened to overturn such an idea would doubtless be rejected by Austrian economists. Such central ideas of schools of thought have been termed 'paradigms' by the historian of science Thomas Kuhn (Kuhn, 1962), while the philosopher Imre Lakatos has called them the 'hard cores' of a body of theory (Latsis, 1976).

7.3 Economic methodologies

This section describes the ways in which economists evaluate theories of profit and enterprise. It indicates that, Professor Blaug's views notwithstanding, economists from different traditions do not invariably accept Popper's reasoning.

Instrumentalism

Perhaps the best-known attempt to apply Popper's falsificationism to economics was made by Professor Milton Friedman in his 'Methodology of Positive Economics' (1953). Since Friedman's views differ slightly from those of Popper, his approach has come to be known not as falsificationism but as 'instrumentalism'. Acceptance of Friedman's views is largely confined to the neoclassical tradition.

Friedman argues like Popper that theories should be evaluated by the performance of their conditional predictions against the empirical evidence: if a theory 'works' then it is to be accepted – at least provisionally. For example, the model of perfect competition can be used to generate the conditional prediction that if the demand for a product rises, the industry will respond by raising output in the long run as new firms enter. As noted earlier, this is the procedure of comparative static analysis.

The point at which Friedman parts company from Popper is over the assumptions of models. Popper lays down no rules about whether or not they can be tested. Friedman, however, asserts that assumptions need not be tested – attention is to be restricted to the conditional predictions. In the example above, the model of perfect competition would have to be accepted as long as its predictions coincided with the empirical results, even if it were being applied to an industry in which products were not homogeneous or which did not have a myriad of small producers.

An implication of Professor Friedman's reasoning is that assumptions about the information which economic agents have should not be questioned. This is of particular importance to neoclassical economics because this school of thought traditionally makes the assumption that economic agents possess complete information. This idea is contested: Austrian economists in particular make much of their alternative view that economic agents act in conditions of uncertainty. Friedman's argument provides a convenient basis on which neoclassical economists can sidestep such criticisms (Machlup, 1967; Boland, 1982).

Conventionalism

This approach to the evaluation of theories developed originally in response to the growing understanding of the impossibility of inductive proof. It is the view that theories are to be looked upon as mere summaries of empirical findings to date. Questions of truth and falsity do not therefore arise for conventionalists – all theories are true in so far as they are confirmed by at least some evidence. Like instrumentalism, it is largely confined to neoclassical economics (Boland, 1982, pt. III).

Conventionalism involves the use of a range of criteria to judge theories. One is the use of a small number of ideas or principles in a theory; another is the requirement that a theory should not contradict other well-accepted theories. Conventionalism also stresses the fact that economists form a social group in which collective judgements are of much importance. Thus the criterion for evaluating a theory is the degree to which it wins acceptance among what Thomas Kuhn called the 'invisible college' of fellow-researchers and theoreticians across the world. Given the multiplicity of criteria, the hallmark of conventionalism is a reluctance to make final judgements upon theories – notably, to reject them as false when not confirmed by the evidence. Rather, theories are left pending – 'the jury is out' indefinitely. This approach is strongly linked to the use of immunising stratagems which allow theories to survive potentially damaging brushes with empirical evidence: theories which can be defended by immunising stratagems can be left pending forever.

A priorism or praxeology

This approach to the testing of theories stems primarily from the writings of Ludwig von Mises, a prominent economist of the Austrian school (see Chapter 5). Von Mises' position was that theories in the social sciences such as economics should be tested by entirely different procedures from those used in the natural sciences (1949). While empirical testing is appropriate for the latter, social scientists have to take account of the fact that the objects of their studies – people – have motivations and values. He thus argued that economic categories like income and price must be related to opportunity costs, and these in turn are inescapably subjective. For example, although a job might carry a pay-rate of $15 per hour, this would not have the same meaning for all applicants: people would clearly have different distances to travel, so that the net income (in terms of both time and money) would differ; different applicants would have to be ready to expend different amounts of effort in acquiring new skills; the job satisfaction which the post offered would naturally differ from person to person depending on personality factors, while applicants would face varying opportunity costs in terms of the benefits forgone from other employment.

As a result, von Mises argued, indicators like prices have no objective meaning whatever, so there is no possibility of using such data to establish the truth or falsity of theories. This can only be done by examining the truth of the basic postulates of an economic theory. These are that choices and actions, when undertaken by competent adults, are the result of conscious, purposive decisions. Thus the truth or otherwise of economic theory, von Mises contended, is known to everyone simply by virtue of having to make choices, and the only accurate test is introspection. Theories in economics are therefore true 'from the first' or *a priori*. *A priorism* is the belief that economics should consist of deductive reasoning from self-evident truths or axioms to consequences or prediction; empirical evidence should play a secondary role at best.

Marxist methodology

Von Mises' repudiation of empirical testing is shared by Marxist economists. Sweezy (1964) and Hollis and Nell (1975), for example, take the view that Marx was able to perform a more insightful analysis of capitalism than his non-socialist rivals because he was able to 'abstract' essential features of capitalism from inessential details. For Marx, the essential relationship was that between capitalist and worker rather than that between consumer and seller or landlord and tenant, and much of Marx's work (as well as that of later Marxist writers) is devoted to describing the historical evolution of such class relationships. The importance of these relationships is taken to be self-evident (Blaug, 1980, p. 126). Like von Mises' assertions about the truth of Austrian theories of economic behaviour, the importance of the capitalist–worker relationship is asserted *a priori*.

7.4   Testing theories of profit and enterprise

The problem with these non-empirical perspectives is that they are not conducive to discussion. It is not possible to assess in open debate the truth or otherwise of their basic propositions since they are simply asserted: one must either take them or leave them. These approaches thus run directly counter to Popper's view that theories should be tested by comparing their conditional predictions with empirical results. Despite the difficulties with Popper's approach, one of its more attractive features is the way in which it treats knowledge as being open to discussion among informed critics, as stressed by the formal term for Popper's philosophy of science, 'critical rationalism'. For Popper, all scientific knowledge is objective and can therefore be the subject of open, free and rational discussion.

It has been urged (Caldwell, 1982) that each paradigm or school of thought in economics should be tested only by the criteria which it sets itself. Nevertheless the importance of the argument that only empirical testing can lead to knowledge which is objective and open to rational assessment is one which many economists find attractive, and this section accordingly discusses the possibilities for assessing the contending approaches to profit and enterprise in terms of falsifiability.

The falsifiability of neoclassical theories

In 1982 Professor Mark Blaug commented that 'of all the contending economic doctrines of the past, it is only the orthodox, timeless equilibrium theory . . . that has shown itself to be willing to be judged in terms of its predictions' (Blaug, 1980, p. 262). The basis of Blaug's argument is his view that modern neoclassical economics is ideally suited to the production of falsifiable hypotheses. As noted above, this is achieved by means of comparative static analysis which involves the comparison of one equilibrium with another. It is plain that explanations based on comparative static analysis can be transformed quite easily into conditional predictions such as: 'If the state raises taxes on cars, then (*ceteris paribus*) the price of cars will rise and the quality demanded will fall.' It might thus appear that such conditional predictions are open to falsification and hence satisfy the criteria laid down by Popper.

In order to assess the validity of this view, it is necessary to look briefly at the characteristics of market equilibrium. This concept lies at the heart of neoclassical economics and, as Chapter 4 showed, it has received so much emphasis that the notion of enterprise is virtually excluded. Equilibrium and enterprise are exclusive states – markets may display one but not both at the same time. What are the characteristics of equilibrium? Essentially, equilibrium is attained when there are no forces for change: when all adjustments to circumstances have been completed, all consumers are maximising their satisfaction levels and all producers are maximising their incomes. Equilibrium occurs, in short, when enterprise has run its full course.

A key element in equilibrium is the idea that all decisions are 'rational', i.e. they are taken on the basis of perfect information. Since the acquisition of perfect information and the completion of all adjustments may require large amounts of time, noeclassical theories tend to involve comparisons between long-run equilibria. In practical terms, of course, neoclassical economists rarely specify the actual time which any predicted adjustment will take: the duration of the long run is rarely disclosed.

These considerations drive towards a conclusion of some importance. It is that while the conditional predictions of neoclassical economics may seem to be falsifiable, in practice they are not. This is because such predictions are usually made on the basis of auxiliary hypotheses which are notably wide in scope, such as the notion that economic agents are fully informed. The effect of these auxiliary assumptions is to give almost infinite scope for the use of immunising stratagems. Defenders of a neoclassical theory can normally argue that their theories have not been disproved because one of the auxiliary hypotheses was violated – for instance, because some economic agent did not possess complete information. Similarly, a threatened theory could be defended on the grounds that the long run was not yet over. In other words, the decision by neoclassical economists to focus upon long-run equilibria in which entrepreneurial processes have run their course leads them to formulate hypotheses which are virtually invulnerable. In consequence, it has been argued (Boland, 1982) that neoclassical economics is incapable of generating knowledge.

The falsifiability of Austrian economics

While neoclassical economics places equilibrium at the centre of attention, Austrian economics lays emphasis upon enterprise and the processes of economic change. There are thus two important points of difference between these two schools of thought. First, while neoclassical economics centres upon the long run when all adjustment processes have run their course, Austrian economics focuses upon the processes which occur during the adjustment period. Second, different assumptions are made about the information which economic agents are assumed to have. In neoclassical theory economic agents are assumed to be fully informed and 'rational' (or can at least compute the probabilities of the consequences of different decisions), while in Austrian economics they operate in a world of uncertainty and are therefore forced to experiment with new products or bundles of consumer goods. Entrepreneurs in particular are assumed in new Austrian economics to be continually trying out new business ventures, exploiting new technological opportunities or developing new markets. In other words, whereas economic agents are assumed in neoclassical economics to be endowed with full information, in Austrian economics they are engaged in a continual process of learning.

It may be imagined that the empirical testing of Austrian theories, although perhaps somewhat difficult because of their dynamic nature, would not be impossible. The established view, however, is that von Mises' praxeology applies to Austrian economics with the result that the conjectures of this school of thought cannot be tested empirically. But more recently the argument has been advanced by Professor Lawrence Boland (1982) that – contrary to the received view – Austrian economics is more capable of generating falsifiable conjectures than neoclassical economics. Boland's argument is that because of its focus upon the short run, new Austrian economics is strongly placed to generate falsifiable hypotheses. This is because the conditional predictions of Austrian economics could, in principle, be framed with respect not to a vaguely defined 'long run' but to specific periods in real time. For example, Austrian economists might conjecture that if prime rates were to rise by three points, business investment would fall by 15 per cent *within* (say) *three years*. Unlike a neoclassical hypothesis about a long-run equilibrium position, this conjecture would be vulnerable to refutation and could thus generate knowledge.

The principal difficulty with Boland's recommendation is that Austrian economics also includes the idea that entrepreneurs are likely to take action on their own initiative rather than in response to external stimuli. For example, although the market for a certain kind of food may be in equilibrium one week, a producer may decide to experiment with something else in the following week, thus disturbing matters. The trigger for such events lies not in the outside world of objective facts but in their subjective perception by consumers and businessmen – coupled, of course, with a willingness to innovate. Whether theories could be framed to capture such mental processes is not clear.

The falsifiability of Marxist theories

Despite the rejection of empirical testing of Marxist economic ideas by Baran and Sweezy, this body of economic thought produces predictions which appear in principle open to falsification. First is the theory that values are related to labour times. This was of course modified by Marx to the idea that products exchanged not at their values but at their 'prices of production', so that the link between labour times and prices was weakened. Moreover, the consistency and adequacy of Marx's law of value as an explanation of prices and profits are still under debate, as Chapter 6 indicated.

Other predictions include the conjectures that profits will tend to fall and that wages will tend to remain at subsistence level. Both have run into difficulties. While rates of profit fell between 1950 and 1980, evidence since then suggests an upward movement in both the United Kingdom and the United States, while living standards in the West rose throughout the period. In the face of such developments, Marxists have often shifted ground. The rising living standards of the working class, for example, were explained by Lenin in terms of the exploitation of the colonies. Lakatos comments acerbically:

> The early predictions of Marxism were bold and stunning but they failed. Marxists explained all their failures: they explained the rising living standards of the working class by devising a theory of imperialism. . . . But their auxiliary hypotheses were cooked up after the event to protect Marxism from the facts. (Lakatos, 1978, vol. I, p. 6)

7.5 Conclusion

Earlier chapters of this book reviewed various theories of profit and enterprise. Adherents of all these theories claim that their particular ideas come closest to the truth. This chapter has examined the problems of testing these claims.

Three difficulties hinder the task. First, each tradition has its distinct view both of the nature of truth and of the evidence which may be used to substantiate its claim. Many Austrian economists, for example, repudiate empirical testing and argue that their theories are correct simply because their truth is known *a priori*. In a similar vein, Marxists affirm that their theories deal with the 'essential' features of the capitalist system; yet the criteria for establishing what is essential are rarely spelled out.

Other economists reject such *a priorism* and pursue the idea that empirical testing offers a definitive and objective method for distinguishing good theories from bad. This perspective has gained many adherents, particularly in the empirically orientated neoclassical school. As the discussion has indicated, however, this approach is hindered by the second of the three problems, namely that empirical testing can succeed only if hypotheses are vulnerable to falsification. If theorists frame their conjectures in such a way as to be invulnerable, as is often the case, then empirical testing cannot work.

The third problem is closely related to the second. It is that the complete and final disproof of an entire body of theory or paradigm like Marxism or neoclassical economics is virtually impossible. This is because 'hard core' ideas can be defended indefinitely by the use of immunising stratagems.

Given the nature of these difficulties it is hardly surprising that incompatible theories of profit and enterprise have managed to survive over the decades. The net result is that economists and policy-makers alike are confronted with a cacophony of conflicting ideas. For those prepared to look hard enough, a justification for virtually any attitude towards profit and enterprise, from the strongest encouragement of profit-seeking to outright suppression, can be found in the writings of economists of different schools. In consequence, politicians in different countries have been able to pursue a wide range of policies towards industry and commerce. The following chapter reviews many of these policies to illustrate their successes and failures.

Further reading

A good introduction to methodological matters in general is provided in Chalmers (1982), while Kuhn (1962) explains the idea of 'paradigms'. Ryan (1970) and Lessnoff (1978) discuss the applicability of empirical testing to the social sciences in general.

A survey of methodology in economics is found in Pheby (1988) and Campbell *et al.* (1989, ch. 1). More comprehensive is Blaug (1980). Besides describing many basic problems, Blaug severely criticises the Marxist and praxeological stances and argues strongly that neoclassical economics is the only school of thought which is capable of being tested empirically. This builds upon the ideas of Friedman (1935, pp. 3–43, reprinted in Breit and Hochman 1968, pp. 23–47).

Blaug's views have not gone uncontested. Boland (1982) argues that neoclassical economics is virtually untestable and that the Austrian approach is, contrary to established belief, capable of generating vulnerable hypotheses. For defences of the praxeological view, see Shand (1984), Littlechild (1986) and von Mises (1949). The Marxist position is set out in, for example, Hollis and Nell (1975), while Campbell (1981) and Resnick and Wolff (1987) offer Marxist critiques of mainstream economics and Keat and Urry (1983) discuss methodological issues in social science from a Marxist point of view. Caldwell (1982) argues strongly for methodological eclecticism.

8
Profit, enterprise and economic policy

Disputes about profit and enterprise have not been confined to academic economists. On the contrary, the divergent ideas reviewed in this book have been a source of persistent contention in national debates on economic policy. Conflicting policies like free trade and protectionism, regulation and privatisation, state subsidies and *laissez-faire* all owe their justification to the different perspectives on profit and enterprise described in earlier chapters. This chapter examines the impact which the different theories of profit and enterprise have upon policy-making today. The analysis includes the industrialised economies, the Communist bloc and the Third World. The chapter shows that while the records of different policies do not provide definitive proof of the truth of the various theoretical approaches – indeed, as the previous chapter showed, this could never have happened – the historical record can nevertheless offer lessons for policy-makers and economists on the efficacy of different policies towards enterprise and profit.

8.1 Policy debates and policy initiatives

Since World War II there has been intense debate in the West over the proper economic roles of the market and the state. Economists have taken a range of positions, some advocating complete freedom in markets, some supporting rigorous state planning and others favouring varying degrees of state intervention. In this debate, the links between policies and schools of economic thought are not simple and direct: pro-market economists tend to draw upon the ideas of classical, neoclassical and Austrian economics, while more interventionist economists use

146

theories from Keynesian economics, neoclassical economics and radical or Marxist analyses. Nevertheless, the different schools of thought all carry, more or less explicitly, a series of implications for economic policy and it will be helpful to review these briefly.

Austrian economists, as previous chapters have shown, are firm advocates of the benefits of markets. The basis for this judgement lies in the dynamic argument that markets allow full scope for enterprise. For Austrians, the virtue of markets is that they promote adjustment, innovation and change. Austrian economists place little faith in the abilities of public organisations to generate better solutions to economic problems than entrepreneurs operating in free markets. This conclusion is based on their view that economic agents – including governments – have but limited information about consumers' needs and the availability of resources. There is thus a necessity for entrepreneurs to explore these matters continually by trying out new ventures. While private entrepreneurs can, in the Austrian view, be relied upon to undertake this searching as they pursue profit, public agencies are likely to neglect it. Moreover, Austrians believe, any interventions which are based on a presumed knowledge of the optimum will very probably be wrong.

The arguments of neoclassical economics also suggest that markets can contribute to the public good when they are perfectly competitive. Although this may resemble Austrian thinking on markets, the basis for the neoclassical finding is rather different. Neoclassical economists see competitive markets as being beneficial because they result in a state of affairs described as the 'optimum allocation of resources'. In general terms, this occurs when the cost of the last item produced is just equal to the value which consumers place upon it. To produce any more would be to squander resources, while to produce any less would be to neglect opportunities to satisfy consumer wants. At the same time, however, neoclassical economists argue that this conclusion only holds under certain circumstances: there must be no monopoly-creating barriers to entry to markets and no external effects like pollution. If these conditions are violated, markets fail to achieve the optimum outcome. Thus parallel to the notion that markets can produce an optimum outcome is another neoclassical idea – market failure.

An important extension to these ideas came with the development in the mid-1950s by Professor Paul Samuelson of the concept of 'public goods' (Samuelson, 1954). These are goods which, once provided, can generate benefits to any number of consumers without any additional costs and which it would be difficult to debar non-payers from using. The classic example is a lighthouse, which can be used by any number of ships regardless of whether they have paid for its construction. Again, the implication is that only public action can secure the benefits of public goods to the economy. Soon it came to be argued that many goods had the attributes of public goods even if they were not pure cases. Health care, housing, transport and education could all be thought of as quasi-public goods having large external benefits. This appeared to provide a rationale for extensive state involvement in markets – an idea which Austrian economists naturally contest.

A further idea of importance in neoclassical economics is the assumption that economic agents possess perfect information. This leads many neoclassical economists to overlook the problems of gathering and evaluating data. The implication is that market failure can be both identified and rectified by public agencies with speed and precision. While neoclassical economists are by no means agreed on the proper degree of state intervention in markets, the paradoxical result of their approach is that the ideas of neoclassical economics can be used both to endorse *laissez-faire* policies and to provide strong arguments in favour of intervention by government. Any problems arising from such intervention tended until the late 1980s to receive relatively little investigation.

Similar arguments have been deployed in relation to macroeconomic phenomena. Here, Keynesian economists have taken the position that the market system can be prone to malfunctions such as inflation or persistent unemployment. Again, some economists have drawn the conclusion that intervention by the state can be beneficial while the costs of such intervention have been neglected, especially in introductory economics texts (Lipsey, 1979, pp. 554–6; McConnell, 1981, pp. 248–9; and Samuelson and Nordhaus, 1985, pp. 176–7).

Radical ideas have also contributed to the debate. Like neoclassical economists, radicals have rarely given strong emphasis to enterprise. While not all radicals share Marx's view that profits arise from exploitation, the work of many like Thorstein Veblen and J. K. Galbraith has given credence to the idea that running business corporations is a largely routine affair which can be as well handled by bureaucrats as by entrepreneurs. These ideas have been used to lend support to government policies such as planning, regulation and public ownership. Through intellectuals like Britain's Fabian socialists, concepts such as market failure and the beneficence of state intervention, alongside the view that the profit motive was not essential for the administration of business, began to be incorporated into the thinking of left-of-centre political parties such as the British Labour Party and the American Democratic Party. During the middle years of the twentieth century these ideas found considerable favour with electorates and politicians on both sides of the Atlantic. The Depression of the 1930s, the apparent successes of Soviet planning and a widespread wish to redistribute income led, in the years immediately before and after World War II, to a trend away from *laissez-faire*. In the United Kingdom many industries were taken into public ownership, others were regulated, an interventionist macroeconomic policy was pursued, large-scale welfare services were set up and taxes raised to pay for them. Similar extensions to state activity were seen in Europe while in the United States regulation, macrointervention and welfare programmes were instituted, notably during the New Deal of the 1930s under the presidency of F. D. Roosevelt (1882–1945) and in the 1960s under the presidency of Lyndon Johnson (1908–73).

During the 1970s, however, events took a negative turn. The economies of the West were increasingly beset by stagflation – a combination of slow growth, high unemployment and inflation. With the apparent failure of interventionist policies, the arguments of pro-market economists including the new Austrians began to gain ground, and many governments began to free markets from public control. These changes were evident both in the fields of general economic management of the macroeconomy and at the level of industrial and competition policies. These are reviewed in turn.

8.2 Economic management

The issues here relate to taxation, welfare services and macroeconomic policy.

Taxation and supply-side economics

Over the decades since World War II, the share of public expenditure in GDP rose in all of the major Western economies. By 1987, the share of GDP taken by government ranged from 26 per cent in Japan to 57 per cent in Sweden. For the United States the figure stood at 33 per cent while for the United Kingdom it was 40 per cent. By 1979 the top marginal rate of tax on salaries in the United Kingdom was 83 per cent; on investment income it stood at 98 per cent. For groups in receipt of welfare benefits, the marginal rate of income loss could be even higher: for some low-income groups in the United Kingdom, a pay rise of £1 might mean tax payments, social insurance contributions and a loss of welfare entitlements with a total value of as much as £1.30.

In neoclassical economics, there is some uncertainty over the effects of tax cuts on an individual's supply of effort. On the one hand, the mere fact of having extra income could allow workers to take life more easily

– the so-called 'income effect'. Certainly the record of the last 150 years demonstrates that higher real rates of pay have been taken in part in the form of extra leisure, with the working week falling in the industrial countries from 60–70 hours in the mid-nineteenth century to around 35–40 hours today. On the other hand, higher net pay rates also have a 'substitution effect' by inducing workers to spend more time working and less in unpaid activities. Thus higher post-tax pay can be expected to induce greater work effort. Neoclassical economists argue that there is no means of establishing *a priori* which of these two effects will be the more powerful. So it is not clear what effect lower taxes will have upon work effort. Austrian economists, however, reject this logic, arguing that the productivity and innovation which have permitted people to enjoy greater leisure as well as higher material living standards are the result of a drive for material rewards. For Austrian economists, it is axiomatic that the substitution effect must be the more powerful: greater post-tax income will call forth more effort, more risk-taking and more ingenuity. For Austrians, lower taxes on incomes and profits are the keys that unlock the entrepreneurial spirit.

During the 1980s the view that taxation ought to be cut in order to increase effort, savings and enterprise began to gain ground (Minford, 1984). Indeed, it was urged that cuts in taxation and welfare benefits would bring such benefits in terms of higher productivity and output that there would be a 'supply-side revolution' – a term coined by Professor A. B. Laffer of the University of California in the late 1970s. He advanced the thesis that a cut in taxation could result in such a surge in output and incomes that government revenues would suffer by far less than the gross cuts implied. For example, a reduction in tax rates from 25 per cent to 20 per cent would not result in a fall in public revenues of one-fifth because national income would rise. After a few years faster growth could, Laffer argued, make up much or perhaps all of the initial revenue loss (Laffer and Seymour, eds., 1979).

The 'Laffer effect' is illustrated in Figure 8.1. Government revenue (plotted horizontally) is clearly zero when tax rates (plotted vertically) are also zero. As tax rates are increased, the government raises more money. After a certain point, however, higher tax rates operate as a disincentive and depress national income, with the result that increases in taxes lead to *lower* tax revenues. Ultimately, at a tax rate of 100 per cent no one produces anything and public revenue is once again zero. Laffer thus argues that if a government finds itself with a tax rate of t_1 it could reduce taxes to t_2 and still enjoy the same receipts OR.

In 1981 Ronald Reagan took office as President of the United States, on a programme which drew heavily on such thinking, and federal income taxes were duly cut from a range of 14–70 per cent to a range of

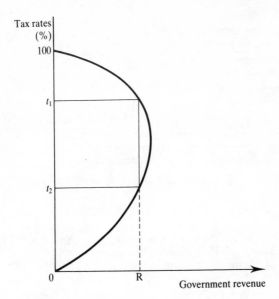

Tax rates (%)

Figure 8.1 The Laffer effect

10–28 per cent between 1981 and 1986. The results of this bold stroke for economic growth were, however, obscured by the simultaneous expansion of the defence budget, which rose from 5.3 per cent of GNP to 6.3 per cent between 1981 and 1986, and by the reluctance of Congress to cut other spending programmes. While federal receipts shrank in relative terms, federal spending remained virtually constant as a proportion of GNP during the early 1980s, leading to a budget deficit of over $212 billion by 1985. In short, while tax reforms designed to stimulate enterprise were coming into effect, the US economy was given a huge fiscal stimulus. The result was economic expansion: after a recession in 1981–2, the American economy grew by 26 per cent between 1982 and 1988, creating over 15 million civilian jobs. Productivity, however, grew by less than 1 per cent per year – well below the rates recorded by other major economies. These trends – growth and job creation combined with slow advances in productivity – were by no means new to the US economy. During the upswing of 1975–8, for example, GNP grew by 15 per cent while employment again advanced by 15 million (see Figures 8.2 and 8.3). The special features of the expansion of the 1980s were first that new businesses were formed at the rate of 600,000 per year – double the average for the 1960s – and second that it has lasted so long. At the time of writing (spring 1990) the expansion is in its eighth year and signs of its weakening are elusive. Whether this prodigious effort has resulted

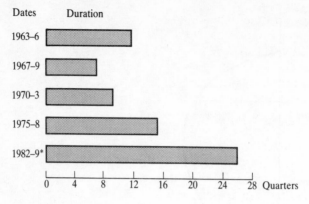

* Upswing incomplete

Figure 8.2 The duration of US economic upswings 1983–89 (Trough-to-peak changes in GDP; measured in quarter years.) (Source: *OECD Leading Indicators and Business Cycles*, OECD, Paris, 1986, Table 13.2, p. 58)

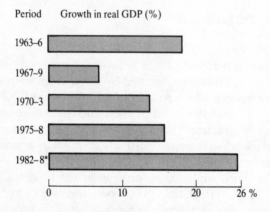

* Upswing incomplete

Figure 8.3 US economic growth 1963–88 (Growth in real GDP in successive economic upswings.) (Sources: *Yearbook of National Accounts Statistics*, UN, New York, 1975; Datastream)

from supply-side improvements as Ronald Reagan preferred to conclude or from old-fashioned Keynesian demand-creation remains, however, a controversial point.

In the United Kingdom, a similar experiment began under the premiership of Margaret Thatcher. Between 1979 and 1989, taxes on income and profit were reduced: the top rate of personal income tax on earnings was cut from 83 per cent to 40 per cent, the basic rate (the only rate paid by over 90 per cent of the workforce) was reduced from 33 per cent to 25 per cent and the main tax on company profits was scaled down from 52 per cent to 35 per cent. At the same time, however, rising social security contributions offset these cuts so that while net marginal rates of income loss for the typical worker fell, the reduction was only from 40 per cent to 34 per cent. But these reforms did not lead to a loss in public revenue, partly because the administration raised indirect taxes (VAT was almost doubled from 8 per cent to 15 per cent) and partly because government receipts were bolstered by sales of public assets such as the telecommunications company, British Telecom, and municipal housing. In line with Professor Laffer's expectations, however, the British economy expanded rapidly, raising tax receipts. The most significant result, perhaps, was a surge in productivity, which advanced by over 2.5 per cent per year from 1980 to 1988 as against annual gains of less than 1.5 per cent during the 1970s (see Figure 8.4). For the first time since World War II, Britain outdistanced its European neighbours in terms of economic growth. Nevertheless, as the 1980s drew to a close the British economy began to be dogged once again by capacity constraints as output failed to match demand. A widening trade deficit and resurgent inflation undermined the thesis that the British economy had thrown off the shackles of the post-war decades. Whether Mrs Thatcher's supply-side initiatives have been sufficient to permit rapid growth in the longer term remains to be seen.

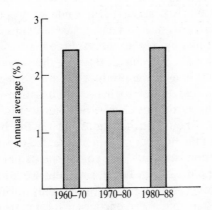

Figure 8.4 Growth in output per person employed, UK, 1960–88 (Sources: *Economic Trends*, Central Statistical Office; Datastream)

Welfare spending

Free or subsidised health care, education and housing together with state-organised social security systems have been provided by governments in the West for well over a century, the pioneer being imperial Germany under Chancellor Bismarck. In the United States, social security and other social insurance programmes advanced from 1.5 per cent of GNP in 1954 to 6.5 per cent (more than the defence budget) by 1980. In the United Kingdom, the Labour government which took office at the end of the World War II consolidated and extended earlier social welfare programmes to create a welfare state comprising free health and education services, state retirement pensions, income support schemes and unemployment benefits. Such programmes accounted for over 20 per cent of GDP by the early 1980s. Although these programmes are motivated in large measure by a wish to redistribute income, a rationale has also often been provided by the neoclassical ideas that housing, education and health have strong 'public goods' characteristics. From the point of view of many economists, however, subsidised services carry two problems. The first is that their delivery may well be inefficient. The second relates to their effect upon personal attitudes and economic behaviour.

The problem with the delivery of subsidised services is that the views of producers can override considerations of cost or consumer preference. Services thus become supply- rather than demand-led. A good example may be Britain's National Health Service (NHS), in which resources are allocated in accordance with doctors' interpretations of needs. While doctors must inevitably play a prominent role in the delivery of medical care, the result, it is argued, is a tendency to perform spectacular but expensive surgery (such as heart transplants) as against cheaper, more routine work like hip replacements. Free market economists see these effects as the direct result of the way the services are organised and financed rather than as the product of poor management *per se*. These economists would prefer to make organisations which provide care compete for the custom of clients. In other words, hospitals, schools and universities should attract funds not on the basis of existing costs but by virtue of the number of patients treated or students educated. Ideally, these economists would like to see clients paying for services with either vouchers or cash (or both), since this would induce providers to offer the services which people want, thus raising the quality of service. Such a system might also encourage local managers to be entrepreneurial in seeking out new services to offer and new, more cost-effective techniques for providing them (Seldon, 1980).

It is also argued that subsidised welfare services have an insidious effect on national life by undermining personal responsibility. The argument is that people lose the habit of saving and insuring to provide for their old age or misfortune when the 'nanny state' (as critics term it) stands ready to assist. Many point to the example of Japan, where welfare provision is limited and people save over 16 per cent of disposable incomes (see Figure 8.5). By contrast, in Norway and Sweden, where welfare provision is extensive, household savings ratios in the late 1980s were actually negative. In the United Kingdom, where welfare provision is also generous, savings in 1987 were low at 5.6 per cent of disposable incomes. Evidence from the United States, however, undermines any simplistic interpretation: despite the fact that welfare provision is less generous, Americans saved only a paltry 3.9 per cent of income in 1987.

Macroeconomic management

Besides state involvement in welfare, health and education, a major departure of the post-war decades has been the use by governments of fiscal policy to manipulate aggregate demand. The intellectual basis of

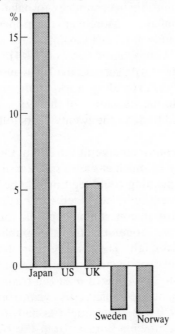

Figure 8.5 Net household saving, 1987 (Net household saving as a percentage of disposable income, selected countries, 1987) (Source: *OECD Economic Outlook*, June 1988, Table R12)

this policy was Keynesian economics. As outlined in Chapter 4, John Maynard Keynes set out an elaborate model of the macroeconomy which tried to demonstrate that private enterprise could not by itself guarantee full employment. Rather, the economy could become trapped in an 'unemployment equilibrium'. This theory appeared to square with the evidence: between 1929 and 1938, unemployment in the United States fluctuated between 8 million (some 20 per cent of the workforce) and 13 million (25 per cent). The equivalent figures for the United Kingdom are 1.4 million (9 per cent) and 3 million (23 per cent). Between 1929 and 1937, world industrial output showed little net growth while world trade declined by 3 per cent in volume terms. Arguing that government action was the only means of breaking out of this stagnation, Keynes lobbied for an active fiscal policy to raise aggregate demand and create jobs.

The idea that markets could fail and that state intervention could be both beneficial and easy was largely accepted by economists after the War. The effect upon economic policy was profound: governments accepted responsibility for securing full employment; the United Kingdom and the United States both passed Employment Acts (in 1944 and 1946 respectively) and began to 'fine tune' their economies to balance the pressures of unemployment and inflation. Moreover, the principle of intervention was extended to include foreign exchange rates (which were 'fixed' under the Bretton Woods agreement of 1944). These efforts, furthermore, appeared to meet with success: the 1950s and 1960s were characterised by rapid growth, expanding world trade and low unemployment, in sharp contrast to the stagnation of the 1930s. Figure 8.6 traces the development of world trade in the twenty years following the War.

Certain problems, however, began to emerge in the 1960s. One was the fact that it proved in practice to be much easier to spend more than to retrench, so that while public spending could legitimately be raised during a recession, it could not so easily be cut when contraction was demanded to control a boom. Partly in consequence, public spending rose as if on a ratchet. Second, the monetary effects of public programmes began to make themselves felt. These arose from the tendency of expenditure to run ahead of taxation: while Keynes had expected the government budget to be balanced over the trade cycle, in the United Kingdom there was a budget deficit every year from 1950 to 1986 (with the exception of 1969–70). These deficits had to be financed by borrowing. When governments borrow from the banking sector, the result is a growth in the money supply. This leads in turn to inflation – a problem which grew in intensity as the 1970s wore on, as Figure 8.7 indicates.

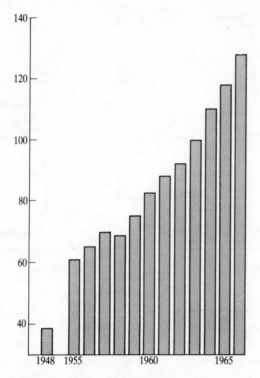

Figure 8.6 The growth of world trade 1948–66 (1963 = 100) (Source: *Yearbook of International Trade Statistics*, 1966, UN, Table C)

In response to the problem of inflation, Western governments turned increasingly to 'monetarist' macroeconomic policies in which the central concern was not the maintenance of full employment but the control of inflation. For monetarists, the key is restraining the growth of the money supply. This in turn was to be achieved by a reduction in public borrowing. Since taxation was already high in most industrial countries, most monetarists favoured a reduction in public spending. While not purely Austrian in origin, such policies clearly dovetailed with Austrian views on the dangers of 'big government' and more specifically of public welfare programmes.

Besides the effect upon inflation, some Austrian economists like Professor von Hayek laid a second charge against Keynesian macro policies. This related to the effects on profit and enterprise. Essentially, Professor von Hayek questioned the basic objective of damping the business cycle. For him, slumps have the useful effect of putting failed businesses into liquidation, so that their assets can be sold off at low prices. By acquiring equipment and premises at knock-down prices, other entrepreneurs can

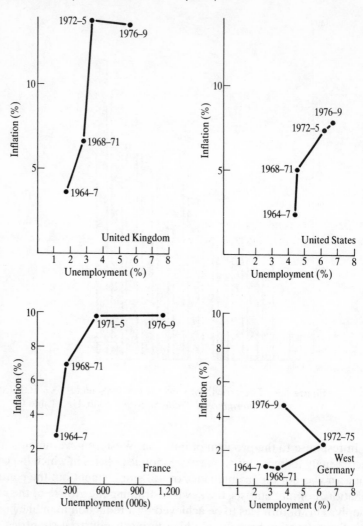

Figure 8.7   Stagflation 1964–79 (Source: *Main Economic Indicators*, OECD, Paris)

initiate new ventures which might not otherwise be profitable. Thus a slump, Professor von Hayek argues, provides the conditions for profitable new business and lays the foundations for the next upsurge in entrepreneurial activity. The major deficiency of Keynesian policies from this perspective is that by preventing these periodic 'shake-outs' in industry, they hinder enterprise and thus impair economic performance.

8.3 Microeconomic policy

Besides involving themselves in general economic management, post-war governments have concerned themselves with the running of particular industries through policies designed to maintain competition as well as through subsidies, regulation and direct ownership. Different theories of profit and enterprise naturally have given rise to fierce controversy over the proper conduct of these policies.

Antitrust or competition policy

A basic theorem of economics demonstrates that monopoly leads to sub-optimum outputs and prices: a monopolist sets a price which exceeds marginal cost and consumers therefore buy rather less of the product than they otherwise would. Moreover, because other firms cannot enter the industry and compete, the monopolist's super-profits persist indefinitely. High profits, in the light of this line of argument, can be an indicator of the exploitation of consumers as much as of successful entrepreneurship. Although large companies may be able to generate economies of scale, it is also argued (Leibenstein, 1976, pp. 207–12) that, without the spur of competition, monopolists may use resources inefficiently since costs may not be controlled firmly. Similar charges can of course be made against other less-than-perfectly-competitive market structures such as oligopoly and 'imperfect competition', restrictive practices (like the controls exercised by many professional bodies and labour unions) and cartels.

The deduction which has often been drawn from the preceding discussion is that competition should be promoted by breaking up monopolistic corporations and by controlling mergers and restrictive practices. Legislative action in pursuance of these ideas came first in Canada in 1889, quickly followed the next year in the United States with the passage of the Sherman Antitrust Act, which attempted to outlaw monopolies and collusive 'conspiracies'. This was followed in 1914 by the Clayton Antitrust Act, which forbade specific practices such as price discrimination, monopolistic mergers and interlocking directorships. The Federal Trade Commission was established in the same year to investigate complaints under this legislation. In Britain the Monopolies Commission was established in 1948. In 1965 it was renamed the Monopolies and Mergers Commission, when its powers were extended to include the review of takeovers. Unlike US law in general, which makes monopolies illegal *per se*, the UK approach is discretionary, requiring the Commission to weigh the advantages of large companies (in terms of economies of scale) against their disadvantages. Most other Western states and the EC have similar agencies to maintain competition.

While the theoretical case against monopolists is fairly clear, the execution of policy presents several practical problems. Three are discussed below; in each case, differing perspectives on profit and enterprise are shown to have important consequences.

The first question relates to the definition of the market. This is not as straightforward as it may appear. For example, a company selling package holidays could be considered part of the package holiday market (in which case it might appear to be dominant) or of the total market for travel including scheduled airflights, weekend breaks by rail and motoring holidays (in which case it might appear to control a smaller part of the market). Similarly, sales of typewriter correcting fluid could be counted either as a single market or as part of a broader market for office supplies which would take in products such as word processors. In many ways the question of defining a market reduces to the selection of a time horizon. On the supply side, a longer perspective allows for greater possibilities of new entry. On the demand side, the critical issue is the degree of substitutability between products. This again relates to time: although a typewriter user may be committed to buying correcting fluid while he still has the machine, in the longer term he could switch to a word processor.

On these matters, economists often divide. Some, using the static analyses which characterise neoclassical theory, tend to adopt short time horizons. This can lead them to measure the intensity of competition by examining the market shares of existing firms either by computing 'five-firm concentration ratios' (the aggregate market shares of the largest five firms) or a Herfindal index score (which takes account of both the number of firms and their size distribution). This approach thus tends to neglect the possibility of new entry (although in the early 1980s this received renewed attention (Baumol, Panzar and Willig, 1982)). The static perspective tends to suggest that monopoly is widespread throughout the UK economy (Campbell, 1981, pp. 59–80, for example). The strong implication of such a result is that there is a need for a firm antitrust policy.

Pro-market economists question the above arguments. Placing emphasis upon the dynamics of enterprise and innovation, they tend to take a longer perspective, stressing the probability that new entrants will overthrow today's monopolies and cartels. From this perspective, monopolies, although commonplace, are mostly temporary and are accordingly not a cause for concern. For these economists, the antidote to monopoly is not state action but entrepreneurship (Shand, 1984, pp. 125–36). Pro-market economists would thus look with favour upon the shift in US policy from one based on narrowly defined markets (US Merger Guidelines 1968) to wider definitions (Merger Guidelines 1982, 1984).

Many pro-market economists go further and argue that a policy of regulating seeming monopolies has the effect of penalising success. An example is the trial of Alcoa under the Sherman Act (*United States* v. *Aluminium Company of America*, 2nd Cir 1945). The company had expanded its production of aluminium in step with rising demand. The effect of this policy was to exclude potential entrants by pre-empting them, and Alcoa was found guilty of monopolisation (Swann, 1979, ch. 6). The attitude of pro-market economists is that such action is overly strict (Kirzner, 1973, pp. 131–5) since the 'monopoly' arose simply from entrepreneurial alertness to consumer demand.

A second issue dividing economists in the area of antitrust policy relates to barriers to entry. At one extreme, the static tradition of neo-classical economics provides a basis for the view that advertising, trade-marks and similar business practices are barriers to entry which need to be controlled. Thus when Britain's Monopolies and Mergers Commission looked into the Unilever/Procter and Gamble duopoly of washing powders in 1968 they concluded that heavy advertising was both wasteful and a barrier to entry by new firms. It accordingly recommended that a non-advertised (and therefore cheaper) brand be placed upon the market by the two firms to compete with their established lines. (It failed to sell and was soon withdrawn.) In a similar vein, Professors Cowling and Mueller counted advertising as one of their 'social costs of monopoly' (1978).

Pro-market economists including Austrians contest this view of advertising, arguing that it is an integral element of the dynamic process of competition (Littlechild, 1981). For such economists, the only barriers to competition which cause concern are those which entrepreneurs cannot circumvent by ordinary business methods. Thus a reputation created by advertising could be assaulted by a rival campaign, while a technological lead could be tackled by licensing or by R & D. Neither could therefore be classed as an absolute entry barrier and neither, in the eyes of pro-market economists, would warrant state action.

Despite a reluctance to see governments intervening, pro-market economists tend to support state action in some areas. This is because for these economists the largest single cause of monopoly power is public policy, as exemplified by the granting of permits and patents. Other examples are the legal privileges gained by trade unions, notably the right to strike without being sued. In Britain, for example, unions had used these rights to establish 'closed shops' in which a certain union had monopolistic control over the supply of labour in a factory or workplace. These practices were paralleled by the control – often backed by law – which many groups such as lawyers, opticians and stockbrokers exercised over entry into their professions. Pro-market economists are particularly sensitive to the damage which such legally based barriers to the free pursuit of profit can cause, arguing that they restrict entrepreneurship. In consequence they support actions like de-regulation, trade union reform and the liberalisation of the professions, which have the effect of undermining these monopolies.

A third problem in antitrust policy which often divides economists concerns takeovers and mergers. On the one hand, many economists who tend to use narrow or static definitions of markets and who tend as a result to perceive monopolies as being endemic look askance at ac-quisitions of businesses by companies already in the industry ('horizon-tal mergers') on the grounds that they diminish competition. They therefore tend to support the monitoring and restriction of takeovers (Hartley, 1977, pp. 157–68). More pro-market economists, however, ar-gue that freedom to acquire firms is important because it is a means whereby entrepreneurs can gain entry into new industries. Furthermore, selling a subsidiary is a means of recovering money which might other-wise be lost; without such freedom of exit, entrepreneurs might consider entry into a new market too risky and enterprise would be restricted. These economists also see takeovers as a mechanism for ensuring that management is kept on its toes by threatening those firms which use resources inefficiently with absorption by a rival (Littlechild, 1986; Chiplin and Wright, 1987). Any attempts to hinder takeovers would, they argue, simply protect incumbent managements from the pressures of the competitive process.

Public ownership

Although never widespread in the United States, public ownership of industrial enterprises is common throughout Western Europe. In the United Kingdom in the 1970s nationalised industries accounted for around 10 per cent of GDP and dominated the supply of electricity, gas, postal services, coal, telecommunications, shipbuilding, aerospace, steel, and bus and rail transport. In many cases, state ownership came about for military or strategic reasons, as in the case of the British govern-ment's purchase of a majority of shares in Anglo-Persian Oil (later BP) in 1912 at the behest of Winston Churchill (1874–1965) who, as First Lord of the Admiralty, wished to ensure that oil would be available for the Royal Navy. In France, several businesses including Renault passed into state hands when the property of wartime collaborators was confiscated. In other instances, however, the justification for the public takeover of private assets was grounded in the radical or heterodox views of profit and enterprise discussed in Chapter 6. Many of the United Kingdom's state industries were nationalised by Labour governments in pursuance of that party's avowedly socialist programme: 'To secure for the producers by hand and brain the full fruits of their industry and the most equitable distribution thereof that may be possible on the basis of the common ownership of the means of production, distribution and exchange'. Much of the thinking behind this programme can be traced to the Fabian socialist Sidney Webb (1859–1947), who shared the view of many radical economists that businesses could be run without private ownership and the profit incentive. Some radicals have gone further and argued that the state can act more entrepreneurially than can private businessmen (Holland, 1972). Such notions are attacked by pro-market economists who, drawing upon other theories of profit and enterprise such as the Austrian approach, have been critical both of the principle of state ownership and of the ways in which it has operated in the United Kingdom and elsewhere (Burton, 1983).

For neoclassical economists, nationalisation presents few problems of principle. Given their relative neglect of enterprise, it is all too easy for them to neglect issues of efficiency as well and to assume that businesses will run at least cost. Costs and revenues should, neoclassical economists often surmise, be known to management regardless of whether those managers serve a state-appointed board or private shareholders. Efficiency, therefore, can be assumed to look after itself, particularly in industries like rail or coal which face competition (cf. Millward and Parker, 1983). At the same time it has been argued that public ownership can promote efficiency in the cases of 'natural monopolies' – industries in which economies of scale and scope can only be reaped by a single supplier. The prime examples are the network industries like gas and electricity, where duplication of pipelines and cables would clearly be wasteful (Parker, 1989).

Austrian economists, by contrast, take the view that private profit-seeking is essential to the conduct of successful business. They stress that costs and revenues cannot be known with certainty but must be continually rediscovered by a process of trying out new organisational procedures, new types of product, new prices and new approaches to marketing. Without a direct interest (a shareholding and the possibility of a dividend) in such entrepreneurial activities, Austrians argue, management is likely to sink into inertia, allowing costs to rise and service to deteriorate. State-owned industries therefore fail to adapt to changing conditions of demand and cost, and inefficiency (and ultimately financial losses) are likely to ensue (Buchanan *et al.*, 1978).

The historical record in the United Kingdom lends some support to both perspectives. On the one hand, Britain's electricity industry with a national grid and high technical standards attained a position of world leadership between the Wars under public control. On the other hand, problems quickly began to accumulate in many British industries which were taken into public ownership after World War II. Some, like coal and shipbuilding, faced declining sales yet found difficulty in trimming capacity, and losses began to mount. The process of adjustment was often hampered by union opposition. Others, like electricity, faced the converse situation of strong demand but tended to allow costs to rise by overinvesting (Monopolies and Mergers Commission, 1981, ch. 4). The management of the nationalised industries was further complicated by government intervention which frequently cut investment programmes or controlled prices in the pursuit of macroeconomic objectives.

In terms of profits, Britain's nationalised industries have had a poor record. As a proportion of net output, profits averaged zero in the 1950s, climbed to 6 per cent in the 1960s and fell to negative values in the 1970s (Millward, 1976). From 1945 to 1979, government subsidies totalled £31.6 billion (at 1979 prices). In terms of productivity, the record was relatively bright between 1958 and 1968, with output per man rising at a compound rate of 5.3 per cent per annum as against 3.7 per cent in privately owned industry (Pryke, 1971). In the 1970s, however, productivity slumped in the nationalised sector. The economist Richard Pryke blamed overmanning, deficient pricing policies, poor plant utilisation and bad management (Pryke, 1981).

Although there is a lack of firm evidence that state enterprises are invariably less efficient than their private sector counterparts (De Alessi, 1980; Parker, 1985), a similar catalogue of problems seems to have dogged public enterprises in a number of other countries. In Italy, for example, the Istituto per la Recostruzione Industriale (IRI), which was established by Mussolini in 1932 to provide long-term development funds for industry, survived the Fascist period to occupy an important position in the post-war Italian economy. Owning over 600 companies and employing 4 per cent of the nation's workforce, it accounted for 100 per cent of cast-iron output, 66 per cent of special steels and 90 per cent of shipbuilding by the late 1970s. From that point on, however, its fortunes declined as the smokestack industries in which it was involved suffered reverses. In 1983 it lost a colossal $2.1 billion, and a period of divestment began. In Britain the Conservative government elected in 1979, influenced by the arguments developed by pro-market economists, began to sell state-owned industries back to the private sector. By 1988, over twenty companies had been sold for more than £20 billion (see Table 8.1). Similar policies have been set in train in the United States,

Table 8.1 Major UK privatisations 1979–90

Shareholdings sold	Date(s)
BP	Various dates 1979–87
National Enterprise Board investments	Various dates 1980–6
British Aerospace	1981, 1984
Cable and Wireless	1981, 1983, 1985
Amersham International	1982
National Freight Corporation	1982
Britoil	1982, 1985
British Rail Hotels	1983
Associated British Ports	1983, 1984
Rover Group (formerly British Leyland)	Various dates 1984–8
British Telecom	1984
Enterprise Oil	1984
Sealink	1984
British Shipbuilders and Naval Dockyards	1985 (not completed)
National Bus Company	1985 (not completed)
British Gas	1986
Rolls Royce	1987
British Airports Authority	1987 (first issue)
British Airways	1987
Royal Ordnance Factories	1987
British Steel Corporation	1988
Regional Water Authorities	1989
Electricity generation and transmission	1990–2 (planned)

France, West Germany, Israel, Japan, New Zealand, Australia and Canada, as well as in a number of developing countries (Hemming and Mansoor, 1988). These policies are naturally welcomed by pro-market economists, particularly the Austrian school.

The British privatisation programme, however, has presented the government with some demanding decisions because many industries were natural monopolies. British Telecom (BT) for example held over 93 per cent of the UK telecommunications market when it was privatised in 1984. Although the possibility of future competition for BT was created when a rival company, Mercury, was permitted to operate, the new company has a small market share and few expect it to exert any real pressure on BT's profit margins for several years. Many pro-market economists argue that in order to give freer rein to enterprise and the pursuit of profit, a better approach would have been to break businesses like BT into competing units. Stung by such arguments, the government took a bolder initiative with the electric power industry: generation plants and the distribution system were to be separated, with initially two generating companies competing to sell power to the latter. New operators were also to be permitted to enter the industry. How this will affect the economic performance of the industry remains to be seen. To compensate for the absence of effective competition in the cases of the privatised 'natural monopolies', a further step – based in part upon American experience – was taken: new regulatory agencies were set up to control tariffs and standards of service.

Regulation

Regulation has a long history in the United States, where regulatory commissions have had responsibility for transportation, energy, banking, telecommunications and other industries. These commissions have, among their other duties, monitored tariffs and levels of service. The basis of such policies is primarily the neoclassical critique of monopoly. Without regulation, it is argued, a sole producer who gains control of a 'natural monopoly' will exploit consumers. Should the industry be fragmented between several producers, however, the situation will be no better, because either the producers will collude to smother competition or there will be a cutthroat price war which will swiftly reduce the number of rivals to one, establishing a monopoly (Swann, 1988, pp. 48–75). As with competition and public ownership, this policy has given rise to much debate among economists in which contrasting perspectives on profit and enterprise have played a role of some importance.

The usual procedure with respect to the regulation of prices and profits has been for regulatory bodies to set a target for the companies in the industry concerned in terms of a permissible rate of return (ROR) on assets employed and to ensure that this is not exceeded. This practice has come under criticism from many sides. Some critics have, for example, alleged that regulatory commissions are prone to being 'captured', turning from consumer watchdogs into protectors of the producers' interests (Stigler, 1971). The critics also include neoclassical economists, who argue that regulation leads to economic distortions (Parker, 1989). For example, as long as the target ROR is above the cost of borrowed funds it will pay the corporation to invest, thereby expanding its asset base and raising total profits (Averch and Johnson, 1962). The probable consequence is again overinvestment. Thus US airlines in the era of regulation competed for passengers by continually investing in more modern aircraft.

Austrian and other pro-market economists have also criticised regulatory systems but for additional reasons. The problem which they perceive in ROR-based regulation is that the profit incentive is obscured. Since owners are not allowed to benefit in terms of higher profits from increases in operating efficiency, there is no incentive to cut waste – much in the way that incentives may be lacking in the state sector. Pro-market economists also criticise regulatory regimes on the grounds that they can operate as barriers to entry by restricting access to markets to licensed operators, thus limiting the scope for enterprise.

In an effort to retain incentives to efficient operation, the British government attempted to control prices rather than rates of return on capital. This has been effected through the RPI – X formula, in which RPI denotes changes in the Retail Prices Index, that is, the rate of general inflation, while X is an integer. For example, for British Telecom for the period 1984–9, X was set at 3, allowing BT to raise tariffs by three percentage points less than the rate of inflation. (In 1989 X was raised to 4.5.) This indicated the scope which policy-makers felt was available for BT's costs to fall in real terms by virtue of advancing technology. The benefit of such a system is that the companies involved are entitled to keep any residual income as profit, thus maintaining the incentive for them to cut costs. Caveats must, however, be entered: first, the formula is not helpful if companies can simply raise profits by reducing the quality of service, and second the rule cannot apply in its original form to industries like power generation where the cost of purchased inputs such as fuel is at once volatile and large relative to value added. In the UK energy sector the formula has accordingly been amended to RPI + $X - K$ where K represents fuel input costs. Critics also point out that since the formula is renegotiated every five years, the government could simply raise the X if the regulated industries were to meet their existing targets and earn large profits (as occurred in the case of BT in 1989). The industries might then lose an incentive to cut costs. The RPI – X formula is not foolproof.

Partly in response to criticisms from pro-market economists that regulation restricts the entry of new competitors, governments on both sides of the Atlantic took steps from the late 1970s to restore competition and enterprise. In the United States, trucking and air transport were deregulated from 1978. The immediate result was a decline in tariffs and fares, demanning, a reduction in union power, pay cuts, the entry of new operators and new methods of service provision – much as pro-market economists had predicted (Bailey, 1986). In trucking, the benefits to consumers were estimated at US$26 billion (Cecchini, 1988, p. 13). The OECD reported (1986, p. 302) that by 1986 the real price of US air travel had fallen by 13 per cent and that flight frequencies had increased. Although some services were curtailed, the net gain to consumers has been estimated at $100 billion over the period 1978–87 (*The Economist*, 4 February 1989). On the negative side, complaints about flight delays are reported to have increased. In a similar move, the United Kingdom deregulated long-distance road passenger transport in 1980. Besides inducing sharp falls in coach fares, the move put competitive pressure on British Rail fares to the benefit of travellers.

The longer-term effects of deregulation nevertheless concern economists and policy-makers. Both American air transport and UK coach transport have, since deregulation, been marked by a growth in concentration. In the United States, the market share of the top eight airlines, which had stood at 80 per cent in 1978, retreated to 74 per cent in 1983 before advancing strongly to 94 per cent in 1988. In some areas where one airline has a dominant position, fare increases have been frequent. It thus appears that while deregulation engenders competition, the result of competition in turn can be consolidation and possibly the creation of local monopolies. Certainly policy-makers need to ensure that markets remain contestable.

Besides the control of prices and profits, regulation has been used to secure social and environmental objectives such as safety in the workplace, the purity of food and drugs, and pollution standards. Such regulations are often called 'holding the ring' since they set limits to the competitive struggle between entrepreneurs: in effect, regulation rules out certain tactics which entrepreneurs might otherwise use to make profit, such as adulterating their products. Although few would defend the worst practices of bygone days like using sawdust in sausages, many pro-market economists argue that these regulatory standards can become barriers to normal entrepreneurial activities. For example, at the time of writing West Germany's beer purity law stipulates that no beverage shall be called 'beer' unless it is made entirely of traditional ingredients. The result is that beers from other countries cannot be sold in West Germany, so that the purity law serves as a barrier to competition (Cecchini, 1988, p. 50). The Friedmans (1980) illustrate the expansion of regulation by reference to the *Federal Register* of US regulations which grew from 2,599 pages occupying six inches of shelf space in 1936 to 36,487 pages occupying over ten feet of shelf in 1978. The Friedmans conclude that this panoply of controls on enterprise was responsible for the deceleration in US productivity during the 1970s (Friedman and Friedman, 1980, pp. 190–1).

Regulation is also used to restrict environmental damage, much of which, it is argued, is attributable to the activities of private entrepreneurs. Profit-seeking businessmen, for example, first began the use of CFCs which damage the ozone layer. Such effects are clearly instances of what neoclassical economists term 'market failure' and many conclude that regulation is the only answer. Pro-market economists dispute this, arguing that in numerous cases the establishment and enforcement of property rights within a market system is the best remedy (Coase, 1960). For example, Cheung (1978) argues that the advance of the Sahara Desert into the Sahel region of Africa can be attributed not to drought – though this has contributed – but to overgrazing. This in turn arises because tribes do not have clear property rights over tracts of land and thus have no incentive to replant or to husband the vegetation. Chandler (1986, p. 18) in a similar vein observes that energy is used far more efficiently in the market-orientated economies of the West than in the centrally planned East, where incentives to economise on inputs are absent. Medvedev (1990) likewise attributes the extensive environmental degradation of the USSR directly to the system of collective ownership: 'Land and other resources . . . are considered free commodities. This not only leads to waste but means that industries are not interested in the conservation of resources' (Medvedev, 1990, p. 29). Whether individual rights of ownership can be established over global resources like the ozone layer, however, is not clear.

Industrial intervention

Besides the formal mechanisms of antitrust policy, privatisation and regulation, governments use a multiplicity of somewhat less formal means with the objective of influencing the decisions of private entrepreneurs. One example is the provision of subsidies which distort costs and prices. Another is the provision of cheap credit or the guaranteeing of loans with the effect that risk premia are avoided. A favoured technique is to protect domestic industry from overseas competition by regulating foreign trade through tariffs or quotas. Other barriers include idiosyncratic labelling laws or policies of restricting public procurement to domestic suppliers. Technology is often the target for intervention, with governments subsidising or coordinating the research efforts of the private sector. In other cases, governments have gone so far as to attempt to 'plan' sectors of industry by publishing forecasts of economic trends in the expectation that these estimates will be incorporated into the decisions of private businesses.

During the 1950s and 1960s the trend in respect of tariffs and the control of overseas trade was away from intervention. Under the General Agreement on Tariffs and Trade (GATT), tariffs and non-tariff barriers to trade were reduced in a series of international negotiations or 'rounds'. In the stagflationary 1970s, however, intervention became more widespread as governments attempted to protect industries from volatile energy prices, turbulent foreign exchange markets and rapid technological change. By 1983, subsidies to industry amounted to 1.87 per cent of GDP for the OECD area as a whole. Foreign trade fared similarly. In the United States, the 1980s saw a succession of Trade Bills going before Congress, with the result that the share of US trade covered by trade barriers rose from 12 per cent in 1980 to 23 per cent in 1987 (figures from the Institute for International Economics, *The Economist*, 25 February 1989, p. 73). Estimates of the cost to American consumers put lost real spending power at some $50 billion per year. By 1988, the proportion of the EC's manufactured imports covered by restrictions stood at 15 per cent, while 30 per cent of exports from Japan and the Asian Newly Industrialised Countries (NICs) faced trade restrictions.

Several different justifications are advanced for these various kinds of state intervention. It is sometimes argued that the short time horizons of private investors prohibit them from investing in advanced technologies with long gestation periods. Public procurement of weapons from national suppliers clearly derives from a desire to maintain a domestic capacity to produce armaments. Other arguments draw on the radical economists' notion that technological change can proceed effectively without the help of entrepreneurs. In yet other cases there is a fear that regional economies will be dislocated or that particular social groups will be disadvantaged by market-driven, profit-directed change. There is often also an unspoken assumption that state intervention will be costless and effective. Ultimately, however, these justifications – with perhaps the exception of the argument about a strategic need for self-sufficiency in arms – have one critical feature in common: they are based upon a suspicion that profit-seeking entrepreneurs will not be able, for whatever reason, to ensure rapid and successful adaptation to changing economic pressures.

In support of this case, pro-interventionist economists can point to several pieces of evidence. First, Germany and the United States both became powerful industrial economies behind tariff barriers during the late nineteenth century. Second, the post-war technological advances of Japan and the United States can be attributed at least in part to the efforts of their governments in sponsoring R & D work (Feigenbaum and McCorduck, 1984; Freeman, 1987). Moreover, interventionists can point to several instances in which industries under the control of private entrepreneurs have failed to meet the challenges of changing circumstances and have lost ground to more innovative producers from overseas. Examples here include the British motorcycle and wool textile industries (National Economic Development Office, 1969).

Pro-market economists naturally contest the idea that state intervention in economic affairs can be fruitful. It is, of course, basic to the Austrian perspective in particular that swift adjustment to changing market conditions can be carried out only by profit-motivated private entrepreneurs. Any forces which hinder such efforts, pro-market economists conclude, will reduce incomes and productivity. The evidence which can be cited in support of this claim consists largely of interventions which have failed to secure their objectives. For instance, large-scale intervention by France and the United Kingdom in three 'ailing industries' – textiles, iron and steel and shipbuilding – failed to stem sharp declines in employment since rationalisation could not ultimately be avoided. Or again, the British government for many years discriminated in favour of the sole domestic computer manufacturer, ICL. As the world began to standardise on IBM technology, however, it became apparent that ICL would never be able to earn a profit on this basis and the policy was abandoned. Perhaps the classic instance is provided by the UK Labour government's National Enterprise Board which had the brief of channelling a billion pounds of public funds into new, growing companies at the forefront of technology during the late 1970s. In the event, most of the funds were used to subsidise 'lame duck' companies in shipbuilding, vehicles and machine tools. Burton (1983) argues that such a diversion of funds was predictable because political pressures and bureaucratic procedures mean that government intervention will more usually serve to retard rather than to accelerate the adjustment process. Politicians and civil servants, he goes on, lack the training and the incentives to make a success of 'picking winners'. Pro-market economists also hold that the influence of the state over Japanese industry is commonly exaggerated and that the mainspring behind Japan's economic success is simply entrepreneurship of the highest quality.

Pro-market economists also have little sympathy with the argument that capital markets are myopic, citing the fact that official inquiries (such as Britain's Wilson Committee, 1978) have found no real evidence of a failure to supply industry's needs. As Wassell concludes, 'It is a reliable rule of thumb that, if an enterprise – whether at birth or close to death – cannot attract private capital, governments step in only at great peril to the taxpayer' (Burton, 1983, p. 9).

Small businesses

Although many governments during the 1980s have shifted away from intervention in business decision-making in general, in one area there is now more state involvement than before. This is the formation of new business enterprises. America has long had a Small Business Administration which attempts to ensure that small firms receive equitable treatment from government in terms of the burdens of regulations and access to public procurement. In the United Kingdom small businesses are now favoured by tax breaks, training grants, free advice, preferential loans and exemptions from form-filling. This policy stance contrasts with the thrust of policy in the 1960s and 1970s, when the British government actively promoted mergers in the industrial sector to form large corporations able to reap economies of scale.

The expectation is that the policy of assisting small firms will create a new generation of entrepreneurs. Although the gains from these policies are difficult to measure, it does appear that they are going with the grain of economic developments in several respects. First, self-employment has risen by 40 per cent in both the United States (between 1972 and 1984) and United Kingdom (1979–85). Second, the number of US and UK firms has been rising more rapidly since the end of the 1970s (*The Economist*, 21 January 1989, p. 89; Stead, 1989). These developments are particularly welcome to new Austrian economists, who argue that what nations need in a competitive world is an 'enterprise culture' – a general willingness to take the initiative, to risk savings and career in new ventures. Many British supporters of this view look, of course, to the United States as one of the foremost examples of a society with such a culture.

8.4 Marxist economics and *perestroika*

Marx's central concern was to analyse capitalism rather than to draw up blueprints for the socialist society which would, he believed, emerge after the workers' revolution. As a result, there was little in his writings which the Russian Bolsheviks could use as a basis for economic policy when they seized power in 1917 and established the world's first Communist state. Nevertheless, the broad principle was clear: since, according to Marx, profit arose from the very fact that labour power was bought and sold like any other commodity, it followed that exploitation could be ended only by the 'abolition of the wages system' (Marx and Engels, 1968, p. 229), that is, by the working class taking collective control of all of society's productive wealth. In short, all resources were to be owned by the workers' state.

The new Communist government of the USSR faced many difficulties, including a lack of experienced industrial managers. During the early 1920s, therefore, private entrepreneurs were allowed to produce and sell. By 1927, however, the Communist Party – now under the leadership of Joseph Stalin – felt able to institute a full-scale system of central economic planning. Business units – 'enterprises' – were placed under the control of individual managers (as opposed to the workers' committees which had flowered after the Revolution), and were grouped into associations. These were then allocated to People's Commissariats or ministries: one for coal-mining, another for textiles and so on. The ministries, which by 1939 numbered twenty-one, then devised plans for their enterprises: managers were given instructions about how much to produce, what resources to use and to whom to deliver their output. Coordination between the various ministries was the responsibility of Gosplan, the Economic Planning Office. Plans were set out in terms of 'materials balances' which described intended levels of production and consumption of physical volumes of goods. The centrepiece of the system was the Five-Year Plan, the first of which came into effect in October 1928. By the early 1980s, around 500,000 prices were set and monitored centrally, absorbing the efforts of over 100,000 state officials. Overall, the state bureaucracy of the USSR employed about 18 million persons – equivalent to some two-thirds of the entire labour force of the United Kingdom.

Profit played little role in the planning system: although goods and services were transferred from one enterprise to another for money, prices were set centrally and bore no systematic relationship to costs. Many prices were frozen while others crept upwards so that by the late 1980s, many basic foodstuffs were being sold at give-away prices, requiring large state subsidies. In 1989 it was estimated by the State Statistics Committee that a rise of 49 per cent in the prices of consumer goods would be needed to bring supply and demand into balance (*Financial Times*, 26 January 1990, p. 20). Because of the arbitrary level of most prices, enterprises could accrue profits or sustain losses regardless of their efficiency so that the government subsidised loss-makers and, at its discretion, appropriated the earnings of the profitable. Rent and interest, being merely forms of surplus value in Marxist theory, were – at least formally – abolished.

The planning mechanism bore the stamp of Marx's approach to profit and enterprise. First, profit was still earned by socialist enterprises, despite being a deduction from wages, because it served the useful purpose of financing investment. Second, Marx had seen no necessary link between profit and enterprise, with profit arising essentially from the exploitation of labour rather than from the economical and inventive running of a business. It seemed to follow that the work of running a business was largely a matter of routine which could be – and was – often delegated by capitalists to paid managers. Under socialism, it was therefore natural that management should become routine administration – the execution of instructions – and that profits, accruing arbitrarily to different business units, should be used for reinvestment at the discretion of the state. Soviet practice followed these ideas to a large extent: although managers were offered incentives in the form of bonuses, these usually related to output rather than value. The result was a distortion of economic activity. For example, in the 1980s oil and gas pipelines were made with uncoated steel pipes which had to be replaced every two or three years because of corrosion. There was no incentive to use more durable pipes because repair and replacement counted as part of the oil and gas industry's output and thus contributed to management bonuses. Similarly the Russian coal industry was known to ship large amounts of slate with its coal to boost its output figures despite the adverse consequences for coal users. It has, indeed, proved impossible to institute and police an incentive system in the USSR that has not distorted output and efficiency (Winiecki, 1988). Soviet bonuses, in short, do not compare with the profit incentive as an encouragement to enterprise.

Even during the heyday of planning, there were many reaches of the Soviet economy where the writ of the planners did not run, such as repair work and the family plots which the peasants retained. Consumers were able to spend their money as they pleased and, importantly, urban workers were able to select their own occupations so that there was, in some ways, a market for labour. Indeed, market forces were even at work during the 1930s, when rapidly growing heavy industries bid for labour so aggressively that money wages more than doubled. The Soviet economy has, moreover, traditionally relied extensively upon incentive payments in the form of output-based bonuses to bring forth greater effort.

The Five-Year Plans oversaw the industrialisation of the USSR during the 1930s, with huge advances in the production of coal, iron and steel and other heavy industries being recorded. This industrial base enabled the USSR to withstand the German assault during World War II and to emerge subsequently as a military superpower. Following the Russian model, the nations which adopted Communism after the War instituted planning systems of their own. Nevertheless, the Soviet economy has faced many difficulties. One of the most important has been that productivity has consistently lagged behind world standards. As a result, consumer goods have continually been in short supply so that durables like cars are relatively scarce: for example, the rate of car ownership in the USSR is about one-twelfth of that in the United States. Even basic items like meat and sugar are often rationed or are simply unavailable. It has been estimated that Soviet housewives spend the equivalent of a working day each week standing in queues (*The Economist*, 11 March 1989). The farm sector, which had been forcibly collectivised by Stalin during the 1920s and 1930s, was notable for its poor productivity record: whereas before 1914 Russian agriculture had been a net exporter of grain, the USSR has been forced to import foodgrains regularly since World War II.

The problems of technical innovation illustrate the difficulties of the planning system. In the West the initiative for creating, say, new machine tools lies with machine tool producers, who undertake their own R & D and develop new products which they estimate will meet their customers' needs. In the Soviet planning system, by contrast, the equivalent organisation

> is less active – one might even say passive. . . . The firm is virtually assured of takers for its product to the limits of its capacity. It does not have to search out markets, invent new types of equipment . . . or engage in a competitive struggle for markets. It is little concerned with the production and commercial difficulties of its customers, does not try to anticipate them and has little interest in supplying follow-up services and technical advice. (Abouchar, 1977, p. 154)

Furthermore, machine-building enterprises typically do not have R & D facilities but rely upon industry-level research institutes. The adoption of new designs from such institutes is, however, often hindered by the fact that, being less familiar, they could slow production and so prevent the enterprise from fulfilling its plan. Abel Aganbegyan, chief economic adviser to the Soviet government, recounts the instance of a new coal-cutting machine which, because of divisions in responsibility in the Soviet planning system, took fifteen years to come into production (Aganbegyan, 1988, p. 93).

These difficulties, compounded by the depletion of natural resources and pressures to divert output away from investment into consumption and military uses, led to a slowdown in economic growth in the USSR during the 1980s (see Figure 8.8). On the initiative of the new Secretary-General Mikhail Gorbachev the reaction was a volte-face in both political and economic policy. In politics, it was promised that the authoritarian, secretive structures of the Communist Party and state apparatus would become more accountable and responsive: the policy of *glasnost* (openness). In economic matters, the new policy was *perestroika* (restructuring).

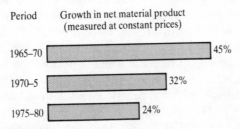

Figure 8.8 Decelerating economic growth in the USSR 1965–80 (Sources: *Yearbook of National Accounts Statistics*, vol. 3, p. 639, UN, New York, 1975; *UN National Accounts Statistics 1983*, p. 1655, UN, New York, 1986)

The intended economic mechanism of *perestroika* was laid down in the Law on State Enterprises which was passed in 1987. As described by Abel Aganbegyan, it was intended to work as follows:

> From now on enterprises and associations will work out and approve their own plans. They will not be subject to the approval of any higher authority and there will be absolutely no allocation of planned work. Enterprises proposing a plan for the following year will firstly build up an order book on the basis of consumer demand. Payment for resources is to be provided for as well as payments into the state budget, the ministerial funds and to local authorities. Where necessary, credit and bank assistance can be obtained – all this so that the working collective can determine its self-accountable income and be individually responsible for its disposal. (Aganbegyan, 1988, pp. 112–13)

Aganbegyan's editor offers the explanation that self-accountable income 'is the income that in capitalist economies would be called profit' (Aganbegyan, 1988, p. 113). A further element in *perestroika* is the establishment of wholesale trading by enterprises in place of the former system of allocating output by administrative order. This is intended to make enterprises compete for orders from buyers. In essence, therefore, *perestroika* is intended to make Soviet enterprises into autonomous business units competing for profit. These profits they will be entitled to keep, either to pay out as bonuses or to plough back as reinvestment.

The USSR is by no means alone in these reforms. Yugoslavia has always given more scope to the private sector than have other East European states, while Hungary adopted a more free market approach in the 1960s and, in 1988, opened a stock exchange. Another important development (but currently suspended) was the adoption of market-orientated reforms (*gaige*) in China under the leadership of Deng Xiaoping following the death of Mao Zedong in 1976. Private enterprises are now reported to employ some 24 million Chinese workers.

The programme of reform proved far more difficult to implement than expected. In the USSR even in the later 1980s, only some 5 per cent of output was being sold at freely negotiated prices (*The Economist*, 14 January 1989, p. 47). More importantly, *perestroika* failed to deliver higher living standards, with but 'fractional rises' in industrial and agricultural output in 1989 according to the State Statistics Committee (*Financial Times*, 26 January 1990, p. 20). These problems doubtlessly were caused at least in part by the relative lack of a class of entrepreneurs ready to take advantage of the new economic conditions. At the same time, people's expectations about consumer goods were raised, and there was widespread labour unrest over demands for better conditions.

In 1989, however, economic events were largely overshadowed by political developments. The loosening of the control of the state apparatus stimulated popular demands for even greater freedom or, in some republics of the Soviet Union, for independence. In Tibet and China, such movements met with bloody suppression. In much of Eastern Europe, however, Communist power was swept away.

8.5   The Third World

The shift towards a greater recognition of enterprise in the industrial countries of both East and West has been paralleled by developments in the Third World in terms of the initiatives of the governments of the developing countries and of the policies of aid donors.

Upon gaining independence, many Third World nations centralised economic power in the hands of governments. One argument put forward was that these countries lacked an entrepreneurial or business class so that the state had to assume responsibility for organising the economy. A further factor, however, was the adoption of economic ideas which were critical of markets by the new controlling groups. In India, for example, the government formed by the Indian Congress Party drew up Five-Year Plans involving state ownership of major industries, price controls and high tariffs, while businessmen wishing to invest were compelled to obtain licences before proceeding. In most Third World countries, state control over the economy was increased by the way in which international aid was disbursed. For much of the post-war period, development assistance took the form of government-to-government aid. The expectation was that Third World governments would, through a rational, planned assessment of the needs of their economies, identify the investments which would bring the best economic and social returns. The alternative of relying upon Western multinational corporations to undertake production and investment was often rejected as 'neo-imperialism'; it was frequently claimed that such investment would lead to the exploitation of local labour while profits would be repatriated to the home state, allowing no benefits to accrue to the host nation.

Although support for these policies was widespread among economists in the 1960s and 1970s, some members of the profession remained sceptical. Professor Peter Bauer (1971, 1981) of the London School of Economics pointed to the wasteful use of development funds in Third World countries on prestige projects such as state-owned airports and national airlines. Often such waste was compounded by incompetence, bureaucracy and corruption. During the 1970s and early 1980s, these 'white elephants' helped to drive many Third World countries deeply into debt. Other economists drew attention to the problems caused by governments attempting to control the prices of foodstuffs. While this boosted the real incomes of the urban population, it deprived farmers of necessary incentives to produce and invest, and thus depressed food output despite food shortages (Crook *et al.*, 1989). Rather than rely upon state intervention, pro-market economists urged Third World governments to create the conditions for successful local entrepreneurship. As early as 1958, Professor Friedman was arguing that 'What is required in underdeveloped countries is . . . an atmosphere of freedom, of maximum opportunity for people to experiment, and the incentive for them to do so' (Friedman, 1958, p. 509). Some of the nations of the developing world that have followed this advice such as Hong Kong, Singapore, North Korea and Taiwan have met with spectacular success. This is not to argue that free markets alone will *guarantee* fast economic growth in the other countries of Asia, as well as Africa and Latin America. The important point, however, is that development strategies which ignore profit and enterprise have rarely achieved the desired results.

In the 1980s the importance of enterprise and free markets in the development of the Third World came to be more widely recognised. By the late 1980s, price controls were being abandoned in countries like India, São Tomé, Mozambique, Madagascar and Guinea, while foreign exchange restrictions were also being liberalised in Uganda, Ghana, Malawi and Senegal. In India in the mid-1980s the incoming government of Rajiv Gandhi cut income tax, abolished many controls and liberalised much of the country's overseas trade. The impetus for such changes has in many cases come from international agencies like the World Bank, which in 1988 was supporting over two dozen economic adjustment programmes in Africa alone (World Bank, 1988, p. 86). Underlining its policy of bolstering free markets, the Bank comments that 'Privatisation and a reduction in the role of parastatals have been important components of public-enterprise adjustment efforts' (1988, p. 88). The social costs of these policies have been high, with welfare, education and health services being reduced as public spending has been cut. Nevertheless, defenders of these policies argue that the cost of failing to adjust and to encourage private enterprise would, in the long term, be even heavier.

8.6 Conclusion

This chapter has reviewed policies which governments have adopted towards industry and commerce. Since policies usually need to be justified in terms of a relevant economic theory, their sheer variety can be taken as an indication of the diversity of theories about profit and enterprise – a diversity which earlier chapters of this book have described.

The broad swing in policy towards enterprise is, as previous chapters have indicated, largely a relearning of the lessons of earlier times. The importance of individual effort and its link to private property was central to Adam Smith's *The Wealth of Nations*. This message was, however, obscured by two factors. One was the dominance of neoclassical economics, which gave little prominence to enterprise and seemed to provide support for state intervention to correct 'market failure'. The second was the pressing need for collective action in the early twentieth century to overcome problems like food adulteration, poverty and unemployment. By the 1970s, however, such ideas came under attack as productivity sagged, stagflation deepened and taxation grew remorselessly. The need for a wholly fresh approach prompted a search for ideas and policies from beyond the conventional wisdom of Keynesian and neoclassical economics. The 1980s saw the emergence in the United States, the United Kingdom and elsewhere of enterprise-based policies which drew especially upon the ideas of Austrian and other pro-market economists. Given the difficulties set out in Chapter 7 of proving or disproving rival interpretations of the evidence, it is inevitable that these debates should often remain inconclusive. One thing, however, is plain: the controversies surrounding profit and enterprise are not confined to university seminar rooms. Rather they are, as they have always been, part of the stuff of contemporary debate.

Further reading

For a general background on schools of thought and their policy implications, see Friedman and Friedman (1980) for a pro-market stance and Meade (1975) for a more radical view. For a good introduction to supply-side economics, see Healey and Parker (1988). More detailed is Bartlett and Roth (1984). Bosanquet (1983) synthesises and critically assesses pro-market policies towards welfare services. On macroeconomic policy the Keynesian perspective is set out in, for example, Dernburg (1985, ch. 17); the Austrian view is argued in von Hayek (1966) and Littlechild (1986). See Ramsey (1977) for the failures of macroeconomic forecasting. For contending perspectives on competition and monopoly, see Kefauver (1966), Hartley (1977) and HMSO (1978) for the narrower, more neoclassical views, and Kirzner (1973, ch. 3) and Schumpeter (1950, chs. V–X) for an Austrian interpretation. Interesting is the exchange between Cowling and Mueller (1978) and

Littlechild (1981). Chiplin and Wright (1987) argue the case for a libertarian policy towards mergers. Good reviews of the issues surrounding public ownership and regulation are in Wiseman (1978) and Rowley (1982). Friedman and Friedman (1980) again is a classic pro-market assault on regulation. A detailed history of deregulation and privatisation is found in Swann (1988). On industrial intervention, Freeman (1987) and Caves and Ueseska (1976) have good accounts of Japanese policy towards technology. Holland (ed.) (1972) argues the case for state intervention; Burton (1983) provides a rebuttal. The OECD (1986) offers a critical overview.

Claims for the employment potential of small firms are found in Birch (1979), while Lloyd (1984) stresses their entrepreneurial role. Storey and Johnson (1987a) and Storey *et al.* (1987b) are sceptical. Stockman (1986) and Anderson (1988) offer contrasting assessments of the success of 'Reaganomics'. On the economic performance of the United Kingdom under the premiership of Margaret Thatcher, see Dornbusch and Layard (1987) or Artis (ed.) (1986).

On the economics of the USSR, Nove (1969) is a good introduction, while Bor (1967) describes the planning system in the late 1960s. Aganbegyan (1988) outlines the Gorbachev reforms of the late 1980s. For policies in the developing countries, see Bauer (1971), Little (1982) and a series of articles in *The Economist*, December 1988–March 1989.

9
Building on the past

This book arose out of a concern about the lack of attention given to profit and enterprise in mainstream economics teaching. This neglect is obvious from an inspection of the textbooks at both introductory and intermediate levels of undergraduate economics courses. The inevitable consequence of this neglect is that generations of economics graduates have entered employment with little or no understanding of how market economies really work.

The neglect of enterprise is curious in the light of two important facts. The first is that many economists have *not* neglected enterprise and profit. Rather several well-developed theories have been produced to account for the role and function of both profit and enterprise. The second is that during the 1980s policy-makers became increasingly anxious to foster entrepreneurship as a way of escaping from stagflation and nurturing economic growth. These two features are taken in turn.

9.1 Approaches to profit and enterprise

A variety of theories of profit and enterprise have been reviewed in this book (these are summarised in Table 9.1). In the early chapters it was shown that the classical economists (Chapter 3) were primarily concerned with the processes of long-run development and growth and with income distribution. Although Smith and his followers took pains to rebut the old mercantilist doctrine of protectionism, enterprise was not central to their concerns and there was a notable failure by most classical writers to distinguish sharply between enterprise and the provision of capital.

Table 9.1   Perspectives on economic topics – a simplified view

	School of economic thought			
Topic	Classical	Neoclassical	Austrian	Marxist
Value	Costs, with emphasis on labour	Demand and supply (subjective valuation)	Demand and supply (subjective valuation)	Labour
Incomes	Population; wages fund; abstinence	Derived demand; marginal product	Derived demand	Class
Profit	Residual; a legitimate reward	Divided into normal and supernormal; only the former is legitimate in the long run	Essential motivator; unquestionably legitimate	Result of exploitation – not legitimate
Enterprise	Accorded implicit importance	Neglected	Central to the market process	One of the dispensable functions of the capitalist
Role of state	'Ring-holding' and *laissez-faire*	*Laissez-faire* BUT intervention in cases of market failure	Active promotion of competition	Under capitalism: maintaining the power of the capitalist class. Under socialism: ownership and the control of means of production; planning

Note: Pre-classical economic thought has been omitted from this table since it cannot easily be reduced to a single set of views.

Late in the nineteenth century, economic theory underwent a significant change in which the classical 'labour theory of value' was abandoned in favour of a subjective, utility-based supply and demand theory. These new ideas were, however, taken up in different ways by neoclassical and Austrian economists, with these two schools of thought adopting distinctive positions with regard to entrepreneurship and profit. For neoclassical economists (Chapter 4), the focus of interest falls firmly on the idea of equilibrium prices and output levels. Markets are analysed in terms of models which are essentially static, with supply and demand moving smoothly into balance. Enterprise plays little part in such models – inevitably so, since enterprise is a dynamic factor which is difficult to accommodate within static theories. Although profit-making is taken to be the objective of firms, businessmen are depicted essentially as *reacting* to fluctuations in prices and profits. Prices and profits change and, as a response, firms adjust their production levels (see, for example, Lipsey, 1979, pp. 248ff; McConnell, 1981, pp. 519ff). Firms, in short, are not portrayed as being run by pro-active, entrepreneurial initiative-takers.

A major rival of the neoclassical school is Austrian economics (Chapter 5). In place of equilibrium, Austrians place entrepreneurship at the centre of attention. For Austrian economists, the market is not a static institution but a search process in which entrepreneurs continually seek out new opportunities for profit. This unending search produces change: new products, new processes, new materials, new approaches to marketing and so on are constantly being tried out. Economists of the Austrian tradition argue that profit originates in an alertness to new opportunities, and go on to emphasise the distinction between interest (the reward of capital) and profit (the reward of enterprise). Austrians argue that the approach to profit in the (largely neoclassical) textbooks is deficient in that it suggests that businessmen make decisions about, for example, the level of production as a reaction to current or past profit levels. Austrians believe that this obscures the essential aspect of profit: that it motivates enterprise. Thus for Austrians the key feature is the expectation of *future* profit.

The Austrian approach to profit stands in marked contrast to a final view of profit which is found in the works of radical and other theorists. This is the theory that the profits of entrepreneurs are made at the expense of other members of society. Some writers of the mercantilist tradition (Chapter 2) of the sixteenth and seventeenth centuries, for example, took the view that profits are made at the expense of buyers. In a similar vein, Karl Marx and other socialists (Chapter 6) argued that profits arise from the exploitation of labour by capital. This analysis has of course been used to support arguments for an increased role for the state in economic affairs, even to the point of the expropriation of privately owned businesses.

9.2 The rediscovery of enterprise

Alongside the compendium of theories of profit and enterprise is a second important factor. During the 1980s governments began to rediscover the importance of enterprise. The search for the contribution of enterprise was prompted by the stagflation of the 1970s, which seemed to present governments with a sterile choice between boosting jobs by raising inflation to new heights or curing inflation by accepting record levels of unemployment. To escape from this dilemma, governments – notably those led by Ronald Reagan in the United States and Margaret Thatcher in the United Kingdom – took steps to improve the supply-side capabilities of their economies. The general thrust of the new policies was to promote flexibility and improve incentives. As Chapter 8 described, in the United Kingdom this meant reversing the interventionist trends of the post-war decades by reducing the levels of income tax, scrapping regulations, selling state-owned businesses and promoting the formation of new businesses. The United States has likewise engaged in tax-cutting and deregulation. Other nations have followed suit, with privatisation programmes being introduced from Holland to Israel. In a major initiative intended to liberate international competition from the shackles of government intervention, the European Community plans in 1992 to scrap all state-maintained barriers to competition, thus instituting a truly free market. The objective is to allow Europe's entrepreneurs full scope to pursue profit on a continental scale.

In the Third World, a similar reversal of policy can be detected. For many years, state 'enterprise' was tolerated or even encouraged by international lending agencies. From the 1980s, however, problems with these state organisations became evident in terms of overmanning and poor management. Bureaucracy often hamstrung the relatively dynamic private sectors of these economies, while development became increasingly hindered by the huge international debts built up by high-spending governments. During the 1980s, in an attempt to retrieve a deteriorating economic situation, many developing countries – often at the behest of creditors like the World Bank – have adopted pro-market and pro-enterprise policies.

In the Communist bloc, the mounting economic problems of the early 1980s took the form of a slowdown in growth and a failure to close the gap with the West in terms of consumer goods. It became apparent that central planning systems were not meeting their targets. Consequently reformers like Deng Xiaoping and Mikhail Gorbachev have now begun to attempt to dismantle state controls and to give wider play to market forces and the pursuit of individual self-interest by profit-seeking entrepreneurs.

9.3 The implications for economics

This change in the direction of policy coincided with a re-examination of economic ideas. Many economists began to question the principle that state intervention, at the micro or macro level, was beneficial. Competition, which had formerly been thought of in static terms (being measured by, for example, the number of firms in an industry), began to be seen as a *process* in which the keys to success are alertness, innovation and sensitivity to consumer preferences. Above all it meant a renewed recognition by economists of the role of profit in motivating the efforts of enterpreneurs. It thus led to a revived interest in the contribution of Austrian economics.

Unfortunately, these changes – evident in the learned journals and the economic press – have yet to be translated into the introductory texts. As Chapter 1 showed, the principles which receive prominence in these texts in the sphere of microeconomics are basically neoclassical ones. With a few exceptions (e.g. Stead and Wisniewski, 1988), markets are portrayed as moving mechanically from one equilibrium to another. Enterprise has no part to play and, not surprisingly, the entrepreneur receives scant attention. It may be objected that introductory texts are already so burdened with material that the inclusion of extra content would be impossible. Nevertheless it is of interest to note that, during the 1980s, texts were extended to take in new (or revamped) theories in macroeconomics such as monetarism and 'rational expectations'.

Typically the approach that is pursued in the macro sections of the texts is one of eclecticism: Keynesian, monetarist and rational expectations analyses are set out in successive chapters and the controversies between them are frankly admitted. A similar course could be followed with regard to the working of markets. As well as equilibrium theories, other approaches which place more emphasis upon profit and enterprise should be given attention. Equilibrium theory could be explained not as though it represented the entire sum of economic truth but rather as just one perspective. By this means, profit and enterprise could usefully be incorporated into the teaching of economics even at the introductory level. Moreover, this approach would do some justice to the rich plurality of ideas on profit and enterprise which earlier chapters attempted to describe.

An important consequence of such an approach would be to focus attention on the role of profit. By setting the alternative theories alongside each other, attention would be drawn to the controversies which surround the issues of profit and enterprise. At the very least, it would be difficult with such an eclectic approach simply to dismiss enterprise from the discussion as is all too often the case at present. If the need to discuss enterprise is placed upon the agenda, then this book will have succeeded.

Bibliography

Abouchar, A., 1977, *The Socialist Price Mechanism*, Durham, NC: Duke University Press.

Aganbegyan, A., 1988, *The Challenge: Economics of perestroika*, London: Hutchinson.

Alchian, A. A. and Demsetz, H., 1972, 'Production, information costs and economic organizations', *American Economic Review*, vol. 62, reproduced in Alchian, A. A., *Economic Forces at Work*, Indianapolis: Liberty Press.

Allen, G. C., 1979, *The British Disease*, Hobart Paper 67, London: Institute of Economic Affairs.

Allen, G. C., 1986, *How Japan Competes*, London: Institute of Economic Affairs.

Amin, S., 1978, *Imperialism and Unequal Development*, Hemel Hempstead: Harvester Wheatsheaf.

Anderson, M., 1988, *Revolution*, New York: Harcourt Brace Jovanovich.

Armstrong, P., Glynn, A. and Harrison, J., 1984, *Capitalism Since World War II*, Harmondsworth: Penguin.

Artis, M. J. (ed.), 1986, *The UK Economy: A manual of applied economics*, London: Weidenfeld & Nicolson.

Averch, H. and Johnson, L. L., 1962, 'Behaviour of the firm under regulatory constraint', *American Economic Review*, vol. 52, December, pp. 1053–69.

Bailey, E. E., 1986, 'Price and productivity change following deregulation: the US experience', *Economic Journal*, vol. 96, March, pp. 1–17.

Bailyn, B. (ed.), 1964, *The Apologia of Robert Keayne: The self-portrait of a Puritan merchant*, New York: Harper & Row.

Bannock, G. and Doran, A., 1978, *Small Firms in Cities*, London: Economists Advisory Group for Shell UK.

Barnes, J. (ed.), 1985, *The Complete Works of Aristotle*, vol. 2, Princeton: Bollingen Series, LXXI.

Barry, N. P., 1979, *Hayek's Social and Economic Philosophy*, London: Macmillan.

Bartlett, B. and Roth, T. P., 1984, *The Supply Side Solution*, London: Macmillan.

Bauer, P., 1971, *Dissent on Development*, London: Weidenfeld & Nicolson.

Bauer, P., 1981, *Equality, the Third World Economic Delusion*, London: Weidenfeld & Nicolson.

Baumol, W. J., 1959, *Business Behaviour, Value and Growth*, New York: Macmillan.

Baumol, W. J., 1968, 'Entrepreneurship in economic theory', *American Economic Review*, vol. 58, May, pp. 64–71.

Baumol, W. J., 1983, 'Towards operational models of entrepreneurship', in J. Ronen (ed.), *Entrepreneurship*, Lexington, MA: D. C. Heath.

Baumol, W. J., Panzar, J. and Willig, R., 1982, *Contestable Markets*, New York: Harcourt Brace Jovanovich.

Baumol, W. J. and Blinder, A. S., 1988, *Economics: Principles and policies*, 4th edn, New York: Harcourt Brace Jovanovich.

Begg, D., Fischer, S. and Dornbusch, R., 1987, *Economics*, London: McGraw-Hill.

Binks, M. and Coyne, J., 1983, *The Birth of Enterprise: An analytical and empirical study of the growth of small firms*, Hobart Paper 98, London: Institute of Economic Affairs.

Birch, D. L., 1979, *The Job Generation Process: MIT study on neighbourhood and regional change*, Cambridge, MA: MIT.

Blaug, M., 1978, *Economic Theory in Retrospect*, Cambridge: Cambridge University Press.

Blaug, M., 1980, *The Methodology of Economics*, Cambridge: Cambridge University Press.

Blaug, M., 1985, *Great Economists Since Keynes: An introduction to the lives and works of one hundred modern economists*, Hemel Hempstead: Harvester Wheatsheaf.

Blaug, M., 1986a, 'Entrepreneurship before and after Schumpeter', in M. Blaug (ed.), *Economic History and the History of Economics*, Hemel Hempstead: Harvester Wheatsheaf.

Blaug, M. (ed.), 1986b, *Economic History and the History of Economics*, Hemel Hempstead: Harvester Wheatsheaf.

Blaug, M., 1986c, *Great Economists Before Keynes: An introduction to the lives and works of one hundred great economists of the past*, Hemel Hempstead: Harvester.

Bohm-Bawerk, E. von, 1891, *The Positive Theory of Capital*, London: Macmillan.

Bohm-Bawerk, E. von, 1949, *Karl Marx and the Close of His System*, New York: Augustus M. Kelley.

Bohm-Bawerk, E. von, 1959, *Capital and Interest*, South Holland, IL: Libertarian Press.

Boland, L., 1982, *The Foundations of Economic Method*, London, George Allen & Unwin.

Bor, M., 1967, *Aims and Methods of Soviet Planning*, London: Lawrence & Wishart.

Bosanquet, N., 1983, *After the New Right*, London: Heinemann.

Bowley, M., 1937, *Nassau Senior and Classical Economics*, London: George Allen & Unwin.

Bradley, I. and Howard, M., 1982, *Classical and Marxian Political Economy*, London: Macmillan.

Breit, W. and Hochman, H. M., 1968, *Readings in Microeconomics*, New York: Holt, Rinehart and Winston.

Brewer, 1980, *Marxist Theories of Imperialism: A critical survey*, London: Routledge & Kegan Paul.

Buchanan, J., 1976, 'General implications of subjectivism in economics', in J. Buchanan (ed.) *What Should Economists Do?* Indianapolis: Liberty Press.

Buchanan, J. M., Rowley, C. K., Breton, A., Wiseman, J., Frey, B., Peacock, A. T. and Grimond, J., 1978, *The Economics of Politics*, IEA Readings 18, London: Institute of Economic Affairs.

Buchanan, J., Burton, J. and Wagner, R. E., 1978, *The Consequences of Mr Keynes*, Hobart Paper 78, London: Institute of Economic Affairs.

Buchanan, J. and Di Pierro, A., 1980, 'Competition, choice and entrepreneurship', *Southern Economic Journal*, vol. 46, pp. 693–701.

Burden, T. and Campbell, M., 1985, *Capitalism and Public Policy in the UK*, London: Croom Helm.

Burton, J., 1983, *Picking Losers . . . ? The Political Economy of Industrial Policy*, Hobart Paper 99, London: Institute of Economic Affairs.

Burton, J., Yeager, L. B., Friedman, M., Brumer, K., Darby, M. R., Lothian, J. R., Wallis, A. A., Minford, P., Beenstock, M. and Budd, A., 1986, *Keynes's General Theory Fifty Years On: Its relevance and irrelevance to modern times*, Hobart Paperback 24, London: Institute of Economic Affairs.

Caldwell, B., 1982, *Beyond Positivism*, London: George Allen & Unwin.

Campbell, M., 1981, *Capitalism in the UK: A perspective from Marxist political economy*, London: Croom Helm.

Campbell, M., Hardy, M. and Healey, N. (eds.), 1989, *Controversy in Applied Economics*, Hemel Hempstead: Harvester Wheatsheaf.

Campbell, R. H. and Skinner, A.S., 1982, *Adam Smith*, London: Croom Helm.

Cantillon, R., 1931, *Essai sur la nature du commerce en général*, London: Macmillan.

Carter, C. F. and Ford, J. L., 1972, *Uncertainty and Expectations in Economics: Essays in honour of G. L. S. Shackle*, Fairfield, NJ: Augustus M. Kelley.

Casson, M., 1982, *The Entrepreneur: An economic theory*, Oxford: Basil Blackwell.

Caves, R. E. and Ueseska, M. 1976, *Industrial Organisation in Japan*, New Haven, CT: Brookings Institution.

Cecchini, P., 1988, *The European Challenge*, 1992, Aldershot: Wildwood House.

Chalmers, M., 1982, *What Is This Thing Called Science?*, Milton Keynes: Open University Press.

Chamberlin, E. H., 1946, *The Theory of Monopolistic Competition*, Cambridge, MA: Harvard University Press.

Chandler, W. U., 1986, *The Changing Role of the Market in National Economies*, Worldwatch Paper 72, Washington, DC: Worldwatch Institute.

Cheung, S. N. S., 1978, *The Myth of Social Cost*, Hobart Paper 82, London: Institute of Economic Affairs.

Chiplin, B. and Wright, M., 1987, *The Logic of Mergers*, Hobart Paper 107, London: Institute of Economic Affairs.

Clark, J. B., 1899, *The Distribution of Wealth*, New York: Macmillan.

Coase, R. H., 1937, 'The nature of the firm', *Economics* vol. 4, November, pp. 386–405.

Coase, R. H., 1960, 'The problem of social cost', *Journal of Law and Economics*, October, reprinted in W. Breit and H. M. Hochman (eds.), 1968, *Readings in Microeconomics*, New York: Holt, Rinehart and Winston.

Coates, A. W. (ed.) 1971, *The Classical Economists and Economic Policy*, London: Methuen.

Collis, J. S., 1975, *The Vision of Glory*, Harmondsworth: Penguin.

Commons, J., 1934, *Institutional Economics*, New York: Macmillan.

Coomarawami, A. K., 1977, *Traditional Art and Symbolism*, ed. R. Lipsey, Princeton: Bollingen Series, LXXXIX.

Cordato, R. E., 1980, 'The Austrian theory of efficiency and the role of government', *Journal of Libertarian Studies*, vol. 4, no. 4, pp. 393–403.

Cowling, K. and Mueller, D. C., 1978, 'The social costs of monopoly power', *Economic Journal*, vol. 88, December, pp. 727–48.

Crook, C. *et al.*, 1989, *Sub-Saharan Africa: From crisis to sustainable growth*, Washington, DC: World Bank.

Culyer, A., 1985, *Economics*, London: Basil Blackwell.

De Alessi, L., 1980, 'The economics of property rights: a review of the evidence', *Research in Law and Economics*, vol. 2, pp. 1–47.

Debreu, G., 1959, *Theory of Value*, New Haven, CT: Yale University Press.

Dernburg, T. F., 1985, *Macroeconomics: Concepts, theories and policies*, New York: McGraw-Hill.

Dietz, J. L. and Street, J. H., 1987, *Latin America's Economic Development – Institutionalist and structuralist perspectives*, Boulder, CO: Lynne Rienne Publishers.

Dobb, M., 1955, *On Economic Theory and Socialism*, London: Routledge & Kegan Paul.

Dobb, M., 1973, *Theories of Value and Distribution Since Adam Smith: Ideology and economic theory*, Cambridge: Cambridge University Press.

Dolan, E. G. (ed.), 1976, *The Foundations of Modern Austrian Economics*, Kansas City: Sheed & Ward.

Dolores, M. T., 1979, 'Alternative views of Mengerian entrepreneurship', *History of Political Economy*, vol. 11, pp. 271–85.

Dornbusch, R. and Layard, R., 1987, *The Performance of the British Economy*, Oxford: Clarendon Press.

Dow, J. C. R., 1964, *The Management of the British Economy*, Cambridge: Cambridge University Press.

Dunsire, A., Hartley, K., Parker, D. and Dimitriou, B., 1988, 'Organizational status and performance: a conceptual framework for testing public choice theories', *Public Administration*, vol. 66, no. 4, Winter, pp. 363–88.

Edwards, C., 1985, *Fragmented World*, London: Methuen.

Ekelund, R. B. jun. and Hebert, R. F., 1975, *A History of Economic Theory and Method*, Tokyo: McGraw-Hill Kogakusha.

Ekelund, R. B. jun. and Saurman, D. S., 1978, *Advertising and the Market Process*, New York: Pripp.

Ekelund, R. B. jun., Hebert, R. F. and Tollison, R. D., 1989, 'An economic model of the medieval Church: usury as a form of rent seeking', *Journal of Law, Economics and Organization*, vol. 5, Fall, pp. 307–31.

Emmanuel, A., 1972, *Unequal Exchange – A study of the imperialism of trade*, London: New Left Books.

Evans, G. H. jun., 1949, 'The entrepreneur in economic theory: an historical and analytical approach', *American Economic Review*, vol. 39, pp. 336–55.

Fay, C. R., 1960, *The World of Adam Smith*, Cambridge: W. Heffer & Sons.

Feigenbaum, E. A. and McCorduck, P., 1984, *The Fifth Generation: Artificial intelligence and Japan's challenge to the world*, London: Pan.

Fetter, F. W., 1969, 'The rise and decline of Ricardian economics', *History of Political Economy*, vol. 1, Fall, pp. 370–87.

Fine, B. (ed.), 1986, *The Value Dimension*, London: Routledge & Kegan Paul.

Fisher, R. M., 1986, *The Logic of Economic Discovery: Neoclassical economics and the marginal revolution*, Hemel Hempstead: Harvester Wheatsheaf.

Flew, A., 1976, 'The profit motive', *Ethics*, vol. 86, July, pp. 312–22.

Frank, A. G., 1975, *On Capitalist Underdevelopment*, Bombay: Oxford University Press.

Frank, A. G., 1979, *Dependent Accumulation and Underdevelopment*, London: Macmillan.

Freeman, C., 1987, *Technology Policy and Economic Performance: Lessons from Japan*, London: F. Pinter.

Friedman, M., 1953, 'The methodology of positive economics', in M. Friedman, *Essays in Positive Economics*, Chicago: University of Chicago Press.

Friedman, M., 1958, 'Foreign economic aid: Means and objectives', *The Yale Review*, Summer, pp. 500–16.

Friedman, M. and Friedman, R., 1980, *Free to Choose*, London: Secker & Warburg.

Friedman, M. and Schwartz, A. J., 1963, *A Monetary History of the US 1867–1960*, New York, NBER.

Galbraith, J. K., 1961, *The Affluent Society*, London: Hamish Hamilton.

Galbraith, J. K., 1969, *The New Industrial State*, Harmondsworth: Pelican.

Galbraith, J. K., 1973, *Economics and the Public Purpose*, Harmondsworth: Penguin.

Garegnani, P., 1984, 'Value and distribution in the classical economists and Marx', *Oxford Economic Papers*, vol. 36, pp. 291–325.

Gide, C. and Rist, C., 1915, *A History of Economic Doctrines*, London: Harrap.

Gilder, G., 1985, *The Spirit of Enterprise*, Harmondsworth: Pelican.

Gill, R. T., 1973, *Economics: A text with included readings*, Hemel Hempstead: Prentice Hall.

Girvetz, H. K., 1963, *The Evolution of Liberalism*, New York: Collier.

Glahe, F. R. and Lee, D. R., 1981, *Microeconomics: Theory and Applications*, New York, Harcourt Brace Jovanovich.

Glynn, A. and Sutcliffe, R., 1972, *British Capitalism, Workers and the Profits Squeeze*, Harmondsworth: Penguin.

Gordon, Barry J., 1964, 'Aristotle and the development of value theory', *Quarterly Journal of Economics* vol. 78, no. 1, pp. 115–28.

Gravelle, H. and Rees, R., 1981, *Microeconomics*, London and New York: Longman.

Hahn, F., 1982, 'Reflections on the invisible hand', *Lloyds Bank Review*, no. 144, April, pp. 1–21.

Hansen, A. H., 1939, 'Economic progress and declining population growth', *American Economic Review*, vol. 29, pp. 1–15.

Hardach, G. and Karras, D., 1979, *A Short History of Social Economic Thought*, London: Edward Arnold.

Hardwick, P., Khan, B. and Langmead, J., 1982, *An Introduction to Modern Economics*, London: Longman.

Hartley, K., 1977, *Problems of Economic Policy*, London: George Allen & Unwin.

Hawley, F. B., 1893, 'The risk theory of profit', *Quarterly Journal of Economics*, vol. 7, pp. 459–79.

Hayek, F. A. von, 1935, *Collectivist Economic Planning*, London: Routledge & Kegan Paul.

Hayek, F. A. von, 1943, 'Scientism and the study of society', *Economica*, vol. 9, pp. 267–91.

Hayek, F. A. von, 1948, *Individualism and Economic Order*, Chicago: University of Chicago Press.

Hayek, F. A. von, 1966, *Monetary Theory and the Trade Cycle*, New York: Augustus M. Kelley.

Hayek, F. A. von, 1972, *A Tiger by the Tail*, Hobart Paper 4, London: Institute of Economic Affairs.

Hayek, F. A. von, 1976, *The Road to Serfdom*, London: Routledge & Kegan Paul.

Hayek, F. A. von, 1978a, *New Studies in Philosophy, Politics and Economics*, London: Routledge & Kegan Paul.

Hayek, F. A. von, 1978b, *Denationalisation of Money – The argument refined*, 2nd edn, Hobart Paper 70, London: Institute of Economic Affairs.

Hayek, F. A. von, 1982, *Law, Legislation and Liberty*, 3 vols., London: Routledge & Kegan Paul.

Healey, N. and Parker, D., 1988, *Current Topics in Applied Economics*, Prudhoe: Anforme.

Hebert, R. F., 1985, 'Was Richard Cantillon an Austrian economist?', *Journal of Libertarian Studies*, vol. 7, pp. 269–79.

Hebert, R. F. and Link, A. N., 1988, *The Entrepreneur: Mainstream views and radical critiques*, New York: Praeger.

Heckscher, E., 1934, *Mercantilism*, London: George Allen & Unwin.

Heilbroner, R., 1980, *The Worldly Philosophers*, Harmondsworth: Pelican.

Hemming, R. and Mansoor, A. M., 1988, *Privatisation and Public Enterprises*, Occasional Paper 56, Washington, DC: International Monetary Fund.

Hey, J. D. and Lambert, P. J. (eds.), 1987, *Surveys in the Economics of Uncertainty*, Oxford: Basil Blackwell.

Hicks, J. R., 1957, *Value and Capital*, London: Oxford University Press.

Hicks, J. R., 1983, 'From classical to post-classical, the work of J.S. Mill', in J. R. Hicks (ed.) *Collected Essays on Economic Theory*, III, Oxford: Oxford University Press, pp. 60–70.

HMSO, 1978, *A Review of Monopolies and Mergers Policy: A consultative document*, London: HMSO.

HM Treasury, 1978, *Committee to Review the Functioning of Financial Institutions*, chairman Sir Harold Wilson.

Holland, S. (ed.), 1972, *The State as Entrepreneur*, London: Weidenfeld & Nicolson.

Hollander, S., 1973, *The Economics of Adam Smith*, Toronto: University of Toronto Press.

Hollander, S., 1979, *The Economics of David Ricardo*, Toronto: University of Toronto Press.

Hollander, S., 1987, *Classical Economics*, Oxford: Basil Blackwell.

Hollis, M. and Nell, E. J., 1975, *Rational Economic Man*, Cambridge: Cambridge University Press.

Hoselitz, B. F., 1951, 'The early history of entrepreneurial theory', *Explorations in Economic History*, vol. 3, reprinted in J. J. Spengler and W. R. Allen (eds.), 1960, *Economic Thought: Aristotle to Marshall*, Chicago: Rand McNally.

Howard, M., 1983, *Profits in Economic Theory*, London: Macmillan.

Howard, M. and King, J. E., 1985, *The Political Economy of Marx*, London: Longman.

Hughes, J., 1986, *The Vital Few: The entrepreneur and American economic progress*, Oxford: Oxford University Press.

Hutchison, T. W., 1981, *The Politics and Philosophy of Economics*, Oxford: Basil Blackwell.

Jacobs, J., 1985, *Cities and the Wealth of Nations*, New York: Random House.

Jevons, W. S., 1970, *The Theory of Political Economy*, Harmondsworth: Penguin.

Jewkes, J., 1978, *Delusions of Dominance*, Hobart Paper 76, London: Institute of Economic Affairs.

Kay, J. A. and Thompson, D. J., 1986, 'Privatisation: a policy in search of a rationale', *Economic Journal*, vol. 96, March, pp. 18–32.

Keat, R. and Urry, J., 1983, *Social Theory as Science*, London: Routledge, Chapman & Hall.

Kefauver, E., 1966, *In a Few Hands: Monopoly power in America*, Harmondsworth: Penguin.

Keynes, J. M., 1936, *The General Theory of Employment, Interest and Money*, New York: Harcourt Brace.

King, M. A., 1975, 'The United Kingdom profit crisis: myth or reality?', *Economic Journal*, vol. 85, March, pp. 33–54.

Kirzner, I. M., 1960, *The Economic Point of View*, Kansas City: Sheed & Ward.

Kirzner, I. M., 1963, *Market Theory and the Price System*, New York: Van Nostrand.

Kirzner, I. M., 1973, *Competition and Entrepreneurship*, Chicago: University of Chicago Press.

Kirzner, I. M., 1979, *Perception, Opportunity and Profit*, Chicago: University of Chicago Press.

Kirzner, I. M., 1981, 'Why the market outclasses the state', *Journal of Economic Affairs*, vol. 1, no. 3, April, pp. 181–3.

Kirzner, I. M., 1983, *Method, Process and Austrian Economics: Essays in honour of Ludwig von Mises*, Lexington: D.C. Heath.

Kirzner, I. M., 1985, *Discovery and the Capitalist Process*, Chicago: University of Chicago Press.

Kirzner, I. M., Hannah, L., McKendrick, N., Vinson, N., Wickenden, K., Knight, Sir A., McFadzean, Sir F., Henderson, P. D., MacRae, D. G. and Pearce, I., 1980, *The Prime Mover in Progress*, IEA Reading 23, London: Institute of Economic Affairs.

Kitch, M. J., 1967, *Capitalism and the Reformation*, London: Longman.

Knight, F. H., 1921, *Risk, Uncertainty and Profit*, Boston: Houghton Mifflin.

Knight, F. H., 1951, *The Economic Organization*, New York: Augustus M. Kelley.

Koutsoyiannis, A., 1979, *Modern Microeconomics*, 2nd edn, London: Macmillan.

Kuhn, T., 1962, *The Structure of Scientific Revolutions*, Chicago: University of Chicago Press.

Lachmann, L. M., 1976, 'From Mises to Shackle: an essay on Austrian economics and the Kaleidic Society', *Journal of Economic Literature*, vol. 14, pp. 54–62.

Lachmann, L. M., 1977, *Capital, Expectations and Market Process*, Kansas City: Sheed, Andrews & McMeel.

Laffer, A. B. and Seymour, J. P. (eds.), 1979, *The Economics of the Tax Revolt: A reader*, New York: Harcourt Brace Jovanovich.

Laidler, D., 1981, *Introduction to Modern Microeconomics*, Oxford: Philip Allan.

Lakatos, I., 1978, *Philosophical Papers*, vol. I, ed. J. Worrall and G. Currie, Cambridge: Cambridge University Press.

Lange, O., 1936, 'On the economic theory of socialism', *Review of Economic Studies*, vol. 4, no. 1, October, pp. 53–71.

Lange, O. and Taylor, F. M., 1938, *On the Theory of Socialism*, Minneapolis: University of Minnesota Press.

Langholm, O., 1979, *Price and Value in the Aristotelian Tradition: A study in scholastic economic sources* Bergen: Universitetsforlaget.

Latsis, S., 1976, *Method and Appraisal in Economics*, Cambridge: Cambridge University Press.

Lavoie, D., 1986, *Between Institutionalism and Formalism: The rise and fall of the Austrian School's Calculation Argument: 1920–1950*, Centre for the Study of Market Processes Working Paper 1986–21, George Mason University.

Leibenstein, H., 1976, *Beyond Economic Man: A new foundation for micro-economics*, Cambridge, MA: Harvard University Press.

Lenin, V. I., 1968, 'The three sources and the three component parts of Marxism', in K. Marx and F. Engels, *Selected Works*, London: Lawrence & Wishart.

Lenin, V. I., 1970, *Imperialism – The highest stage of capitalism*, Moscow: Progress Publishers.

Leslie, T. E. C., 1888, *Essays in Political Economy*, London: Longmans, Green.

Lessnoff, M., 1978, *The Structure of Social Science*, London: George Allen & Unwin.

Lipsey, R. G., 1979, *Introduction to Positive Economics*, London: Weidenfeld & Nicolson.

Little, I. M. D., 1982, *Economic Development: Theory, policy and international relations*, New York: Basic Books.

Littlechild, S. C., 1981, 'Misleading calculations of social costs of monopoly', *Economic Journal*, Vol. 91, June, pp. 348–63.

Littlechild, S. C. 1983, 'Subjectivism and method in economics', in J. Wiseman (ed.), *Beyond Positive Economics*, London: Macmillan.

Littlechild, S. C., 1986, *The Fallacy of the Mixed Economy*, 2nd edn, Hobart Paper 80, London: Institute of Economic Affairs.

Lloyd, T., 1984, *Dinosaur and Co.*, London: Routledge & Kegan Paul.

Loasby, B. J., 1976, *Choice, Complexity and Ignorance*, Cambridge: Cambridge University Press.

Loasby, B. J., 1982, 'The entrepreneur in economic theory', *Scottish Journal of Political Economy*, vol. 29, no. 3, November, pp. 235–45.

MacFarlane, A., 1978, *The Origins of English Individualism*, London: Macmillan.

Machlup, F., 1955, 'The problems of verification in economics', *Southern Economic Journal*, pp. 1–21.

Machlup, F., 1967, 'Theories of the firm: marginalist, behavioral and managerial', *American Economic Review*, vol. 57, pp. 1–83.

Machlup, F. (ed.), 1977, *Essays on Hayek*, New York: New York University Press.

Mack, M. P., 1963, *Jeremy Bentham: An odyssey of ideas*, New York: Columbia University Press.

Malthus, T. R., 1960, *An Essay on the Principle of Population, as It Affects the Future Improvement of Society with Remarks on the Speculations of Mr. Godwin, M. Condorcet and Other Writers*, New York: Random House.

Mandell, E., 1978, *Late Capitalism*, London: Verso.

Mangoldt, H. von, 1855, 'The precise function of the entrepreneur and the true nature of the entrepreneur's profit', in F. M. Taylor (ed.), 1907, *Some Readings in Economics*, Ann Arbor: George Wahr.

Marris, R., 1964, *The Economic Theory of 'Managerial Capitalism'*, London: Macmillan.

Marshall, A., 1966, *Principles of Economics: An introductory volume*, London: Macmillan.

Marx, K., 1960, *Capital*, vol. III, London: Lawrence & Wishart.

Marx, K., 1963, *Poverty of Philosophy*, New York: International Publishers.

Marx, K., 1965, *Capital*, vol. I, Moscow: Progress Publishers.

Marx, K., 1968, *Wages, Price and Profit*, in K. Marx and F. Engels, *Selected Works*, London: Lawrence & Wishart.

Mathias, P., 1969, *The First Industrial Nation: An economic history of Britain 1700–1914*, London: Methuen.

McClelland, D., 1961, *The Achieving Society*, Princeton: Van Nostrand.

McClelland, D., 1973, *Karl Marx, His Life and Thought*, London: Macmillan.

McCloskey, D. N., 1981, *Enterprise and Trade in Victorian Britain*, London: George Allen & Unwin.

McConnell, C., 1981, *Economics*, New York: McGraw-Hill.

Meade, J. E., 1975, *An Intelligent Radical's Guide to Economic Policy*, London: George Allen & Unwin.

Medvedev, R., 1990, 'The environmental destruction of the Soviet Union', *The Ecologist*, vol. 20, no. 1, January–February, pp. 24–9.

Meek, R. L., 1954, 'Adam Smith and the classical concept of profit', *Scottish Journal of Economics*, vol. 1, pp. 138–53.

Meek, R. L., 1977, *Smith, Marx and After: Ten essays in the development of Economic Thought*, London: Chapman & Hall.

Menger, C., 1950, *Principles of Economics*, Glencoe, IL: Free Press.

Mill, J. S., 1875, *Principles of Political Economy*, London: Longman, Green, Reader and Dyer.

Mill, J. S., 1948, *Essays on Some Unsettled Questions of Political Economy*, London: London School of Economics.

Millward, R., 1971, *Public Enterprise Economics*, London: McGraw-Hill.

Millward, R., 1976, 'Price restraint, anti-inflation policy and public and private industry in the UK', *Economic Journal*, vol. 86, pp. 226–42.

Millward, R. and Parker, D., 1983, 'Public and private enterprise: comparative behaviour and relative efficiency', in R. Millward, D. Parker, L. Rosenthal, M. T. Sumner and N. Topham, *Public Sector Economics*, London & New York: Longman.

Minford, A. P. L., 1984, 'State expenditure: a study in waste', supplement to *Economic Affairs*, vol. 4, no. 3, April–June.

Mises, L. von, 1949, *Human Action: A treatise on economics*, New Haven: Yale University Press.

Mises, L. von, 1951, *Profit and Loss*, South Holland, IL: Consumers–Producers Economic Service.

Mises, L. von, 1974a, *Planning for Freedom*, South Holland IL: Libertarian Press.

Mises, L. von, 1974b, 'The economic nature of profit and loss', in L. von Mises, *Planning for Freedom*, South Holland, IL: Libertarian Press.

Mokry, B. W., 1988, *Entrepreneurship and Public Policy: Can government stimulate business startups?* Westport, CT: Quorum Books.

Monopolies and Mergers Commission, 1981, *Central Electricity Generating Board*, London: HMSO.

Morita, A., Reingold, E. M. and Mitsuko, S., 1987, *Made in Japan: Akio Morita and Sony*, London: Collins.
Moss, L. S. (ed.), 1976, *The Economics of Ludwig von Mises*, Kansas City: Sheed & Ward.
Myers, M. L., 1983, *The Soul of Modern Man: The ideas of self-interest – Thomas Hobbes to Adam Smith*, Chicago: University of Chicago Press.
Napoleoni, C., 1972, *Economic Thought of the Twentieth Century*, London: Martin Robertson.
Nasr, S. H., 1976, *Man and Nature*, London: George Allen & Unwin.
National Economic Development Office, 1969, *The Strategic Future of the Wool Textile Industry*, London: HMSO.
Niel, T. P., 1949, 'The physiocrats' concept of economics', *Quarterly Journal of Economics*, November, pp. 532–53.
Nove, A., 1969, *An Economic History of the USSR*, Harmondsworth: Penguin.
Nozick, R., 1977, 'On Austrian methodology', *Synthese*, pp. 353–92.
O'Brien, D. P., 1975, *The Classical Economists*, Oxford: Clarendon Press.
O'Connor, J., 1973, *The Fiscal Crisis of the State*, London: St James Press.
OECD, 1986, *Structural Change and Economic Performance*, Paris: OECD.
Oser, J., 1970, *The Evolution of Economic Thought*, New York: Harcourt Brace & World.
Panic, M. and Close, R. E., 1973, 'Profitability of British manufacturing industry', *Lloyds Bank Review*, July, pp. 17–30.
Parker, D., 1985, 'Is the private sector more efficient? A study in the public v. private debate', *Public Administration Bulletin*, vol. 48, pp. 2–23.
Parker, D., 1986/7, 'What profit in teaching economics?', *Economic Affairs*, vol. 7, no. 2, December/January, pp. 38–40.
Parker, D., 1987, 'The new right, state ownership and privatization: a critique', *Economic and Industrial Democracy*, vol. 8, pp. 329–78.
Parker, D., 1989, 'Controlling natural monopoly in the UK: is regulation the answer?' in M. Campbell, M. Hardy and N. Healey (eds.), *Controversy in Applied Economics*, Hemel Hempstead: Harvester Wheatsheaf.
Pasour, E. C., 1978, 'Cost and choice: Austrian v. conventional views', *Journal of Libertarian Studies*, vol. 2, no. 4, pp. 327–37.
Pheby, J., 1988, *Methodology and Economics*, London: Macmillan.
Pigou, A. C., 1920, *The Economics of Welfare*, London: Macmillan.
Pollard, S., 1968, *The Genesis of Modern Management*, Harmondsworth: Penguin.
Pryke, R., 1971, *Public Enterprise in Practice*, London: MacGibbon and Kee.
Pryke, R., 1981, *The Nationalised Industries: Policies and performance since 1968*, Oxford: Martin Robertson.
Ramsey, J. B., 1977, *Economic Forecasting – Models or markets?*, Hobart Paper 74, London: Institute of Economic Affairs.
Redlich, F., 1966, 'Toward an understanding of an unfortunate legacy', *Kyklos*, vol. 19, pp. 709–16.
Reekie, W. D., 1984, *Markets, Entrepreneurs and Liberty: An Austrian view of capitalism*, Hemel Hempstead: Harvester Wheatsheaf.
Resnick, S. and Wolff, R., 1987, *Knowledge and Class: A Marxian critique of political economy*, Chicago: University of Chicago Press.
Ricardo, D., 1955, *Works and Correspondence*, ed. Pierro Sraffa, Cambridge: Cambridge University Press.
Ricardo, D., 1971, *Principles of Political Economy and Taxation*, Harmondsworth: Penguin.

Rima, I. H. (ed.), 1970, *Readings in the History of Economic Theory*, New York: Holt, Rinehard and Winston.

Rima, I. H., 1978, *Development of Economic Analysis*, Homewood, IL: Richard D. Irwin.

Roberts, E. B. and Wainer, H. A., 1971, 'Some characteristics of technical entrepreneurs', *IEEE Transactions on Engineering Management*, EM–18, pp. 100–9.

Robertson, H. M. and Taylor, W. L., 1957, 'Adam Smith's approach to the theory of value', *Economic Journal*, vol. 67, June, pp. 181–98.

Robinson, J., 1933, *The Economics of Imperfect Competition*, London: Macmillan.

Robinson, J., 1966, *Economic Philosophy*, Harmondsworth: Penguin.

Roover, R. de, 1963, 'The scholastic attitude toward trade and entrepreneurship', *Explorations in Entrepreneurial History*, vol. 3, pp. 76–87.

Roover, R. de, 1988, 'The concept of the Just Price: theory and economic policy', *Journal of Economic History*, vol. 18, pp. 418–34.

Rothbard, M., 1970, *Man, Economy and State: A treatise on economic principles*, Los Angeles: Nash Publishing.

Rothbard, M., 1970, *Power and Market*, Kansas City: Sheed, Andrews & McMeel.

Rothbard, M., 1982, *Ethics of Liberty*, Melo Park, CA: Institute for Humane Studies.

Routh, G., 1975, *The Origin of Economic Ideas*, White Plains, NY: M.E. Sharpe.

Rowley, C., 1982, 'Industrial policy and the mixed economy', in Lord Roll (ed.), *The Mixed Economy*, London: Macmillan.

Ryan, A., 1970, *The Philosophy of the Social Sciences*, London: Macmillan.

Sahlins, M., 1974, *Stone Age Economics*, London: Tavistock.

Samuelson, P. A., 1954, 'The pure theory of public expenditure', *Review of Economics and Statistics*, vol. 36, November, pp. 387–9.

Samuelson, P. A. and Nordhaus, W. D., 1985, *Economics*, New York: McGraw-Hill.

Say, J. B., 1821, *A Treatise on Political Economy*, 2 vols., Boston: Wells & Lilly.

Scherer, F. M., 1980, *Industrial Market Structure and Economic Performance*, 2nd edn, Chicago: Rand McNally.

Schumpeter, J. A., 1934, *The Theory of Economic Development*, Cambridge, MA: Harvard University Press.

Schumpeter, J. A., 1939, *Business Cycles*, 2 vols., New York: McGraw-Hill.

Schumpeter, J. A., 1950, *Capitalism, Socialism and Democracy*, 3rd edn, London: George Allen & Unwin.

Schumpeter, J. A., 1954, *History of Economic Analysis*, London: Oxford University Press.

Schumpeter, J. A., 1961, *The Theory of Economic Development*, New York: Oxford University Press.

Seckler, D., 1975, *Thorstein Veblen and the Institutionalists*, London: Macmillan.

Seldon, A. (ed.), 1980, *The Litmus Papers*, London: Centre for Policy Studies.

Sen, A., 1983, 'The profit motive', *Lloyds Bank Review*, January, no. 147, pp. 1–20.

Senior, N. W., 1938, *An Outline of the Science of Political Economy*, London: George Allen & Unwin.

Shackle, G. L. S., 1949, *Expectations in Economics*, Cambridge, Cambridge University Press.

Shackle, G. L. S., 1970, *Expectations, Enterprise and Profit*, London: George Allen & Unwin.

Shackle, G. L. S., 1972, *Epistemics and Economics*, Cambridge: Cambridge University Press.

Shackle, G. L. S., 1979, *Imagination and the Nature of Choice*, Edinburgh: Edinburgh University Press.

Shackle, G. L. S., 1982, 'Means and meaning in economic theory', *Scottish Journal of Political Economy*, vol. 29, November, pp. 223–34.

Shaikh, A., 1981, 'The poverty of algebra', in I. Steedman *et al.*, *The Value Controversy*, London: Verso/NLB.

Shand, A. H., 1984, *The Capitalist Alternative: An introduction to neo-Austrian economics*, Hemel Hempstead: Harvester Wheatsheaf.

Silver, A. D., 1983, *The Entrepreneurial Life*, New York: John Wiley.

Skinner, A. S. and Wilson, T. (eds.), 1975, *Essays on Adam Smith*, Oxford: Clarendon Press.

Smith, A. 1950, *An Inquiry into the Nature and Causes of the Wealth of Nations*, London: Methuen.

Smith, A., 1979, *The Wealth of Nations*, Harmondsworth: Penguin.

Spengler, J. J., 1959–60, 'Adam Smith's theory of economic growth', *Southern Economic Journal*, vol. 25, pp. 397–414 and vol. 26, pp. 1–12.

Spengler, J. J. and Allen, W. R. (eds.), 1960, *Economic Thought: Aristotle to Marshall*, Chicago: Rand McNally.

Sraffa, P., 1926, 'The laws of returns under competitive conditions', *Economic Journal*, vol. 36, December, pp. 535–50.

Sraffa, P. (ed.), 1951–5, *The Works and Correspondence of David Ricardo*, 10 vols., Cambridge: Cambridge University Press.

Sraffa, P., 1960, *Production of Commodities by Means of Commodities*, Cambridge: Cambridge University Press.

Stead, R., 1989, 'Enterprise in economics', in M. Campbell, M. Hardy and N. Healey (eds.), *Controversy in Applied Economics*, Hemel Hempstead: Harvester Wheatsheaf.

Stead, R. and Wisniewski, M., 1988, *Using Economics*, London: McGraw-Hill.

Steedman, I., 1977, *Marx After Sraffa*, London: New Left Books.

Steedman, I. *et al.*, 1981, *The Value Controversy*, London: Verso/NLB.

Stewart, M., 1972, *Keynes and After*, Harmondsworth: Penguin.

Stigler, G. J., 1958, 'Ricardo and the 93% labor theory of value', *American Economic Review*, vol. 48, June, pp. 357–67.

Stigler, G. J., 1961, 'The Economics of information', *Journal of Political Economy*, June, pp. 213–25.

Stigler, G. J., 1971, 'The theory of economic regulation', *Bell Journal of Economics and Management Science*, vol. 2, pp. 3–21.

Stiglitz, J. E., 1985, 'Information and Economic analysis: a perspective', *Economic Journal*, conference papers, vol. 95, pp. 21–41.

Stockman, D., 1986, *The Triumph of Politics: Why the Reagan revolution failed*, New York: Harper & Row.

Storey, D. J., 1982, *Entrepreneurship and the New Firm*, London: Praeger.

Storey, D. J. and Johnson, S., 1987a, *Job Generation and Labour Market Change*, London: Macmillan.

Storey, D. J., Keasey, K., Watson, R. and Wynarcyk, P., 1987b, *The Performance of Small Firms*, London: Croom Helm.

Streissler, E., 1972, 'To what extent was the Austrian school marginalist?', *History of Political Economy*, vol. 4, pp. 426–41.

Swann, D., 1979, *Competition and Consumer Protection*, Harmondsworth: Penguin.

Swann, D., 1988, *The Retreat of the State*, Hemel Hempstead: Harvester Wheatsheaf.

Sweezy, P. M., 1964, *Theory of Capitalist Development*, New York: Monthly Review Press.
Taussig, F. W., 1915, *Principles of Economics*, New York: Macmillan.
Tawney, R. H., 1936, *Religion and the Rise of Capitalism*, London: John Murray.
Taylor, A. J., 1972, *Laissez-faire and State Intervention in Nineteenth Century Britain*, London: Macmillan.
Turgot, A. R. J., 1898, *Reflections on the Formation and the Distribution of Riches*, New York: Macmillan.
Walker, A., 1866, *The Science of Wealth*, Boston: Little Brown.
Walker, D. A., 1986, 'Walras' theory of the entrepreneur', *The Economist*, no. 134, pp. 1–24.
Walker, F. A., 1884, *Political Economy*, New York: Henry Holt.
Walras, L., 1954, *Elements of Pure Economics*, Homewood, IL: Irwin.
Warren, B., 1981, *Imperialism – Pioneer of capitalism*, London: New Left Books.
Weber, M., 1976, *The Protestant Ethic and the Spirit of Capitalism*, London: Unwin University Books.
Weiss, J. W., 1988, *Regional Cultures, Managerial Behavior and Entrepreneurship*, Westport, CT: Quorum Books.
Westergaard, J. and Resler, H., 1975, *Class in a Capitalist Society*, London: Heinemann Educational.
White, L. H., 1977, *Methodology of the Austrian School*, New York: Centre for Libertarian Studies.
White, L. J., 1981, 'What's been happening to aggregate concentration in the US?', *Journal of Industrial Economics*, vol. 29, no. 3, March, pp. 223–30.
Wicksell, K., 1935, *Lectures on Political Economy*, vol. 1, London: George Routledge.
Wicksteed, P., 1894, *An Essay on the Co-ordination of the Laws of Distribution*, London: Macmillan.
Wiener, J., 1981, *English Culture and the Decline of the Industrial Spirit 1850–1980*, Cambridge: Cambridge University Press.
Wieser, F. von, 1927, *Social Economics*, New York: Adelphi.
Winiecki, J., 1988, *The Distorted World of Soviet-type Economies*, London and New York: Routledge & Kegan Paul.
Wiseman, J., 1978, 'The political economy of nationalised industries', in J. Buchanan, *et al.*, *The Economics of Politics*, IEA Readings 18, London: Institute of Economic Affairs.
Wolff, R. D. and Resnick, S. A., 1987, *Economics: Marxian versus neoclassical*, Baltimore and London: Johns Hopkins University Press.
Wood, A., 1975, *A Theory of Profits*, Cambridge: Cambridge University Press.
Wood, J. C. (ed.), 1986, *Thomas Robert Malthus: Criticial assessments*, London: Croom Helm.
World Bank Annual Report, 1988, Washington, DC: World Bank.
Young, S. and Lowe, A. V., 1974, *Intervention in the Mixed Economy: The evaluation of British industrial policy 1964–72*, London: Croom Helm.

Index

199